AMERICANS IN THE TREASURE HOUSE

AMERICANS IN THE TREASURE HOUSE

Travel to Porfirian Mexico and the
Cultural Politics of Empire

JASON RUIZ

Dear Kathy,

You're more than a "work wife" — you're a life line. Thank you for the support + love thru the years. Here's to many more!

Love,
Jason

UNIVERSITY OF TEXAS PRESS   *Austin*

Requests for permission to reproduce material from this work should be sent to:
Permissions
University of Texas Press
P.O. Box 7819
Austin, TX 78713-7819
http://utpress.utexas.edu/index.php/rp-form

⊗ The paper used in this book meets the minimum requirements of
ANSI/NISO Z39.48-1992 (R1997) (Permanence of Paper).

LIBRARY OF CONGRESS CATALOGING-IN-PUBLICATION DATA

Ruiz, Jason.
    Americans in the treasure house : travel to Porfirian Mexico and the cultural politics of empire / Jason Ruiz.
        pages   cm
    ISBN 978-0-292-75380-8 (hardback)
    ISBN 978-0-292-75383-9 (paperback)
    1. Americans—Travel—Mexico—History—19th century.   2. Tourism—Mexico—History—19th century.   3. Investments, American—Mexico—History—19th century.   4. Mexico—History—1867–1910.   I. Title.
    F1392.A5R85   2014
    917.2'04—dc23   2013017381

doi:10.7560/753808

FOR MARIANNA AND CASSIE, MY FAVORITE
LITTLE TRAVELERS IN THIS BIG WORLD

CONTENTS

ACKNOWLEDGMENTS

Enrolling in graduate school at the University of Minnesota was a life-changing decision, in large part because it allowed me to work with my advisor, Roderick Ferguson, and with Kevin P. Murphy. I owe Rod and Kevin many more thanks than I can enumerate here. Reluctantly, it will have to suffice to thank them for serving as my guides through academia and life. I also thank Louis Mendoza (who deserves an extra thanks for putting me in touch with the University of Texas Press), Edén Torres, Jennifer Pierce, and many other faculty members at the U for gently guiding me in the right directions throughout graduate school. Grad school friends also played a tremendous role in shaping how I think about the issues examined in this book, and I am grateful to Jenn Blair, Pamela Butler (who remained a friend and beloved colleague for three years at Notre Dame), Jill Doerfler, Anne Martínez (who also belongs in the mentor category), Matt Martinez, David Monteyne, Soojin Pate, Mary Rizzo, Heidi Stark, Amy Tyson, and many others who shared ideas and fun throughout our grad school years. I also need to thank Colleen Hennen for so many favors and laughs throughout the years.

My training did not stop when I received my Ph.D. but has continued, thanks to the hard work of valued mentors who have continued to guide me through the process of establishing an academic career, especially Heidi Ardizzone, Laura Briggs, Nicole M. Guidotti-Hernández, José Limón, David Serlin, Deborah R. Vargas, and the many fine folks involved with the Tepoztlán Institute for the Transnational History of the Americas. Lynn Hudson and Jane Rhodes have shown me that the academic life can also be the good life. I thank them for their unending meals, laughs, and advice. I also thank George Lipsitz for reading and providing extensive feedback on Chapter Three. Members of my working group, namely, Amanda Ciafone, Dan Gilbert, Sarah Haley, Naomi Paik, and Shana Redmond, have offered friendship, inspiration, and critical but loving feedback. As my cofacilitators of the Newberry Seminar in Borderlands and Latino Studies, Gerry Cadava, John Alba Cutler, and Benjamin Johnson have also helped me conceptualize and articulate my ideas. Colleagues at Notre Dame, including my American Studies colleagues Annie Gilbert Coleman, Kathleen Sprows Cummings (and our beloved and life-saving "BC"), Erika Doss, Ben Giamo,

Bob Schmuhl, and Sophie White, as well as Laurie Arnold, Jolene Bilinski, Tobias Boes, Gil Cardenas, Cynthia Velazquez Duarte, Ken Garcia, Karen Graubart, Tim Matovina, John McGreevy, Richard Pierce, Yael Prizant, and Katie Schlotfeldt from across the College of Arts and Letters, have provided endless measures of support. At Notre Dame, I am also grateful to the Institute for Scholarship in the Liberal Arts and the Institute for Latino Studies for providing financial and intellectual support for this project. Kate Marshall at Notre Dame has been a friend, confidante, good neighbor, and camper all in one.

Research for this project was funded in part by the Department of American Studies and the MacArthur Program at the University of Minnesota, the Getty Research Library, the Autry National Center, the Latino Studies Fellowship Program at the National Museum of American History, the National Endowment for the Humanities, Macalaster College and the Consortium for Faculty Diversity, and the Ford Foundation. I thank the many generous committee members and administrators who have invested in my work, especially Agustín Fuentes, the staff of the NMAH, and the many anonymous readers. I also thank the staff of the University of Texas Press, especially Nancy Bryan; Leslie Tingle; and the fabulous, legendary Theresa May, as well as the anonymous readers who suggested revisions that greatly strengthened this book. Andrew Deliyannides, who carefully edited the nearly complete manuscript, helping transform flabby prose, along with my graduate assistants Felicia Moralez and Melissa Dinsman, who helped me to prepare it for submission to the Press, deserve special praise, as does Nancy Warrington, who copyedited this book for the University of Texas Press.

I am especially grateful to friends and family who have helped shape this book. My parents, Leon and Linda Ruiz, taught me the pleasure of travel early in life, showing me that a single tank of gas could lead to adventure. I thank them for that and just about everything else. I also thank my aunt Fran Hobson, cousin Heather Hobson, and grandmother Mary Lipka (born in 1918, near the end of the period examined in this book, and a treasure to our family), as well as the large and ever-growing Ruiz clan. My brother, Tom, and sister-in-law, Jackie Ruiz, have provided more assistance than I can ever pay back, especially when it comes to loving and supporting me through the process of completing this book. They also brought me the pure joy of knowing Marianna and Cassie Ruiz, my very favorite girls. As the best of friends, Mike Amezcua, Christian Bracho, Brandon Lacy Campos, Korey Garibaldi, Jonna

Kosalko, Vige Millington, Bethany Moritz, Jecca Namakkal, Sheela Namakkal, Ian Newman, Daniel Reid, Jill Trembczynski, Adam Waterman, and Crystal Whitlow have all earned my heartfelt gratitude.

My biggest thanks go to two people who have helped me grow as a scholar and as a person in the course of researching and writing this book. Sonjia Hyon has proven a steadfast friend and confidante, providing both the cheerleading and the academic *chisme* that has kept me going since we started graduate school together. And finally, Aaron Carico was a generous intellectual guide, devilishly clever editor, and true friend as I took this project from dissertation to book.

Because American travelers to Porfirian Mexico rarely spoke or wrote Spanish, they made frequent spelling and grammatical mistakes in representations of their journeys. To maintain the historical integrity of quoted material and to avoid frequent interruptions in this text, I do not correct original sources with diacritical marks or italics. In the same spirit, I also leave intact certain common mistranslations from Spanish and spellings that are no longer preferred in either Mexico or the United States. For example, most writers spelled Veracruz as two words, which I do not correct when citing historical references to the city or state of "Vera Cruz."

With a few exceptions, I use the term "American" to refer to citizens of the United States who lived, worked, and traveled in Mexico in the late nineteenth and early twentieth centuries. I do so reluctantly, since this term inadequately distinguishes U.S. citizens from other residents of the Americas and does not necessarily connote U.S. citizenship in other parts of the world (including in Mexico, where most people refer to us as *norteamericanos*). Even so, other possible terminology—such as "North American," "United Statesian," and "U.S. American"—prove too awkward or technical. Furthermore, U.S. citizens in Mexico universally referred to themselves simply as Americans. For these reasons, I stick with "American" to describe travelers, with quotation marks implied throughout this book.

Finally, I employ several terms to refer to Mexico's native population, but mostly settle on the term "Indian." While *indio*, its Spanish equivalent, is no longer the preferred term in Mexico, "Indian" is more or less the only historical term that American observers used to refer to Mexico's indigenous populations. I use the term "Indian" with implied quotation marks in the pages that follow but also want to stress that it is important to confront and challenge the lumping of a hugely diverse group of people under a single umbrella term. The government of Mexico currently recognizes sixty-two indigenous language families, speaking to the internal diversity within the term "Indian" that I grudgingly use in the pages that follow.

AMERICANS IN THE TREASURE HOUSE

KEEP CLOSE TO A KICKING HORSE

Mexico is a marvelous conglomerate of the ancient and the modern—the pathetic and the ludicrous.
J. HENDRICKSON MCCARTY, *TWO THOUSAND MILES THROUGH THE HEART OF MEXICO* (1888)

Mexico, in short, is the coming country.
MARIE ROBINSON WRIGHT, *PICTURESQUE MEXICO* (1897)

IN THE OCTOBER 1909 EDITION OF *The American Magazine,* muckraking American journalist John Kenneth Turner published the first in a series of scintillating articles detailing the oppressive practices of Porfirio Díaz, the dictator who had ruled Mexico with an iron fist and an eye toward foreign capital for more than thirty years. According to Turner, Díaz was not the great modernizer of Mexico, as American writers had been claiming for decades in hagiographic books and articles, but was in reality an anti-democratic tyrant who had fostered only the illusion of modernity in his country. Despite being dropped by the magazine that had commissioned them, Turner's articles scandalized and galvanized readers on both sides of the U.S.-Mexico border, helping to foment anti-Díaz activism in Mexico and to reshape perceptions of Díaz in the United States. Published together as *Barbarous Mexico,* these articles finally convinced many American readers that U.S. economic inroads in Mexico had come at a dangerously high cost—namely, through the backing of a ruthlessly oppressive regime. Even today, Turner's journalism stands out as a testament to the power of the press to shape popular opinion. But the manner in which Turner's articles began is almost as interesting as what they inspired. The first installment of the series, which boldly asserted that chattel slavery was alive and thriving in the Yucatán, began with a simple but provocative question: "What is Mexico?"[1] Americans had taken for granted for decades that Mexico under Díaz constituted a burgeoning and legible "sister republic" from which the United States might soon draw great profit, a nation—and a dictatorship—that every American should embrace. Upon their publication, Turner's articles forced them to rethink everything they thought they knew about their southern neighbor.

It is by now a tourist brochure cliché to answer Turner's question by deducing that Mexico is a "land of contrasts," but Americans have always seen their southern neighbor as a place where contradictions collide with one another. As one traveler put it a few years before Turner went to Mexico, "In some respects Mexico is highly civilized, but in others it remains utterly barbaric. Truly a land of paradox. It is most interesting, always picturesque, sometimes blood-curdling, and often sad."[2] This traveler's inability to describe Mexico without using contradictory terms typifies how Americans have seen that nation from the Porfiriato (the term that refers to the long reign of Díaz, 1876–1911) to the present.[3] Mexico is certainly easy enough for just about any American to identify on a map, but its location in the popular imagination of the United States is a far more complicated matter; the country is familiar and alien, close but inaccessible, desirable and ruined. In the words of one primer for American schoolchildren published in 1902, Mexico is one of the "strange lands near home."[4]

Just as it was for Turner, who journeyed throughout the country in an attempt to reveal what Mexico really was, travel is one of the most important practices through which foreigners attempt to define Mexico.[5] Travel brings the traveler face-to-face with difference, but it also creates sites of knowledge that linger long after the journey is over, whether in the form of a diary, a snapshot, a postcard sent home or tucked into a guidebook, a memory, a rumor, or a way of thinking and talking about a place. In this sense, travel is not just a personal act but is, in fact, an ideology. In other words, travel is a practice with tremendous power to create and shape knowledge formations across cultural, racial, ethnic, and national boundaries. So it is to travelers' accounts that I turn in this book. *Americans in the Treasure House* examines a wide array of travel discourse associated with Porfirian Mexico, focusing chiefly on the interplay between representations of travel and the politics of U.S. imperialism. It treats travel as, to borrow Mary Louise Pratt's term, a "contact zone," a social and discursive space "where disparate cultures meet, clash, and grapple with each other, often in highly asymmetrical relations of domination and subordination," and travelers as the cultural workers who construct and reinforce those asymmetrical relations.[6] Whether they went as journalists, venture capitalists, photographers, or pleasure seekers, travelers imagined Mexico as a nation in a state of intense flux, constantly striving to live up to the Porfirian motto of "order and progress" but also thwarted by a profound sense of backwardness. The Mexico that appeared in travelers' representations *required* intervention at a historical moment when the United States was ready to expand its territory and influence. Their Mexico allured because it represented a source of cheap labor and natural resources, a growth market, and a pleasure zone; it was a nation whose leaders were looking for development just when business and political forces were looking to expand beyond the borders of the United States. In the process of imagining and representing this Mexico, travelers exposed their desires to reshape that nation in their own image—and their expectations that they would profit from Mexico's tremendous potential. This book does not provide a straightforward history of their travel; instead, it asks how travel discourse, deeply bound to racialized and sexualized accounts of Mexican bodies, functioned as a site of knowledge production and empire. Ranging from travelogues and literary representations to picture postcards and snapshots, the sources analyzed in this book tell a critical but overlooked part of the story of U.S.-Mexican cultural relations.[7]

I have limited this study to the Porfiriato (and, in the final chapter, its aftermath) in part because it coincided with a period of massive investment of U.S. capital in Mexico. American firms, from small-scale operations to some of the most powerful and profitable in the nation, had more than $1 billion invested in Mexico by the time Díaz finally abdicated his office in 1911. Turner claimed that the "partnership of Diaz and American capital [had] wrecked Mexico as a national entity" by the start of the Revolution, the culprits being both the president and the foreign investors who had, over the years, staged a friendly takeover of the Mexican economy and now wielded undo influence beyond the border. "While Wall Street has more or less conflicting interests in the looting of the United States," Turner claimed, "Wall Street is ONE when it comes to the looting of Mexico."[8] As David Pletcher put it in the 1950s, "by 1911 Mexico was truly an economic satellite of the United States."[9] More recently, Chicano scholar Gilbert G. González has referred to this massive investment and the cultural forms that it inspired as the "economic conquest" of Mexico, a process whereby Díaz ceded the sovereignty of his nation in order to modernize it. González contends that during this period "the United States launched a concerted effort to economically dominate Mexico and subordinate that nation to the corporate interests of the United States," an effort that was debated in the U.S. public sphere.[10] In contrast to Hawaii and the territories formally given over in the wake of the Spanish-American War, "Mexico rose to prominence in U.S. foreign policy not as an annexed territory, but as an economically conquered territory, an example of imperial relations of a new type."[11] Following González, I contend that this economic conquest was inextricably linked to the cultures of U.S. imperialism that also coincided with the Porfiriato. Unlike González, however, I emphasize that travelers did the cultural work of justifying and popularizing economic conquest as a lucrative and worthwhile project for the American public. In this sense, I pay close attention to travelers as the instigators of a large-scale act of seduction. Furthermore, I turn to discourses of race, gender, and sexuality that were interwoven with imperialist practices in Mexico. I will show, for example, that American anxieties about the inabilities of native Mexicans to assimilate into capitalist modernity reflected concerns that Indians could not conform to American ideals regarding health, labor, family size, monogamy, and gender differentiation.

This book is indebted to a generation or so of scholarly works that explore the cultures of U.S. imperialism that emerged in the late nineteenth century, notably those works by Amy Kaplan, Laura Briggs, Ann Laura Stoler, Eric Love, Laura Wexler, and Vicente Rafael. These scholars, along with the many others whose work helped to instigate and advance the "transnational turn" in American studies and related fields, demonstrate that American empire building was never simply a militaristic or political endeavor in places like Hawaii, Cuba, Puerto Rico, and the Philippines; rather, U.S. imperialism depended on a domestic popular culture keenly aware of and interested in the expansion of American power.[12] But this book also asserts that Mexico, a nation omitted from most considerations of American empire building at the end of the nineteenth century, remained an important object of the imperialist fascination long after the Treaty of Guadalupe Hidalgo. Although historians consider American aggression against Mexico in the 1840s a foundational moment in the history of U.S. empire, the accepted historiography of U.S. imperialism tends to shift away from Mexico following the Treaty of Guadalupe Hidalgo (1848) and the Gadsden Purchase

(1853–1854). Following works by González and Shelley Streeby, who has explored the discursive production of Mexico and Mexicanness in the American imagination of the mid-nineteenth century, *Americans in the Treasure House* inserts Mexico into the ongoing scholarly debate about American empire, arguing that the United States revised but did not abandon its expansionist tactics decades after the Mexican-American War. This story, like many in Mexico's history, begins with a foreign invasion.

THE AMERICAN INVASION

The completion of the Mexican Central Railway in 1884 marked a dramatic shift in social and economic relations between the United States and Mexico, which had been strained in the decades following the Mexican-American War. Now, for the first time, Americans of middle-class means could board Pullman cars in such distant cities as Chicago, New York, or Washington, D.C., and disembark thousands of miles later in the heart of Mexico City. Many Americans speculated that this new accessibility would heal the long-standing rift between the two nations.[13] Mexico had suffered tremendously in the war and ceded some 530,000 square miles (more than half of its territory) to the United States for a mere $15 million under the Treaty of Guadalupe Hidalgo. Two decades later, the U.S. government had been reluctant to recognize Díaz, who, in 1876, had seized office in a coup against Sebastián Lerdo de Tejada, as the rightful president. For these reasons and more, resistance to the "colossus of the north" was still a source of pride in Mexico. But the completion of the Mexican Central, which linked El Paso, Texas, with Mexico City, was supposed to change this sentiment.

Prior to 1884, a trip to Mexico was too arduous for most Americans to undertake, so very few had been south of the border.[14] What is more, their popular culture constructed that nation as a dangerous backwater, very close to the United States but quite alien.[15] In dime novels, melodramas, and other popular forms, Mexico was most closely associated with lawlessness and brigandage.[16] *Life in Mexico during a Residence of Two Years in That Country*, an epistolary memoir by an Anglo-American diplomat's wife who lived in Mexico in the late 1830s and early 1840s, was widely read in the United States throughout the mid-nineteenth century (and remains a classic in travel writing), but its author's impressions of Mexican high society did little to disabuse its readers of the notion that Mexico was a beautiful but ultimately primitive country. This remained the general view of Mexico for decades. However, starting in 1884, a flood of words and pictures began to appear in American popular culture that depicted Mexico as a struggling but viable "sister republic" to the United States, one that might be cultivated through increased commercial and cultural influence from its northern neighbor. Instead of focusing solely on backward peons and ruthless *bandidos*, travel discourse now also included the markers of modernity: telegraph lines, paved roads, opulent new buildings in the capital and other major cities, and a population capable of capitalist discipline.

The railroads, perhaps the ultimate symbol of modernity, served as the impetus for these shifts in perceptions and representational practices. Besides actually bringing Americans to Mexico, the rail companies actively worked to shape popular opinion by producing an abundance of photographs, brochures, travel guides, and souvenirs—all of which they distributed to travelers for free as an attempt to undo Mexico's image problem. American rail companies had much at stake in promoting rail travel, since these American firms owned Mexico's ever-expanding railways; the Mexican Central was, in fact, a subsidiary of the Santa Fe Railroad. By 1896, American stockholders owned 80 percent of Mexico's railroad stocks and bonds.[17]

The executives of the Mexican Central used a variety of methods to reframe Mexico as a desirable destination for the American pleasure travelers. In 1883–1884, for example, the company commissioned well-known American photographer William Henry Jackson, the "picture maker of the old west," to document the route. Over the course of two trips on the Mexican Central, Jackson made more than five hundred images that showed potential tourists the visual wonders that awaited them south of the border, from quaint villages and exotic but docile natives to the engineering marvels that were the rail lines. He was the first of many North American travelers who would record this period of Mexico's railroad era and profit from the intense popular interest in this newly accessible nation. Around the same time, the company hired a writer named James W. Steele to promote its service between El Paso and Mexico City. "Mexico," Steele wrote, "save to the very few, has until recently been an almost unknown country. . . . [But] the republic is now open for the entrance of whomsoever will, and her chiefest cities are connected by a continuous line with the entire railway system of the United States."[18] In *To Mexico by Palace Car*, Steele grandly claimed that the coming of the railroad to Mexico was unquestionably the greatest event, save one, in the stormy and sombre [sic] history of our sister state, and to Americans themselves is of only secondary importance. Fenced by impassable barriers for some three hundred years, this rich, old, quaint, and isolated empire has suddenly become the country of the capitalist and the tourist; a land in which, by the invitation of its people, we have already begun an endless series of beneficent and bloodless conquests.[19]

Through Steele's words, the company promoted Mexico as a country that was full of resources and welcoming to the capitalist and the tourist alike. What is more, Steele, like many of his compatriots, constructs the Mexicans as grateful for the presence of Americans, whose "beneficent and bloodless conquest" would help modernize the nation. Steele's use of the term "conquest" in a company-sponsored travelogue speaks to the fact that the company and its audience understood the push of capitalists and tourists into Mexico as a driving force in the eco nomic conquest of Mexico. Although subsequent materials produced by the Mexican Central were less blunt than Steele's travelogue, the company continued to promote Mexican travel for decades. By 1890, the company began producing pamphlets that touted Mexico as the "Egypt of the New World," and in 1893 widely disseminated an almost three-hundred-page travelogue titled *Mexico?: Sí, Señor* to promote its routes to tourists.[20]

Over time, the American public grew accustomed to having Mexico marketed by the rail companies in this way. Responding in part to the flood of brochures and booklets that appeared on the American scene each winter, thousands of Americans began to take advantage of the international lines, arriving en masse to a winter destination that now rivaled Florida in sunshine and accessibility. Unlike Florida, however, Mexico seemed exotic to those unused to foreign travel. As W. E. Carson put it in 1910, "To most of these people Mexico must certainly seem a land of wonders; they have never been to Europe and for the first time they see old churches, cathedrals, and ruins, and mingle among people who have a different language and strange customs."[21] Delighted with a country that was nearby but exotic—a "land of wonders," the tourist had arrived in Mexico. Observers on both sides of the border wryly referred to the touring hordes that descended upon that nation each year as a "foreign invasion."

Countless photographs document this invasion. One arresting example captures the desire among tourists to see and understand Mexico,

FIGURE I.1. Couple with camera. Nettie Lee Benson Latin American Collection, University of Texas Libraries, University of Texas at Austin.

to answer the question "What is Mexico?" for themselves. Placed in a scrapbook by an American mining engineer named Chase Littlejohn, it depicts a middle-aged white man and woman pausing to have their photographs taken on a rutted street (Figure I.1). They wear typical Victorian summer garb, she in a crisp white dress. Overhead telegraph lines almost seem to emanate from their parasol. The man and woman, in turn, are in the process of making their own photograph, one of a small Indian boy who, like the foreigners he faces, pauses to have his picture taken. Standing at the extreme right of the frame, the boy wears an expression of amused patience, as if he is used to having strange-looking foreigners request to take his photograph. While there exist more overtly provocative photographs depicting tourists in Porfirian Mexico, this photograph stands out in my mind as a symbol of Americans' fascination with photographing Mexico in the late nineteenth and early twentieth centuries. Tourists and longer-term travelers took many thousands of photographs throughout the Porfiriato, creating an extensive record of what Americans found interesting in Mexico. As this particular photograph suggests, Mexican people, especially natives and children, occupied a prime position in the visual spectacle that the country provided. Rail travel fostered encounters with people who, as we will see in the pages that follow, often became *objects* of fascination.

This photograph's meaning is deepened by how it appeared in Chase

Littlejohn's photo album. It is sandwiched between photographs depicting a windowless hut made of sticks and grasses (above) and the tidy clapboard buildings of an American firm (below), both probably near where the encounter in the middle takes place. The hut is loosely constructed and appears to consist of just one small room, typical of the *tierra caliente*. In contrast, the freshly whitewashed American buildings boast crisp striped awnings to protect from the tropical sun, shingled roofs, and gutters for the rainy season. Telegraph wires, a rich symbol of the modern age at the time, connect these buildings to the outside world—a crucial factor for Americans living in hot, remote territories such as this. Their placement gives the photographs a sense of narrative. As in most descriptions of travel mentioned in this book, this narrative connotes the civilizing mission that travelers brought with them to Porfirian Mexico. In this case, the hut and the American buildings function as symbols of what Mexico might look like before and after its economic transformation.

Tourists were not the only "invaders" carried into Mexico by the railroads. Pullman cars also transported Americans looking for longer-term opportunities—including a sizable number of American workers and speculators in the mining, petroleum, agricultural, and rubber industries—who went not to discover the pleasures of that country but to draw profits from its newly opened resources.[22] Pletcher argued in the 1950s that the Porfirian development scheme relied partly on American promoters, who served as boosters for the regime and who recruited American workers with the intent of transforming Mexico through American capitalism.[23] Promoters, in turn, relied on the railroads and sometimes heavily invested in them or even ran them.[24] One rail executive named Epes Randolph wrote in the *Los Angeles Times*, a newspaper that frequently dedicated space on its pages to promoters, that the "steel rails of [his] great highway will bring to the very threshold of Los Angeles a fair and fruitful land heretofore isolated, and will develop an immense volume of business in a new field for your merchants and businessmen, if they will but stretch to grab it."[25] Most famously, Ulysses S. Grant, who had served among the occupying forces during the Mexican-American War, was named the president of the ill-fated Mexican Southern Railway in 1881. From everyday Americans who published their letters in the newspapers back home to prominent citizens like Grant, promoters performed the important work of framing Mexico as a logical place for capitalist expansion.

As it was with tourists, it looked to some as if Porfirian Mexico was teeming with promoters and speculators. As early as 1883, a traveler described the Hotel Iturbide in Mexico City as being crowded with "projectors," all seeking their fortunes south of the border.[26] In the decades that followed, travel writers constantly noted their encounters with a diverse array of working men and fortune seekers just about everywhere that rail lines had been laid.[27] A geologist named N. H. Darton described the influx of capital and profit-seekers in Mexico in a 1907 edition of *National Geographic*:

> Foreign capital has flowed into the Republic, especially in later years, and many investors, confident of a continuance of the present stable conditions, are eagerly taking advantage of the many mining, railroading, manufacturing, and other openings which are available. Colonists are coming slowly, but as the conditions become better known they will undoubtedly take advantage of the large areas of public lands that are easily obtainable and in many regions can be utilized with great profit.[28]

Darton's words capture the sense that the economic conquest of Mexico depended on the spread of information about that country and, more specifically, the discursive construction of Mexico as an exploitable field for capitalist expansion. American "colonists" could remake Mexico, as they had done in the western United States, but first they had to see and understand the many opportunities that it offered. Tellingly, Darton's article is titled "Mexico—the Treasure House of the World," an allusion to those opportunities.

Other kinds of American entrepreneurs also resettled south of the border. Historian John Mason Hart notes that by 1902 there were more than eleven hundred American-owned small businesses operating in the country, in addition to the mines, farms, and ranches operated by U.S. citizens.[29] These were not large-scale industrial operations or attempts to develop the nation's mineral resources but small-scale businesses such as photography studios, shops, and tour companies. Most catered to Americans and other tourists passing through Mexico City. D. S. Spaulding, who operated a successful handicraft shop in the capital, was among them, as was Philip Terry, who owned the Sonora News Company, one of the most successful purveyors of curios, antiques, and souvenirs in the capital. Terry also wrote the famous guidebook *Terry's Guide to Mexico*, which went through several editions in the early twentieth century.[30] In 1903, also in the capital, two brothers from

California founded Sanborns, a pharmacy and soda fountain catering to tourists. Today it is the ubiquitous restaurant, pharmacy, and department store chain controlled by Carlos Slim, the richest man in the world. The presence of these small- to medium-scale businesses indicates that some who took part in the American invasion facilitated by the railroads stayed to set up shop and put down roots in Porfirian Mexico.

The Mexican body politic, however, was not immediately content with its newfound accessibility or the gestures of friendship from its northern neighbors, no doubt in part because the military invasion and occupation was so recent in Mexican memory. Marie Robinson Wright, a native of Georgia who made several trips to Mexico, Central America, and South America during the Porfiriato and proved herself to be an indefatigable Díaz supporter in her published travelogues, made it clear that many Mexicans viewed the international rail line with suspicion. "When the first international railway was projected," one of her travelogues claimed, "alarm and apprehension were felt throughout the country. It was thought that the Americans were about to penetrate into the country through that opening, into which Uncle Sam would insert the thin end of the wedge that was to split Mexico from top to bottom."[31] As Wright described it, the railroad was doubly symbolic; it represented both an opportunity and, for Mexicans, a threat. Her prose also implies the sexual undertones of conquest, in which one country becomes a body with the ability to "penetrate" another until the penetrated country splits "from top to bottom." Certainly this was a woman who understood the politics and perils of economic conquest. Nevertheless, despite this loaded language, Wright assured her readers that "a few years have proved to the contrary, and shown that Mexico is strong enough to stand alone."[32]

Wright was not alone in glossing over the fact that some Mexicans did not look kindly upon the influx of American visitors. Many travel writers—even the ones who, like Wright, acknowledged that some Mexicans wondered if the influx of American bodies and capital threatened their national sovereignty—joined her in claiming that Mexicans gratefully welcomed American "colonists." One 1902 article from the Los Angeles Times, which focused on the mining opportunities of "Wealthful Sinaloa," claimed that "all she needs is American enterprise and capital to make Sinaloa the paradise of the rancher and the mecca of the miner; and recognizing this fact, her people welcome the arrival of every American of character and integrity."[33] With representations such as this one so common in travel discourse of the period, it is not surprising that many Americans imagined themselves in self-congratulatory terms and expected a hero's welcome while traveling abroad.

Travelers were right, however, in noting that Mexico was increasingly open to foreign investment. This was, in fact, a key tenet of the Porfirian regime's plan to develop the nation. But the question of what that meant for both Mexicans and Americans remained up for debate. In an 1888 travelogue titled *Mexico: Our Neighbor*, John H. Rice suggested that Díaz had made a devil's bargain by opening his nation's economy to American influence. Díaz, he wrote, "wisely foresaw that the sure paths of safety and progress were those leading through enlarged business and social relations with their northern neighbor. There is wisdom in the old adage, 'keep close to a kicking horse.'"[34] Rice explicitly connected the present economic push to the rather unneighborly actions of the 1840s:

> Every intelligent Mexican has very accurate knowledge of our government and people and just appreciation of our resources and power. . . . This, added to recollections of the past, quite naturally engenders apprehensions of further aggressions by our government, and so nourishes and fosters feelings of antagonism.[35]

As in Wright's depiction of Mexican anxieties regarding the international rail lines, Rice suggests that Mexicans had every reason to fear their northern neighbor. Rice, for one, is impressed that his nation had engendered such feelings.

Mexicans were not the only ones who experienced mixed feelings about the expansion of U.S. capitalism into Mexico. Rice's book reveals a deep ambivalence about the meanings and ends of economic conquest. The tone of *Mexico: Our Neighbor* was, on its surface, anti-imperialist. Rice claimed, for example, that one of Mexico's "principal dangers" was its proximity to the United States, and that "neighboring nationalities and peoples may reasonably view with apprehension and distrust our great and rapidly growing resources and power."[36] Later, he explicitly addressed the question of territorial expansionism by firmly advocating that Mexico's "present boundaries should be absolutely assured against danger from us."[37] However, despite his argument that Mexican sovereignty should be protected in the face of expanding U.S. power, Rice joined scores of other Americans by portraying the eco-

nomic conquest in heroic terms. He reveled, for example, in Díaz's liberal policies that opened the nation for foreign investments (a hallmark
of *porfirismo*) and what he saw as the civilizing effect of U.S.-style capitalism. These policies, he wrote, resulted in "investments amounting to
. . . uncounted millions of American capital in [railroads and] other industries there; all following these great pioneers of civilization, development, and progress."[38] Rice was among the countless Americans who
saw capitalist expansionism rather than annexation or other modes of
formal empire building as America's imperial future, and who couched
this ethos within the intertwined discourses of "civilization, development, and progress."

Other travelers expressed similar misgivings about the American
presence in Mexico but also nonetheless saw opportunities for expansionism. More than two decades after the publication of Rice's travelogue, Protestant minister James G. Dale, who hoped to win souls
rather than dollars, described the push of American fortune seekers
into Mexico:

> The influx of Americans into the country has been enormous. Fully
> 50,000 are scattered over the country. Capitalists have come, investing
> $800,000,000. As a rule, these have set their heart on gold and silver
> mines, rubber plantations, orange groves, bales of henequen, grazing
> lands for cattle, and to reach their goal, they seem willing to trample
> under foot all those high virtues of America's best manhood.[39]

Dale saw the presence of Americans as an impediment to his missionary work, describing the majority of Americans in the country (including the tourists) as criminals and thrill seekers who "follow tricks of
the trade that would bring the blush of shame to every true American."[40] Still, despite this critique of American greed in Mexico, Dale's
book argues for the expansion of American Protestantism. *Mexico and
Our Mission* points to the civilizing effects of Protestant conversion on
native Mexicans and calls for a greater push of missionaries to counter
what he saw as Catholicism's deadening effects on the Mexican population. Like other travelers, Dale understood that the fifty thousand
Americans who had settled permanently or semipermanently throughout Mexico were in the process of transforming the nation, whether
they went for riches or souls. Mexico no longer appeared to be solely
in the hands of the Mexicans; neither were the nation's rich and varied
natural resources.

NATURAL RESOURCES

The period from the late 1880s through the first decade of the 1900s saw a spate of books and articles aimed specifically at potential investors who might take advantage of the rail lines and the opening of business relations between the two republics. A small but dedicated genre of travel books appeared on the American scene with such tantalizing titles as *The Riches of Mexico and Its Institutions* and *Mexico: Its Progress and Commercial Possibilities*, works designed to entice investment and economic growth south of the border.[41] While they lacked the romance that permeated so many travelogues of the day, these books provided practical information for those Americans interested in exploiting Mexico's splendiferous natural resources. Many included information on the Mexican legal system, directories of prominent businessmen (Mexican and foreign), and ads for commercial machinery ranging from portable ovens to cotton gins, making them comprehensive guides for those interested in conducting business south of the border. One book in this genre put it succinctly in stating that "a thorough acquaintance with Mexico and its people is what the businessman wants."[42] Indeed, following the mass arrival of Americans via the international rail lines, it seemed that just about everyone wanted to know how they might draw profit from "the world's treasure house."

As such, natural resources became one of the dominant tropes found in American travel discourse associated with Porfirian Mexico. This emphasis started several decades prior to the Porfiriato, with the publication of Alexander von Humboldt's famous descriptions of New Spain just prior to Mexican independence, but accelerated following Díaz's rise to power, as this president grew increasingly eager to develop his nation's resources and the United States became increasingly interested in expanding its economy beyond its political boundaries. Depictions of the nation's mines, fruits, fields, plantations, and fauna appeared in a wide array of forms, from the books devoted exclusively to them to picture postcards, travelogues, snapshots, and magazine articles, all of which presented Mexico as a fecund and prolific field for investment, a place from which a profit could be drawn with very little effort. Unlike Mexican people, whom travelers treated with a marked ambivalence, abundant, untapped natural resources provided a straightforward rationale for economic conquest.

This fixation on natural resources helped to construct Mexico as a logical extension of the American frontier. According to the logic of the day, espoused most influentially by Frederick Jackson Turner at the World's Columbian Exposition in Chicago in 1893, American exceptionalism was defined by the so-called winning of the West, specifically by the ability of white Americans to create order and profit from an untamed western wilderness. This was the historical process that was supposed to have made America great throughout the better part of the nineteenth century but that was lamentably (for Turner) coming to a close by the end of the century. To many who similarly mourned the closure of the frontier, Mexico presented an opportunity. "There no longer being any 'Great West' to which trade and travel may flow," claimed one 1887 travelogue, "it is believed that our country of the future lies in the South,—the greater south,—in Mexico, Central and South America."[43] In other words, Mexico was the future of the United States, it was "the coming country." By opening up Mexico, both countries would benefit, but in different ways. "Mexico is in need today," Marie Robinson Wright wrote, "of many of the things which people in the United States have already wrested from the hand of nature, while the restless spirit of the American is equally in need of the sphere of mental activity which many of the partially developed resources of Mexico offer."[44] For Wright and many other Americans who wrote about Porfirian Mexico, economic conquest presented a way to keep the frontier alive and to exercise the "restless spirit of the American."

Whereas Wright championed economic conquest for its salubrious effect on the American spirit, others claimed that the unprogressive nature of the Mexican national character demanded intervention from a more advanced race or nation. One 1883 *Los Angeles Times* article, published just before the advent of the international rail line and typical of how writers linked natural resources to national character, claimed that Mexicans were

> a contented, pleasure-loving, easy-going people who delight in music, and dancing and shows, and whose love of pleasure and ease shall yet prove the means of dispossessing their race of the rich territories it holds in such easy hand, whose hidden riches have waited for centuries for the aggressive force of the Anglo-Saxon.[45]

According to the article, Mexico is indeed a treasure house, but one lying dormant under such faulty stewards of natural resources as the Mexicans. This racialized view of natural resources suggests that economic conquest is the inevitable result of a well-endowed but complacent population residing next to the "aggressive force" of white America. Simply put, the nation's natural resources were too valuable to entrust to the Mexicans—and too tempting for the Americans to resist.

The intense focus on natural resources and the idea that it was the destiny of white Americans to profit from them was not limited to published materials. Scores of American tourists and "colonists" assembled scrapbooks illustrated with snapshots documenting the astounding resources found in Mexico and the lifestyles afforded to foreigners there.[46] Americans in Mexico took the time to make snapshots of mineral and agricultural resources and paste them into their scrapbooks or send them to the folks at home. At times, these materials took on strange appearances. Take, for example, the photographic montages created by the maker of a scrapbook detailing the lives of American workers in Mexico in the first two decades of the twentieth century. This book, the property of a man named W. Lincoln Wilson, combined published prints with snapshots, lovingly cut and pasted together. One image superimposes a photograph of a white woman in crisp white riding clothes onto a photograph of indigenous men, women, and children who work as coffee pickers assembled in a sorting house for the beans. As a result of this cut-and-paste work, it appears that the white woman oversees the Indian labor, standing in a place of privilege and power over the locals. In another image, photographs of a white woman and three healthily plump white babies are pasted into a backdrop that features a mélange of strawberries, coffee, melons, bananas, mangoes, and other tropical fruits (Figure I.2). This image captivates because it speaks to the fascination with Mexico's natural bounty and to how American "colonists" might gain from conquest of Mexican resources. Intentional or not, the juxtaposition of the woman and the babies with fruit implies something about reproductivity.[47] Whereas many Americans looked at Indian fertility in Mexico with deep suspicion throughout the Porfiriato (a trope examined in Chapter Three of this book), some white settlers there celebrated their own fecundity. Settlers and travelers alike celebrated Mexico as a fertile territory, rife with possibilities and ripe for exploitation. As this image suggests, the good life was waiting for Americans who had the wherewithal to tap its amazing resources. In other words, with access to land and resources facing increased competition in the United States, Mexico became a place to find the American Dream.

Although the mechanics of rail travel and the extraction of natural resources provide a logical starting place for this book—and could in-

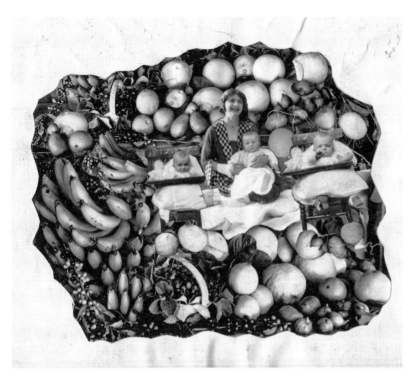

FIGURE I.2. Montage of woman, babies, and fruits. W. Lincoln Wilson Photographic Album, Center for Southwest Research, University of New Mexico.

spire studies of their own—the chapters that follow focus instead on how travel discourse constructed the promises and perils of expanding capitalist modernity in Mexico.[48] I turn in these chapters to a diverse set of themes that dominated in these representations of travel, including the desire to see Mexico through photographic media, descriptions of Porfirio Díaz as a "logical patriarch" for a modernizing state, the so-called problem that Indian difference posed for economic conquest and the construction of the mestizo body politic as its solution, and the city of Veracruz as a symbol of the excesses of the Mexican Revolution and an inspiration for what I call "Porfirian nostalgia" in the years following Díaz's fall. There was never a single cohesive view of Mexico in the late nineteenth or early twentieth century, but the case studies that follow expose many of the dominant modes of representation that constructed that nation as an object of imperialist desire. These chapters illuminate some of the countless ways in which Americans have responded to the question "What is Mexico?" and incited many others of their own.

CHAPTER 1

DESIRE AMONG THE RUINS: CONSTRUCTING
MEXICO IN AMERICAN TRAVEL DISCOURSE

". . . photographs alter and enlarge our notions of what is worth looking at and what we have the right to observe."
SUSAN SONTAG, *ON PHOTOGRAPHY*

IN JANUARY OF 1911, an American named Frank Hamilton dropped into the mail a letter accompanied by a photograph featuring the ruins of Mitla in the state of Oaxaca. This complex of ruins, as the sender might have known, was the most important religious site in ancient Zapotec culture and a well-known symbol of Mexico's pre-Hispanic heritage by the turn of the twentieth century. Famous Mexican archaeologist and ethnologist Leopoldo Batres created a sensation in 1901 and 1902 when he uncovered and restored many important buildings at the site. Photographers scrambled to capture its splendors, including intricate friezes, rare mosaics, and the Salón de las Columnas, the beautiful remains of the antechamber of the main temple at the site. An easy day trip from the colonial city of Oaxaca, Mitla was an important destination for American tourists who ventured into Southern Mexico. Although remote, its architectural wonders and seclusion from the crowds that gathered around similar sites in Central Mexico richly rewarded those who ventured there.

Hamilton's photograph features a barefoot Zapotec girl, wearing a rebozo and simple white shift, standing against one of the massive monoliths in the Salón de las Columnas (Figure 1.1). The girl's face is barely discernible in the deep shadows created by the position of the sun. This glare and the girl's distance from the camera make it difficult to guess her age, but she looks about ten or twelve years old. This picture is unremarkable except for two facts. First, Hamilton sent the letter and photograph to none other than Porfirio Díaz, writing to him in

Foto 66. "Mitla."

FIGURE 1.1. Photograph of a young girl in the Salón de las Columnas, Mitla. Photo by C. B. Waite. Archive of the Centro de Estudios de Historia de México, Mexico City.

English. Hamilton's relationship to the president is unclear, but the act of a private citizen initiating personal contact with the president underscores the image of Díaz as an approachable dictator, friendly both to U.S. capital and to individuals from the United States who presented themselves as allies to the modernization of the nation (a topic that is explored at length in Chapter Two). Whether Díaz ever saw Hamilton's letter is not part of the historical record, but it is held at a Mexican archive.[1]

Second, on the back of the photograph, Hamilton wrote a rather surprising message:

Dear Sir,
I have a very serious question and a favour to ask of you hoping that you will oblige me the same. I would like you very much to find out where this young lady is. If she can't be found look for one that [looks] like her as I love her dearly and wish to communicate with her. My one hope and wish is that she is from a poor family. Thanking you very much with my best wishes and sincere thanks.
    Frank Hamilton[2]

While the details of Hamilton's life and broader interest in Mexico are unknown, his brief note serves as a fascinating and insightful shred of evidence regarding Porfirian Mexico's place within the popular imagination of the United States, one that might be read as a metaphor for American views of Porfirian Mexico under the conditions of economic conquest. To begin with, Hamilton's interest in this girl connects desirability with poverty ("My one hope and wish is that she is from a poor family"), a trope at play again and again in colonialist and neocolonialist representations of conquerable nations and peoples. To desire an impoverished, conquered person reinforced the broader politics of domination. However, despite Hamilton's profession of love, girls like the one pictured here seem to have been interchangeable to him. Any impoverished native Mexican could inspire in Hamilton the complex forms of desire that are at play in his short note to President Díaz.

As this chapter will show, Hamilton's view of the girl at Mitla, however shocking to the contemporary reader, is consistent with dominant representational patterns established by photographers and other creators of travel discourse throughout the Porfiriato. Mexico dazzled, but its appeal depended in part on its poverty. Its beauty was ubiquitous but also elusive. Mexico was veiled but knowable. Its living Indians, positioned among ancient ruins, served as a primary site of contact that showed Americans how to look at—and how to desire—Mexico. This chapter asks how photographic and other representational practices like the ones observable in this photograph shaped American perceptions of Porfirian Mexico, especially in relation to the growing sense shared by many citizens of the United States that their nation should extend its economic and political influence south of the border. To get at this question of representation and popular perceptions of Mexico, I examine a diverse set of visual forms developed by American photographers and cultural workers during the Porfiriato, including postcards, illustrated magazine articles, and travelogues. Taken together, these texts animate Hamilton's desires for Mexico and demonstrate that Mexico's place in the popular imagination of the United States during the late nineteenth and early twentieth centuries was inextricably linked to America's growth as an imperial power.

C. B. WAITE'S MEXICO

The image that Hamilton found so compelling was captured by American photographer Charles Burlingame (C. B.) Waite, who toured Mitla in 1901, taking pictures of women, ruins, and his fellow tourists in equal measure. The trip generated hundreds of images, some published in *El Mundo Ilustrado* and some sold to tourists as souvenirs. C. B. Waite was born in Akron, Ohio, in 1861. After working as a photographer in California, he moved to Mexico, along with his wife and children, in search of inspiration and opportunity in the 1890s.[3] In doing so, Waite found himself among the countless developers and promoters who went south of the border seeking new opportunities and markets during the Porfiriato. As Francisco Montellano puts it, his life "corresponds with that of adventurers, brave explorers with romantic spirits and materialist outlooks, who toured the hitherto unknown world, discovering their riches and inventing paradises."[4] Indeed, Waite found much in common with the adventurers and prospectors who flocked to Mexico (and sometimes purchased his postcards), for he spent a good part of his career speculating in Mexico's growing rubber industry. He also achieved a certain degree of respect in Porfirian society, evidenced by the fact that he photographed official state visits like those of U.S. Secretary of State Elihu Root in 1907. As a well-known photographer who was deeply embedded in Porfirian society, Waite was uniquely positioned to provide a closer view of the world that Americans traveling through and living in Porfirian Mexico created for themselves.

At the time, photography was still an almost exclusively commercial endeavor in Mexico, one that represented a growth industry for an enterprising young man like Waite, who approached it with great energy and an eye toward profit. Unsatisfied with the limitations of the studio, Waite sometimes transported his heavy equipment through Mexico's rugged terrain to places his studio-based peers would not have dared to venture. One photograph from his trip to Mitla shows that his equipment was dragged to the ruins on an oxcart.[5] Waite fearlessly tackled subject matter that was difficult to photograph at the time, from the *tierras calientes*, where plates spoiled quickly, to the iconic Popocatépetl, where he made a particularly lovely photograph of some native men sledding down a snow bank.[6] Instead of dragging vendors and other "street types" into the studio, as many of his predecessors had done, Waite went outside and attempted to capture Mexican subjects in more natural surroundings. Judging from his photographs of traveling writers, ethnographers, and botanists, Waite was also a tireless host to visiting foreigners.

Not long after he arrived in Mexico, Waite's images became ubiquitous on both sides of the border. His photos of ruins, to name just one common motif, illustrated popular Mexican magazines like *El Mundo Ilustrado* and sold at the National Museum, where the nation's most precious artifacts, such as the Aztec Calendar Stone, were then on display. His views of Mexico were so generally likable that they found audiences among the *porfirista* press and tourists alike. He displayed and sold pictures at the "Streets of Mexico" display at the 1901 Pan-American Exposition in Buffalo and turned his photos into lantern slides that illustrated professional globetrotters' lectures throughout the United States. For decades, writers relied on his photographs of popular tourist sites, railroad lines, Mexican "types," and the other stock motifs associated with travel to Mexico. Few of these writers credited the photographer, but his handwritten captions and crisp, straightforward style frequently marked the illustrations in travelogues and other printed matter as his work.

While Waite does not qualify as a "traveler" per se, since he established himself in the capital for more than a decade, his work contributed significantly to the touristic gaze that framed Porfirian Mexico in the popular imagination of the United States. Although he copyrighted his images in Mexico, Waite wrote almost all of his captions directly onto his negatives in English, strongly suggesting that his primary audience consisted of tourists. American-owned firms such as the W. G. Walz Co. Souvenir House, located in the heart of Mexico City at San Francisco Street No. 2, sold Waite's images as five-by-seven-inch prints that tourists could later paste into scrapbooks. Because Waite was so prolific, tourists had thousands of images from which to choose when browsing at shops or newsstands.

Prior to Waite's arrival in the 1890s, few Americans had ever been to Mexico or even seen a photograph of that country. However, starting in the 1870s, photographs of Mexico became ubiquitous in the United States, thanks to Waite and his cohort of photographers, writers, editors, and printers. The Americans who created and disseminated photographic representations of Mexico performed important cultural work, namely, the framing of Mexico as a backward but beautiful country right next door, a place in desperate need of modernization where the American dollar could be stretched and the intrepid investor richly rewarded. This is to say that photographic conventions associated with travel to Porfirian Mexico helped to justify, and even require, the politics of economic conquest, as suggested by Hamilton's bold note to Díaz. The picture postcards, book illustrations, and other photographic representations examined in this chapter easily traversed international borders, meaning that Waite was an able and influential contributor to a transnational system of knowledge production about Mexico. In other words, Waite not only circulated two-dimensional images depicting that nation and its inhabitants; he also taught Americans and others how to see and know Mexico through the photographic conventions that he established and reproduced. To extend the Sontag epigraph that opens this chapter, Waite showed Americans what was worth looking at in Mexico and what Americans had the right to observe when traveling south of the border.

In less than two decades in Mexico, Waite became the country's most prolific commercial photographer and a wealthy man. By the start of the Mexican Revolution, he had amassed a huge catalogue of images and seven thousand hectares of beautiful and lucrative agricultural land in the state of Veracruz (which, of course, he photographed profusely). Montellano notes in *C. B. Waite, fotógrafo* that "this paradisiacal place was considered a strategic enclave for many years because of construction plans for a transoceanic railroad that would unite Puerto México on the Gulf to Salina Cruz on the Pacific."[7] The location of his landholdings speaks to his financial foresight as well as the fact that Waite belonged to the throngs of American speculators who went to Mexico during the Porfiriato. Waite not only contributed to the visual culture of economic conquest, he bought into it.

Waite continued to flourish in Mexico until the country began to change around him in 1910. In what must have been a crushing blow to the photographer, his brother, who had joined him south of the border and had become the manager of an American mining company in Veracruz, was murdered by insurrectionist campesinos in 1912. Nonetheless, Waite rode out this catastrophic loss and the general chaos of the revolution and stayed in Mexico until 1913.[8] Between the start of the war and his departure he made few photographs, except for about forty that documented the aftermath of fierce fighting in Mexico City that unfolded in February 1913 and ended in the execution of President Francisco Madero.[9] In making these final images, Waite contributed to the new but rapidly expanding field of photojournalism, the field that would eventually make Agustín Casasola, the pioneering photojournalist and editor who documented the Mexican Revolution, famous in Mexico and abroad.[10]

Waite was, of course, not alone in establishing the visual conventions associated with Porfirian Mexico. He was one of several prolific foreign photographers who worked in Mexico during the late nineteenth and early twentieth centuries, including Guillermo Kahlo, François Aubert, Hugo Brehme, and Winfield Scott. In addition to satisfying the craze for photo portraits among the urban middle class in Mexico City, these men were commissioned variously by the government, railways, and mining firms to photograph the nation and its people, always in the interest of advancing the Porfirian agenda. Responding to the Díaz regime's desire to emulate European and American manners and technologies, including the blending of art and science through photography, they documented "progress" as it was iterated in private settings (portraiture) and public settings (e.g., infrastructure, factories, public works). Despite their status as foreigners, these men helped establish, reinforce, and justify the Díaz regime through pictures that presented Mexico as a nation at the cusp of modernity, with many markers of progress of which it might boast.[11] Waite and his fellow photographers not only documented what it meant to be modern in Porfirian Mexico; they helped create that modernity.

But at the same time, each of these men also sought subject matters that diverged from the agendas of their clientele, producing huge numbers of images that reflected the contradictions of the Porfiriato. For example, each made hundreds of photographs of Indian people, a move that contradicted elite attempts to construct Mexico as a modern mestizo state. When William Henry Jackson was commissioned by the Mexican Central Railway to photograph the rail lines connecting El Paso and Mexico in 1883–1884, he was inspired to photograph native people living in dire poverty in the village of El Abra, directly transgressing the company's intent of showing potential tourists the wonders that they would find along the Mexican Central's path.[12] These images of ragged men, women, and children and their adobe homes sharply contrasted with his pictures of shiny locomotives, spectacular rail bridges, and modern stations—the types of images favored by every rail company and anyone else interested in showing how modern Mexico had become. For its part, the company never published or displayed the El Abra photographs or others like them made by Jackson, attesting to the fact that this alternative view of life alongside the Mexican Central did not cohere with the company's vision of itself or its celebrated route.

This contrast between the Mexican Central's self-image and the one favored by Jackson represents a tension that characterized photographic practices throughout the Porfiriato, as photographers reconciled their patrons' visions of the modernizing nation with their personal and artistic attractions to the so-called primitive aspects of Mexican life. Like Jackson, most other non-Mexican photographers found native people to be among the most compelling subjects for the camera. So while American and other foreign photographers proved themselves adept at documenting the markers of Mexican modernity (and profited handsomely from these efforts), they also documented the limits of the Porfirian agenda. However, this was probably not because they harbored serious reservations about that agenda or the effects of economic conquest, but because they saw themselves as artists drawn to the more picturesque parts of Mexico.

Throughout the Porfiriato, images made by this cohort of foreign photographers circulated widely in Mexico and dominated American views of travel there. Granted, this was before gifted foreign art photographers like Tina Modotti and Edward Weston traveled to Mexico in the 1920s and before Mexican photographers began to approach photography as a serious artistic endeavor, and the work of earlier foreign photographers looks rather unimaginative to contemporary eyes. Their styles tend to be straightforward and denotative rather than evocative or explicitly emotive. For this reason, despite some interest among Mexican scholars, American art historians and photography enthusiasts have mostly overlooked Waite and other American photographers who worked in Porfirian Mexico. Olivier Debroise, the great chronicler of the photographic medium in Mexico, somewhat grumpily describes them as "simply pragmatic camera operators."[13] Such a dismissal probably stems from the fact that Waite and many of his contemporaries did not adhere to conventions of the pictorialist movement, which utilized painterly techniques (such as soft focus) to advance the medium's artistic possibilities. Still, these photographers amassed a prodigious body of work, some of it quite beautiful, which dominated visual culture in and about Mexico for decades and set the stage for subsequent ways of seeing *lo mexicano*. Their influence on how the world came to see Mexico—and how Mexicans saw themselves—cannot be overstated.

A TRIP TO THE RUINS

Unsurprisingly, ruins proved to be one of the most popular motifs for foreign photographers in Mexico, including Waite. While many of the images that he captured at Mitla focus on the ruins themselves, others document a large party of white American tourists among the ancient

FIGURE 1.2. Tourist party with local girls, Mitla. Photo by C. B. Waite. DeGolyer Library, Southern Methodist University, Dallas, Texas.

treasures. It is undocumented whether Waite himself was part of the group or became friends with its members, as compatriots are apt to do while abroad, but he exhaustively captured the progress of the tourists, who were delighted by the presence of a professional photographer, through the ruins complex. The snapshot era had only just begun, but members of the party already knew how to pose for a tourist picture. They pause and stoically return the camera's gaze. They lean against walls decorated with Mitla's distinctive relief work. They pose with their companions to prove that they all made it to the ruins together. In other words, they engage in touristic activities like those performed by contemporary visitors to the impressive site. What American tourist to Mitla or similar locations has not posed like this? Doing so proves that one has made it to an important and remote ancient site. Perhaps most surprisingly, the party of tourists also engages with Indian people in a number of the images. In several of them, Mitla emerges as a contact zone where white tourists encountered ancient ruins and living Indians.

For one photograph, several of the Americans posed with indigenous boys and girls in a courtyard. Except for two women tourists, the entire group—white tourists and Indian children—lined up to have their pictures taken together as if they are one party (Figure 1.2). Tourists rarely posed with native people during the Porfiriato, so this image, along with similar shots created that day, represents a compelling record of contact with native people. Interacting with the native people was a regular part of the touristic experience in Mexico, and native people appear everywhere in travel discourse, yet travelers seldom paused to have their pictures taken with indigenous people. Despite the feeling of camaraderie conveyed in this photograph, certain signs demarcate the tourists from the locals and indicate how social difference was mediated in the act of posing for a photograph. It is telling, for example, that the touring party chose to pose with children for this picture. A mysterious face, which appears to belong to an adult Indian woman, peers from inside a doorway behind one of the white tourists, quietly disrupting this vision of Mitla, however. One wonders if she is attempting to insert herself into the official record of the visit. Indigenous women appear in several of the images made of the touring party, but it is clear that the tourists—or Waite—favored children as photographic subjects. The overall effect is to make Mitla appear to be populated by poor but sweet-natured women and children. The caption inserted onto the image by Waite reads "Among the Ruins of Mitla," but its creator does not clarify whether the Indian people were among the ruins or *part of* the ruins. As several scholars have recently noted, ruins increasingly fascinated foreign travelers throughout the Porfiriato. Some Americans who traveled to places like Mitla saw indigenous Mexican women as somehow left behind by time and progress, so positioning such women among ruins would have been meaningful on several levels.[14]

Another photo, in which sixteen of the tourists appear, finds the group looking surprisingly relaxed against a backdrop of beautifully carved walls.[15] Three Indian girls appear with the foreigners in this second image. At the far left of the image sits another barefoot girl with very dark skin and a plaintive expression. She is almost certainly the girl depicted in Hamilton's photograph. To her left a mustachioed white man with a porkpie hat on his knee looks at her with keen interest.[16] One of the white women sits on the ground and holds a small Indian girl in her arms in an unusual gesture of intimacy captured between foreign tourists and Mexicans. This type of encounter was exceedingly rare, as photographs almost never depict tourists touching native Mexicans. Instead, most tourists were careful to distance themselves from Mexicans—especially native people. Why, then, was this member of the tourist party comfortable enough with a small native girl to hug her so closely to herself? What does this act say about the place of native Mexicans—especially women and children—in the imperialist imagination of the United States?

At first glance, there is something almost touching about the woman embracing the young girl in this way. Unlike contemporary tourists posing for snapshots, who tend to hug their friends closely, the members of the tour group commemorated in Waite's photographs never seem to touch or embrace one another. But here, one of a number of instances in which members of this party reach out and touch Indian children, the woman's arm tenderly enfolds the little girl. For this reason and because of the sweetness with which the woman smiles at the camera, the photograph suggests warm feelings across the lines of race, class, and culture. Despite the fact that I mention her image in the context of a book about economic conquest and the politics of representation, one surmises that the American woman would not have seen herself as an imperialist presence at Mitla.

Still, this image might be read another way. It brings to mind bell hooks's argument that representations of racial difference, even ones that appear sympathetic to those whose racial difference is highlighted, reflect power relations between dominant and subordinate groups. "When race and ethnicity become commodified as resources for pleasure," hooks writes, "the culture of specific groups, as well as the bodies of individuals can be seen as constituting an alternative playground where members of the dominating races . . . affirm their power . . . in intimate relations with the other."[17] Hooks implies that it is sexual desire that makes cultures and bodies constitute an "alternative playground," but this image suggests that maternal affection might also arise "when race and ethnicity become commodified as resources for pleasure." Although maternal or paternal interest looks benign in photographs, these forms of attachment reinforce the politics of paternalism that were central to the project of economic conquest.

One of the more remarkable photographs documenting Waite's trip to Mitla brings us back to the same location as Hamilton's photograph and to the theme of interracial contact (Figure 1.3). In this photograph more than two dozen people—American tourists, along with indigenous women and children—crowd into the Salón de las Columnas for a group photo. Unlike the images mentioned above, Indian women join the children in posing for Waite's camera. A small cluster of them appears to the left of the image's center.[18] They are joined by many of the tourists who appear in the other pictures. Leaning against a column, one of the male tourists wears a Mexican-style hat with his three-piece

FIGURE 1.3. Tourist party with indigenous women and girls, Mitla. Photo by
C. B. Waite. DeGolyer Library, Southern Methodist University, Dallas, Texas.

suit (one of two men who don a sombrero in the image). He holds the
hands of two girls who look slightly younger than the girl who appeared
in Hamilton's photograph. Another small girl stands nearby, with her
shawl wrapped protectively around herself. A white woman stands at
the far right of the frame, staring down at the young girl. A white man
in a cap stands to the left of the man in the sombrero and also looks
away from the camera, seemingly to stare at one of the Indian women
who stand nearby.

While not as boldly desirous as other Waite pictures, this image is
notable for what it says about contact between travelers and Indian
people and for what it subtly says about Indianness in general. Its
scale, for one thing, challenges other representations of the Salón de las
Columnas. In the vast majority of photos, the Salón takes on a monu-
mental scale, as if it is some sort of hall of giants. In the image from
Hamilton's photograph, for example, the front column looks gigan-
tic next to the small girl who leans against it. That photo was taken
from farther away, heightening the sense that the space is huge. But in
this image, the columns and the courtyard, crowded with people, appear to be on a much more human scale. The Salón becomes an intimate space, one where intimate contact between local Zapotec people
and white people from the United States is once again made possible.

Within this space, the travelers and the locals appear to mix freely with one another.

Most provocative is the physical contact displayed between the white man in the sombrero near the center of the frame and the two Indian girls who flank him. Like the image of the white woman holding a small Indian girl closely to her chest, the man makes physical contact with the girls, holding their tiny hands in his own. These girls represent Waite's favorite type of girls to photograph: small, Indian, and dressed in ragged clothing, but alert and willing to return the camera's gaze. The strange presence of an older white man among them is jarring, considering how infrequently travelers posed with Indian people and the extent to which white travelers distanced themselves from Mexico's natives. But his presence might also make it clear that pretty and docile-looking girls like these were part of the pleasure of traveling to Mexico, as we have seen.[19] Whether the pleasure exhibited here is paternal or erotic in nature is up to the viewer, but it is clear that the men and women of this touring party found themselves more willing than most travelers to cross the racial, ethnic, and linguistic barriers that typically separated tourists from the locals. The result is a more complicated depiction of the touristic encounter than found in most representations of travel to Porfirian Mexico, which present native people as objects to be looked at but not as people who might be engaged or known. This photograph also speaks to one of the key tropes that emerged again and again in the visual culture of travel to Porfirian Mexico, namely, the use of poverty to represent Mexico's desirability.

PICTURING MEXICAN BODIES

One of the elements that stands out in Waite's images of the tourist party and the Zapotec women and children at Mitla is the stark contrast between the well-dressed Americans and the locals. It is immediately apparent that the women and children bear a markedly ragged appearance compared to the tourists. But it is also unsurprising that the indigenous people should look this way, considering their position at the bottom of Porfirian society. My point is not to highlight the vast material differences between tourists and indigenous people in photographs like the ones described above, which should be self-evident. More pertinent to the study at hand is the fact that poverty was such a pervasive theme in the photographs of American tourists and the makers of travel discourse. Images of poor, often naked, women and children frequently appeared on American postcards and in travelogues and magazine articles throughout the Porfiriato. This fascination speaks to American perceptions that Porfirian Mexico, though rapidly modernizing, still required rescue from a more advanced, progressive nation. Poverty, often embodied by nakedness, constructed Mexico as a seemingly faraway place, one that required economic interventionism in order to fully emerge as a modern nation.

John Mraz has intimated that poverty appeared early in the history of mass-produced photographs in Mexico, but that the Porfirian state actively suppressed portrayals of the poor for political reasons.[20] As I will show, the regime intervened against foreigners who looked too closely at Mexican poverty, using its sway with the postal service to prevent them from posting questionable photographs of shockingly abject poverty to the United States and other countries. Still, travelers could not ignore the fact that poverty affected so many Indian people in Mexico. Every Mexican travelogue noted the presence of beggars and thieves on the city streets and abject poverty in the villages.[21] Waite, like most of the foreign photographers who worked in Porfirian Mexico, attempted to convey in visual form the notion that, as he etched on one photograph, "the poor are always with you."[22] While this was undoubtedly the case in a nation with a class divide as wide as Porfirian Mexico's, travel discourse also aestheticized the nation's poverty problem.

Children provided particularly powerful symbols of Mexican poverty throughout the Porfiriato, just as they do today, and foreign photographers like Waite consistently fixated on poor children as subjects. In postcards and other media, poor children in ragged clothing beg on urban streets and stand in desolate fields in the campo. Tiny girls carry their siblings on their backs and stare longingly at the camera. They seem all but abandoned by their parents. When parents do appear, as in one of Waite's images from Mitla described above, it is clear that they do not embody Victorian or Progressive Era ideals of parenthood. In some instances, for example, entire families pick lice from each other's hair, a motif that became popular fodder for American picture postcards.[23]

Many representations of Mexican children from the Porfiriato suggested that, like the girl in the Mitla photograph, the impoverished child needed to be rescued. Waite proved himself a serious student of the genre and subtly encouraged his viewers to see indigenous girls as objects of desire. Take, for example, a beautiful but problematic picture, made into a postcard in 1907, that features a young Indian girl weav-

FIGURE 1.4. One of Waite's favorite subjects, young girls. Photo by C. B. Waite. Rene D'Harnoncourt Photograph Collection, Nettie Lee Benson Latin American Collection, University of Texas Libraries, University of Texas at Austin.

ing palm fronds (Figure 1.4). The image, like countless others produced by foreign photographers, is manifestly intended to celebrate Indian handiwork. Yet, like many of Waite's pictures of girls, the image also betrays a latent eroticism. Waite positions the camera low, so that it appears that the photographer has literally stooped down to the girl's level. A rebozo clings to one of her shoulders but seems to be falling off or to have been pushed back to show more of her body. Her loose-fitting blouse slides down the other shoulder to expose the top part of her chest. The girl appears to be about ten years old.

Though Waite's published photographs enjoyed tremendous popularity during his lifetime, a brief episode in his career illustrates that his vision of Mexico did not appeal to all. In 1901, he was briefly jailed in Mexico City under suspicion by postal authorities that some of his photographs qualified as pornography. According to *El Imparcial*, which mistakenly listed the photographer's name as J. G. Wheite, Waite had been detained for attempting to send a packet of photographs titled "Indigenous Children of Mexico" via certified mail. The newspaper claimed that the subjects of these scandalous photographs included "two dirty boys in a state of absolute misery, corroded by disease" and, vaguely but suggestively, "children in different poses." It also accused

Waite of including in the package negatives in which children were "completely nude, presenting deformed bodies completely unveiled."[24] While the newspaper was reluctant to describe the pictures in fuller detail, it referred to some of Waite's many images of poor women and girls (and, in a few instances, boys) who appear in the nude or in dire poverty. Of course, the two frequently went hand in hand. But was the problem with these particular pictures the fact that the children were naked or that they were poor and deformed?

Mexican critic Georgina Rodríguez Hernández, for one, suggests that Waite's photos posed a danger to Victorian sensibilities by eroticizing Indian women's bodies, though she concedes that Waite's motive for making images that exemplified the idea of the "sensual native" remain "something of a mystery."[25] In contradiction to Debroise's claim that photographs of naked Indian women almost never appeared in U.S. or Mexican visual culture, Rodríguez Hernández shows in a brief article on the social meanings of pictures of naked bodies during the Porfiriato that Waite, along with Winfield Scott, made dozens of prints of women and girls bathing completely in the nude or engaging in everyday activities, such as grinding corn at the metate or combing their hair, with their chests exposed. Though these photographers specialized in landscapes emphasizing the results of the Díaz regime's modernization efforts, they seem to have harbored keen personal interests in this more intimate subject matter.

Waite spent three days in jail and paid a fine of four hundred pesos for possessing the pictures, but it appears that the matter was subsequently dropped.[26] Press coverage of the affair, however, shows that criticism of the photographer's work extended beyond his interest in nude girls, contrary to Hernández's assumption that it was nudity in particular that aroused the suspicion of postal authorities.[27] *El Imparcial*, the semiofficial voice of the Porfirian regime, used the occasion of Waite's arrest to complain about photographers and tourists in general:

> One of the reasons that we are not well regarded abroad is because excursionists seek out the most recondite aspects of the country, the most ridiculous details and individuals, the most degenerate and miserable displays of a barbarous and cultureless state that we fortunately do not know.[28]

Given some of the representations of Mexico examined in this book, the writer of the *El Imparcial* article had good reason to complain. Even

so, he or she omitted the fact that tourists also went to Mexico looking for the signs of Porfirian modernity. Waite himself contributed in-
numerable photographs in this vein, including some commissioned by
the government, that circulated within and outside of Mexico. In fact,
no other photographer contributed more to the American impression
of Mexico as a modernizing state. His arrest nonetheless serves as an
interesting testament to some Mexicans' frustrations with the fact that
tourists continued to fixate on symbols of the nation's supposed backwardness. *El Imparcial*, like many of its middle-class readers and the
ruling elite, blamed the touristic gaze for the nation's poor reputation
abroad.[29]

Poverty was just as dangerous a subject matter as overt sexuality,
especially when photographs intended for international distribution
put destitute Mexicans on display. Quite simply, representations of
poverty threatened to expose the limits of the Porfirian agenda. Despite
the countless visual reminders of progress that permeated the visual
culture of the era, material conditions for Mexico's poor actually deteriorated during the Díaz administration, a fact that imperiled both its
potential to attract foreign investors and the regime's ability to claim
that its "scientific" approach to governance meant that Mexico was a
modern, progressive state. Even so, as *El Imparcial* complained, visitors from abroad constantly wrote about and photographed Mexican
poverty, seeing the nation's rather public display of poverty as both a
striking contradiction to Mexico's material improvements and a source
of scopic pleasure. Poverty in fact became one of the leading tropes
of American photographic representations of Mexico. Ample visual
evidence shows us that Waite made a habit of documenting extreme
poverty, framing it especially through depictions of indigenous girls.

Waite's arrest also speaks to the broader intersections of poverty
and desire in nineteenth- and early-twentieth-century photography.
Wilhelm von Gloeden, the connoisseur of Sicilian adolescents whose
work paralleled Waite's in some ways, relied on poor male models whose
deeply bronzed skin rendered them racially ambiguous. Von Gloeden's
work reflected the practice of fetishizing working men in representations of same-sex desire, one common among middle-class and elite
men in Europe with sexual interest in other men. Scholars in queer
visual and literary studies have shown that crossing class lines enabled
men of means to eroticize the bodies of other men. (Von Gloeden had
the additional alibi that he was depicting classical scenes.) Likewise,
Waite's ability to photograph Indian people undressed relied on differ-

ences in race and class that distanced him from his models. As Montellano has noted, almost all of his nudes and seminudes feature dark-skinned Indian girls of about twelve to fourteen years old. In dozens of his pictures, some of which must have been among those that led to his arrest or at least established his reputation as a pornographer, girls of this type appear bathing in rivers and performing their daily chores.[30] Like von Gloeden, Waite might have "differentiated his production, maintaining a public line of photographs for general purchase while reserving the more risqué pictures for special clients."[31] Certainly, his more explicit shots never made it into the pages of travelogues or even *National Geographic*. Still, Waite turned some such images into postcards. Whether he sold them to a specialized or general market is unclear. Either way, he was able to maintain his connections to the Porfirian elite—and to win lucrative government commissions—until the downfall of the regime.

It is tempting to make guesses about Waite's personal agenda in making these photographs, but the photographer's personal sexual proclivities are not part of the historical record. Nonetheless, his photographs do illuminate the imperialistic gaze that framed many American representations of Mexico during the Porfiriato. It would be fitting to read images of poor Mexican children in relation to what Malek Alloula called the "Colonial Harem" in his now-classic study, for they reflect a similar politics of desire for rescue that permeated French postcards depicting Algeria in the late nineteenth and early twentieth centuries.[32] As Alloula shows, these postcards imagined Algeria as a colony filled with demure but sensual women on display for the French (and European and North American) gaze. Woven throughout these fantasies of a feminized colonial Algeria is the notion that women in the harem required rescuing from their captors. The postcard provided a space for the French (or other imperial) onlooker to see himself as a potential rescuer. Gayatri Spivak rails against the politics of rescue in "Can the Subaltern Speak?" pointing to the long-standing colonial and postcolonial practice of intervening in indigenous gender relations, discursively constructing that act as "white men . . . saving brown women from brown men."[33] Images of destitute, naked, parentless children raised the question about whether, to paraphrase, brown children needed rescuing from brown parents. They also conjure complex questions about the roles of sex and desire in the project of economic conquest.

Take, for example, an arresting Waite photo of two young girls, probably sisters (Figure 1.5). Again, this image is not as explicit as Waite's

FIGURE 1.5. Two young girls, probably sisters. Photo by C. B. Waite. Black Photograph Album, Nettie Lee Benson Latin American Collection, University of Texas Libraries, University of Texas at Austin.

nudes but nonetheless exemplifies the intersections of poverty and desire in his work. Barefoot, dusty, and dressed in tattered clothing that contrasts with their dark brown skin, the prepubescent girls return the camera's gaze. The seated girl holds a basket of chipped pottery. The look on her face suggests that she is annoyed with or frightened by the man pointing the camera at her, but she nonetheless returns his gaze. The standing girl wears a self-confident smile on her face that contrasts sharply with her poverty (and with the more stoic expression worn by her companion). The standing girl's dress is so torn that part of her chest is visible. Waite posed the girls against the wall of an ancient edifice, perhaps during his trip to Mitla, once again demonstrating the close relationship between native women or girls and ruins.

The image of these young sisters corresponds with the photograph of the girl in the Salón de las Columnas, but it has a much more intimate feel, given the closeness of Waite to his subjects and the somewhat tender expressions on their faces. Unlike Hamilton's photograph, this one suggests that the photographer attempted to establish an air of familiarity between the girls and the viewer. While the question of whether these girls inspired romantic interest in American viewers is difficult to answer, it is possible to infer that, like other images discussed above, this photograph represents the American impulse to see poor Mexican women and girls as inherently desirable. What is more, we might presume that some white observers would have seen indigenous women and girls in Mexico as inherently more sexual—and more exploitable—than nonnative women and girls. In a provocative study of sexual violence and American Indian genocide, Andrea Smith has argued that white people have long imagined indigenous women as innately perverse and innately exploitable in sexual terms. As Smith puts it, "In the colonial imagination, Native bodies are . . . immanently polluted with sexual sin . . . . Because Indian bodies are 'dirty,' they are considered sexually violable and 'rapeable,' and the rape of bodies that are considered impure or dirty simply does not count."[34] Smith's work helps explain why American popular and legal cultures have constructed the rape of an Indian woman as a natural and even inevitable act. The possibility of these girls' perversity or "rapeability" need not be manifest in Waite's image. Even without an explicit reference to eroticism, images of native women and girls must be read within the broader context of the sexual politics of colonialism.

Whether or not one agrees with Smith, it is clear that Waite and other Americans found one form of pleasure or another in putting the

FIGURE 1.6. "Buster Brown-Skin." DeGolyer Library, Southern Methodist University, Dallas, Texas.

native body on display. Indian bodies functioned in American travel discourse as sites of interest, desire, disgust, and, sometimes, humor. This last point, that humor could color how foreigners saw the Indian body, is evident in one of the images pasted into one American's travel scrapbook (Figure 1.6). This remarkable photograph shows a young girl standing with an even younger boy, who appears to be her brother, in a scrubby landscape. The barefoot girl wears shabby clothing, including a rebozo that lends her the appearance of an Adelita, one of the iconic women soldiers that would appear during the Mexican Revolution. She looks like one of the countless dusty children that one encounters in Mexican travel discourse from the Porfiriato, but the small boy who is her companion is completely naked, his hand clasped in his sister's. She seems to steady him, for he looks as if he has been crying and would prefer not to have his picture taken. Both children look to their left, as if they are taking directions from an out-of-frame adult.

It is unknown whether this picture was a snapshot or a commercial image purchased by the creator of the scrapbook (or one of his associates), but a handwritten caption in the scrapbook provides insight into how Americans saw and interpreted images of Mexican poverty. Playing on the popular character that began appearing in newspapers in 1902, someone wrote "Buster Brown-skin" in blue ink near the bottom of the photograph. The joke is, of course, that the boy in the photograph was the antithesis of the well-to-do rascal with the blond pageboy haircut from the funny pages. Humor, however feeble, provides a lens for seeing and knowing Mexican poverty. Despite the fact that this real boy is about the same age as the cartoon character, he embodies foreigners' impressions of the abject Mexican child. Their social difference lies not only in their class and social positions (Buster Brown was a rich city kid with pretty clothes and a mischievous streak) but in their very bodies, hence the emphasis on skin in the caption. Mexican racial difference, embodied by native people and symbolized through a variety of representational strategies, posed a serious threat to the project of economic conquest, and this attempt at humor exposes just how wide that gulf was during the Porfiriato. The Mexican boy and the iconic character, whose copyright was purchased by Brown Shoe Company to sell shoes to middle-class American families in 1904, could not have been more racially distinct.

This image and its caption also reflect the ways in which Americans in Mexico distanced themselves and their children from Mexicans. Travelers and U.S. citizens living in Mexico frequently described feelings of sympathy for the poor children they encountered, but they also used images like this one to highlight material and cultural differences. The appearance of "Buster Brown-skin" is especially poignant, given the presence, several pages later in the same album, of some photographs of a young blond girl around the same age as the naked boy. Presumably the daughter of a mine manager, she appears to live a privileged and pampered life, as if her parents have re-created their comfortable middle-class lives in a tropical climate. One of the pictures, sent as a postcard to Mrs. S. H. Reed of Raton, New Mexico, playfully asks:

"Have you seen anything of a little girl who looks like this? I am missing one here." This is an example of the common (and understandable) practice of exchanging images with the folks back home, practiced by many Americans who found themselves living and working in Porfirian Mexico, but the juxtaposition of images also reveals how those expatriates imagined themselves in relation to the locals. The presence of the naked boy and his ragged sister within the same album heightens the viewer's sense of this girl as the beloved and privileged daughter of an American working abroad. The supposedly humorous caption for that image underscored the idea that the naked boy and the well-dressed girl might have shared proximity to one another but would have nonetheless inhabited different worlds.

Another encounter with a naked Indian boy, which appears in a travelogue published by an American woman in 1907, further attests to the American fascination with naked children in Porfirian Mexico. It appears in *The Tour of the 400 to Mexico*, a strange but sporting travelogue that detailed the journey of Grace Owen Brown, her husband, six of their friends, and two African American servants through Mexico in a private train car named "The 400." The book, illustrated by Brown's own snapshots, is written as a diary and, in the words of the author in the introduction, intended as a souvenir for her fellow travelers. In one vignette, Brown describes the act of looking for picturesque people and places in a town called Cerro Prieto as "hunting":

> I took the camera and went hunting and had some mighty good sport. There were brown-skinned boys bathing in a pool down in the ravine, challenging the camera (literally, in Spanish). There were hillsides with the mining works; the ceaseless procession of pannier donkeys; there were little Mexican cabins and, best of all, I shot a cherub! . . . A little bronze cupid—of all the captives of my bow and spear he is the prize trophy. Like Solomon in all his glory, he 'was not arrayed,' as the anthem declares. The little creature tried to fly when he saw me aiming at him, but he didn't even have his wings on![35]

Here Brown is more explicit than most of her compatriots about the pleasure of looking for and at a naked Indian child. The accompanying photograph features a small boy of about four years looking timid but scowling at the photographer.

Brown's tone in this vignette is typically breezy, but there are once again more serious representational politics at play in how she narrates the encounter with her reluctant photographic subject. The author intends the metaphor of hunting for the young boys to be humorous, but the boy's expression in the photograph, as well as Brown's description of the boy attempting to "fly," indicates that even those who drew pleasure from photographing nude "cherubs" must have been aware that the camera, that cherished accoutrement of the tourist (then and now), could also function as a weapon. Here I am reminded of Sontag's famous claim that "there is something predatory in the act of taking a picture. To photograph people is to violate them, by seeing them as they never see themselves, by having knowledge of them that they can never have; it turns people into objects that can be symbolically possessed."[36] The predatory aspect of taking a picture would have been especially powerful in the early decades of the medium, especially in a place like Mexico, where Americans traipsed through the countryside pointing their cameras at people who very likely had never seen a camera or a photograph. For Brown and the cadre of American men who made their livings making photographs in Mexico, native people, whether clothed or unclothed, might have seemed like easy prey.

TIPOS: ETHNOGRAPHY AND ENTERTAINMENT

Poverty and nakedness helped Americans make sense of their relationship to Porfirian Mexico but should also be understood within a broader genre of photography that fixated on Mexican difference. The "Buster Brown-skin" and "cherub" images belong to a large body of images that circulated within the orbit of popular ethnography. A few notes on the ethnographic photograph are in order, for in fact the majority of photographs of human subjects in Mexico might have claimed as their purpose the need to record the physical aspects of the nation's indigenous people. This was especially true during the Porfiriato, a period in which observers contradictorily erased, lamented, and romanticized Indian difference in their portrayals of the nation. Writers of all political stripes from both sides of the U.S.-Mexico border claimed that Indian culture was endangered, as implied by the photographs depicting temporal encounters described above, and that it needed to be recorded before it disappeared altogether. For this reason, Porfirian modernity posed a double-edged sword for the nation's Indians in the eyes of foreigners and Mexican elites. On one hand, "progress" would ease Indian poverty by modernizing Indian people. But on the other, this very progress meant the potential eradication of Indian difference.

Accordingly, the creators of travel discourse set out to record, in words and images, Indian Mexico before it was too late.

Ethnographic impulses were especially apparent in the work of Frederick Starr, who founded the iconic program in anthropology at the University of Chicago, and other anthropologists who saw Mexico as a place where scientists could still observe the "vanishing race" before the onslaught of industrial capitalism. If the temporal encounters described below marked Mexico as a nation in flux, then foreign anthropologists, who were also in the process of creating a new academic field as they went along, undertook the technical work of documenting Indian difference before it was too late. Starr, for one, took a physiognomic approach to native difference, and his book *Indians of Southern Mexico*, published in 1899, catalogued Indian difference through photographic means. This "ethnographic album," as it is described in the book's subtitle, consists almost entirely of images of indigenous people formally posed for the anthropological gaze. Indeed, many of the book's plates take on the appearance of mug shots, combining straightforward portraits with profile pictures of the same Indian person. Starr's photographer, Charles B. Lang, positioned these "specimens," as the preface calls them, in front of a decontextualizing blank white screen. None look happy to be photographed. Instead, they grimace, frown, glare, and cast their eyes away from the camera. Starr and Lang also posed groups of people to make a point about physical consistency among native groups. In an image exemplary of this technique, six Mixtec women, similarly dressed and carefully arranged by height and age, stand together in front of a building (Figure 1.7). Each of these women looks miserable, especially the youngest of the group, who cowers behind what appears to be a frowning sister. Starr offers no explanation for any of this emotional state, perhaps because he presumed the camera to be the most powerful ethnographic tool.[37] Despite this empirical stance, the author's politics are clear: Starr dedicated the book to Porfirio Díaz and Manuel Fernández Leal, Díaz's Minister of Development.

Whereas Starr's work represents an academic gaze pointed at indigenous people in Mexico, C. B. Waite cultivated a far more popular audience for his photographs. Waite's body of work hardly qualifies him as an ethnographic authority, but he must be given credit for paying attention to Indians at all during a time when most Mexican commercial photographers were interested only in the work and play of the nation's elite.[38] In addition to studio photography and government commissions,

MIXTECS: SAN BARTOLO.

FIGURE 1.7. Six Mixtec women. Frederick Starr, *Indians of Southern Mexico: An Ethnographic Album.*

Waite made thousands of prints of Indian people over the course of almost two decades in Mexico. Even when photographing monuments to Porfirian modernity, such as rail trestles or extravagant new buildings, he frequently included native people in the frame. In this sense, Waite painted a much fuller portrait of Mexican life than the photographers who limited their activities to the comfort of their studios. This does not mean, however, that Waite brought a self-conscious political agenda to his depictions of *lo indígena* (like, say, subsequent photographers such as Tina Modotti, who famously tapped into the indigenous revival of the 1920s). Instead, Waite's politics were much more subtle, since he, like most photographers of the era, approached native Mexicans as picturesque—and often pathetic—local color. Indians were also convenient human subjects for men like Waite, since, under the banner of ethnological inquiry, photographers had more or less free rein with the Indian body. Still, because his pictures were some of the only images of Mexico's indigenous people encountered by everyday people in the United States, he exercised tremendous power in shaping American visions of the Mexican Indian.

One particular style of popular ethnographic image merits some attention. Waite took hundreds of *"tipos"* (types) images throughout his career, contributing to a genre that served as a key way for Americans to make sense of Mexican society in general and Indian difference in particular. The *tipos* photograph was introduced during the French Intervention, when European photographers responded to an intense interest in Europe in images of France's excursion in Mexico.[39] François Aubert traveled to Mexico from France in the 1850s and spent part of the 1860s documenting the French Intervention in photographs, from the lavish entertainments held at court to the assassination of Maximilian and the ouster of the French. A shocking image of the emperor's bloody and bullet-ridden shirt following his execution by firing squad in 1867 is attributed to Aubert. The photographer's access to Maximilian and his court allowed him to make pictures of the ultraelite, but he was also intrigued by those at the bottom of the social ladder: working people, the poor, and Indians. Thus, he catalogued Mexican difference by producing and cataloguing images of a wide array of Mexican "types."

Photographic types were not, of course, exclusive to representations of Mexico, but were in fact an important early use of the photograph. As several historians of visual culture have noted, photographers have attempted to categorize general types of people through images since the advent of the medium. Government officials and proto–social scientists frequently used photographs to conceptualize two particular aspects of human character during the second half of the nineteenth century: criminality and race. The makers and users of photographic types thought they could make better sense of seemingly unknowable (and perhaps dangerous) populations by documenting exactly what someone of that type looked like. This reflected the nineteenth- and early-twentieth-century belief that personality and character were reflected through corporeal difference.[40] In contrast to the middle-class photographic portrait, which denoted the sitter's individuality, the "type" image used individual people to represent a larger population of people who shared the identity of the person in the photograph. Whether a typological image depicted what a murderer or a milkmaid was supposed to look like, it served as a sort of visual shorthand for understanding the social world of both the subject and the viewer of the photograph. Although the photographic type was not specific to Mexico, those who worked or traveled there made a particularly compelling use of this style of image.

Aubert began to publish pictures of exemplary specimens of the common folk in the 1860s, making him the first photographer to portray "popular types" in Mexico.[41] Aubert's *tipos* became popular among domestic consumers of photographs in Mexico, a nation that has always been deeply interested in mapping internal social differences.[42] Still, the photos were crudely rendered. Aubert frequently placed models in front of a plain wall or canvas sheet. Many of these models look as if they had been brought in off the streets of Mexico City (or away from their market stalls, as vendors were a favorite subject matter). This is certainly the case in the photograph of an elderly Indian woman carrying a large bundle of grasses (Figure 1.8). Other *tipos* included market vendors, *tortilleras*, and *tlachiqueros*, the men and boys who harvested sap from maguey plants for the production of pulque. Aubert left Mexico for Algeria (another, more enduring object of French imperialism) shortly after Maximilian's execution, leaving behind a large body of images that were then a key part of Mexican popular culture.[43]

In the 1880s, however, another French photographer named Abel Briquet took up making *tipo* photographs, this time under the patronage of the Díaz administration. The government had already commissioned Briquet to photograph the Mexican National Railway, which linked Mexico City to the Gulf of Mexico, in 1876. In the following decade, it hired him again to record "typical" scenes and people throughout the nation. The best of these images were sold as *cartes de visite* or included in commemorative albums released by the administration. Like Aubert, Briquet was intrigued by campesinos and urban working people, so *tipos* frequently appeared in his published work. For decades, Briquet's *tipos* illustrated postcards and travelogues created for American audiences. One image in particular, which depicts a boy using a gourd to draw pulque from a maguey plant, appeared ubiquitously throughout the Porfiriato.

As Debroise has noted, for Mexican audiences, *tipos* reflected and reinforced the apparent naturalness of social hierarchies. By seeming to say "this is what a *tortillera* looks like" or "this is what street vendors look like," the *tipos* made social stratification appear natural, even inevitable. They also fixed the individuals in the photographs as static objects, frozen in time and space, rather than as active human agents. Unlike Progressive Era images of the urban poor in the United States, there was no sense of social or economic uplift in the *tipo* image. It should be emphasized, however, that Americans viewed *tipos* in slightly different ways from Mexican audiences, for *tipos* helped them to understand racial and ethnic difference as well. Travelogue and magazine writers,

FIGURE 1.8. Studio portrait of a female burden bearer. François Aubert, "Anciena mexicana cargando leña," between 1865 and 1867, The Getty Research Institute, Los Angeles.

for example, frequently used *tipo* images to illustrate their thoughts on Mexican racial groups. Writers and their editors frequently captioned *tipo* images depicting specific jobs like vendors, water carriers, or the aforementioned *tortilleras*, simply as "Indian Types," suggesting that the Indian was defined by the labor that he or she performed. Although they were created to catalogue various types that one encountered in everyday Mexican life, *tipo* images came to represent a more general view of Indianness in American eyes.

BURDEN BEARERS

The most common figure in travel discourse during this time was the *cargador* (carrier), a Mexican type that Americans saw as a source of curiosity and delight. "In the land of the Montezumas everything portable from pins to pianos is carried on the backs of the humble descendents of the proud Aztecs," wrote the *Los Angeles Times* in a special article on the *cargador*—"a character familiar to tourists"—in 1902. "The handbag

FIGURE 1.9. *Carboneros* postcard. Author's collection.

and trunk of the traveler, the merchandise of the shopkeeper, furniture and household effects, building stones from the quarry, cement in barrels and sand in sacks, are all conveyed in this manner."[44] One American traveler, writing near the start of the Porfiriato, claimed that the *cargadores* "have a peculiar dog-trot, which they keep hour after hour and day after day. . . . Their ordinary load for a long journey is from seventy-five to a hundred pounds, but in the mines they climb up the primitive ladders—merely notched poles—bearing four and even five hundred pounds of ore."[45] Americans with firsthand experience saw the *cargadores* as a primitive but useful means of moving things. Perhaps above all, they found the *cargador* picturesque. Images of Mexicans carrying huge, often comically oversized loads appeared in a variety of media throughout the Porfiriato, from stereoscope and magic lantern slides to magazine writing. Men, women, and children all appeared in this large body of visual materials, in what I will call the trope of the "burden bearer." In one image frequently reproduced as a postcard and to illustrate travelogues and magazine articles, to cite just one example, two *carboneros* carry two large loads of charcoal wrapped in straw (Figure 1.9).

While the contents of burden bearers' loads varied widely, the carriers were always indigenous people. This was, of course, a historical reality, since native people performed the most menial labor in Porfirian Mexico (a class and racial hierarchy that persists today). The burden bearer was one of the earliest tropes associated with commercial photography in Mexico. François Aubert made many such images, including his haunting studio shot of an elderly, barefoot Indian woman carrying a large bundle of sticks or grasses (see Figure 1.8, above). The barefoot woman wears a bright but ragged white skirt and blouse that contrasts sharply with her dark brown skin. Her expression is particularly disarming. Despite the fact that her face is frozen in what looks like pain or disgust, she plaintively and directly returns the camera's gaze. In *Mexique*, Aubert's two-volume album of photographs, the image of the old woman appears alongside pictures of famous landmarks, other Mexican "types," and panoramic cityscapes.

Images of burden bearers enjoyed their greatest popularity as the subjects of picture postcards. A variety of American and Mexican firms produced these cards, thousands of which circulated in U.S. popular culture during the postcard craze that swept the United States and Europe following the turn of the twentieth century. In general, they depicted men, women, and children carrying things in what seems like endless configurations. Popular motifs within this genre included men with huge loads of baskets or jars for sale, women carrying goods for market or their babies on their backs, and both men and women burdened with loads intended to surprise the American viewer, such as coffins or giant cages stuffed with live chickens. Other postcards featured children as burden bearers. One popular postcard, for example, pairs a photograph of a boy with a pigskin sack on his back drawing pulque from a maguey (the ubiquitous image mentioned above) with an image of a small girl with a baby tied to hers. This particular card seems to imply that native Mexicans were born carriers, and that being a burden bearer was a natural, intrinsic part of being an Indian.

What did the image of the burden bearer mean to Americans? Why were Indians carrying loads such a popular motif for foreign photographers in Mexico? And what does it mean when a class of laborers becomes the fodder of aesthetic objects created, purchased, and circulated across national borders by American actors? Travelers to Mexico saw Indians in ambivalent terms—as both the objects of pleasure and the impediments to modernization. Their representations of Indians and Indianness were accordingly complex and often contradictory. The burden bearer's ubiquity in travel discourse suggests a particular fantasy about Mexican labor that was crucial to the politics of economic conquest, namely the idea that a large and docile pool of labor resided south of the border. Capitalist expansionism required a large labor force, and the burden-bearer image suggested that native Mexicans were not merely savages, as previous generations of travelers had claimed, but another of Mexico's natural resources from which pleasure and profit could be drawn.

This should not suggest, however, that the popularity of the burden bearer softened American views of Indian racial inferiority. In 1897, an article in the *New York Times* claimed: "The longer one stays in Mexico the more convinced is he of the fact that the modern descendants of Montezuma are a race of burden bearers."[46] This description, like many representations of the burden bearer, implied that the Mexican Indian was racially suited to primitive forms of labor—and that the subordination of Mexicans in general was justifiable on racial grounds. Some writers and photographers took this further by explicitly conflating the burden bearer with beasts of burden. The *Los Angeles Times* explicitly compared *cargadores* to animals when it claimed:

[I]n his brawny arms and sturdy legs are combined horse, wagon, driver, all, for there horseflesh costs more than human muscle, man exists on less than does a beast. The cargador, trained from birth to carry burdens on his back, can transfer as much as any ordinary express outfit in the States; and in the struggle for existence the horse has been forced to suspend business.[47]

The claim that horses were more valuable (and better cared for) than peons in Mexico frequently appeared in travel writing around this time. Many representations like the one above ostensibly praised the *cargador* but ultimately dehumanized native laborers by describing exactly how cheap their labor was in the context of Porfirian Mexico. To compare the labor of indigenous people to that of animals was an old representational practice within colonial discourse, intended in part to suggest the exploitability of natives as a laboring population that would facilitate expansion and profit. For American travelers to Porfirian Mexico or the editors of the *Los Angeles Times*, the apparent cheapness of Indian labor would have served as a rationale for economic expansionism. However, such an argument depended on the animalization of the native worker.

Three years earlier, the *Los Angeles Times* ran a photo spread and article detailing Mexico's "three classes of burden bearers: burros, oxen, and men."[48] Two of the photos depicted a team of oxen pulling a load of straw and two burros dwarfed by huge loads of their own. Alongside these images are two images of men, one carrying waste cotton and one carrying large water jugs. The article decried cruelty against animals in Mexico but suggested that hard work was good for indigenous people. "Men are about as heavily worked beasts of burden in Mexico as any four-footed animals," claimed George A. Benham, the author of the piece, "yet they thrive under the work." Benham's view was widely held, and travelogue writers like W. E. Carson described Indians as domesticated animals. Carson wrote that it was "as much to the advantage to keep the peon in good health as it is in the interest of a sheep farmer to keep his flocks from foot-rot, so that, after all is said and done, the easygoing, sweet mannered peon is little more than a beast of burden."[49]

The conflation of the burden bearer with animals constructed the *cargador* as both useful and a source of pleasure. Part of this pleasure was visual, for again and again the *cargador* appeared in American travel discourse as an illustration of Mexico's old-fashioned and backward charm. Another, perhaps more complex, part of the pleasure derived from the burden bearer related to his or her subordinate relationship to travelers themselves. Harriott Wight Sherratt described the novel experience of being carried to an isolated mountain village by local "chairmen" in her 1899 travelogue *Mexican Vistas*. An innkeeper provided Sherratt's husband, Ahasuerus, a horse, but the author was furnished a team of local Indian men and a chair:

> This chariot was a high-backed chair with a wooden foot rest, and a white canopy which could be drawn over the face or thrown back. I seated myself in the chair, the Indian porter knelt, placed one of the two bands around his forehead, and the other around his shoulders, rose slowly like a camel and trotted off with me. The motion was delightful—much like the easy canter of a pony—and many a sly nap I took under my white canopy as the day wore on. . . . These were all strong, robust Indians accustomed to burdens of at least two hundred and fifty pounds, so that my conscience did not reprove me, though I must confess that I had all the time the feeling that I was making a human soul a beast of burden. The beasts of burden, however, bore their loads cheerfully; for the first one carried me, in spite of my protests, straight up the mountain five miles without stopping.[50]

Sherratt clearly enjoyed this close encounter with animal-like Indian burden bearers, who rise like camels and trot like ponies in her description. Unlike the vast majority of travelers, who appreciated burden bearers from a distance or only briefly noted the presence of *car-gadores*, Sherratt makes the porters a key part of the narrative of her journey up the mountain. In an accompanying photograph, she smiles broadly from under the white canopy installed in the chair to shield her from the tropical sun. In making herself part of the Indian's "burden," Sherratt subtly draws a connection between her own privilege as a white American visitor and the generations of travelers who had been carried around Latin America by native people. The trope of the burden bearer shared much in common with descriptions of Indian *mozos* that authors almost always mentioned in their travelogues. The term *mozo* refers to hired servants who performed a wide variety of tasks for travelers during the Porfiriato. They served as porters, tour guides, house servants, and valets. Because he played a multifaceted role in serving the traveler, the *mozo* differed from the *cargador*, who only carried things (at least in the minds of the American observers who wrote about them). Gilbert G. González identifies the "omnipresent and indispensible *mozo*" as a colonial figure, suggesting that American travelers "closely resembled British colonials in their dependence on servants."[51] Travelers complained about *mozos* constantly and frequently used them as comic foils, but, like the burden bearer, the *mozo* also reflected deeper fantasies about Mexico and what it offered the tourist. The *mozo* suggested, for example, that servitude came naturally to Mexicans. This might have been a nostalgic image for postbellum readers, especially since travelers frequently referred to *mozos* in possessive and infantilizing terms, calling them, as one traveler wrote, "our boy" and "our Mexican boy."[52] These phrases remind one of slavery days, and it is not difficult to imagine that the social and economic systems of Porfirian Mexico might have looked familiar to travelers from the South just a generation after abolition.

With the exception of the Yaqui (the indigenous group so vilified and brutalized by the Porfirian regime, and that Americans also saw as hostile and barbarous), American travelers almost always described native people as backward but ultimately harmless because of their natural indolence and willingness to serve. Above all, the *mozo* represented the Indian docility that Americans found so appealing throughout the Porfiriato. During the early part of the railroad era in Mexico, for example, traveler Frederick A. Ober described the *mozo* as follows:

> I like the *mozos*; they are honest and faithful. In the number I have employed, I have not had a faithless one. And then they are so humble;

they will hardly address you without touching their hats, and they are so grateful for a kindness. Poor fellows! . . . This one had trotted by my side for several miles, and when I gave him a piece of silver he could not understand why I should do so; it was only two reales, yet he was so profuse in his thanks that I galloped away from him to escape them.[53]

This description is accompanied by a drawing of an old *mozo* hunched under a heavy load and weighed down further with two more baskets. The most famous representation of a *mozo* would appear almost two decades after the Porfiriato in the form of Rosalino, the simple and indecisive servant in D. H. Lawrence's *Mornings in Mexico* (1927). Tellingly, Lawrence meditates on the differences between native and white people in a chapter dedicated to Rosalino, reiterating the long-standing view of Indians as people with little understanding of the meaning of time and money, and then he projects his impressions of the flighty *mozo* onto the entire native population of Mexico. Lawrence went to Mexico in the late 1920s, but the tropes of the *mozo* with which he plays date back to Porfirian travel discourse. Unlike the iconic British writer, photographers rarely found photographic inspiration in the *mozos*, but, like the burden bearer, they were an important part of travel discourse representing Porfirian Mexico. While the *cargador* fulfilled a particular niche in popular representations of Mexico, we will see in subsequent chapters that some travel writers interpreted the burden bearer as a strikingly contradictory representation of Mexican Indians' inability to modernize.

TEMPORAL ENCOUNTERS

Travelers have long seen the markers of Mexico's past as the most photogenic thing about the nation. Some of the very first widely circulated photographs of Mexico, dating from the French Intervention, featured ruins and native people photographed in styles that evoked Rome and Athens. Travelers who took part in the American "invasion" that began in the 1880s were no exception, for they frequently photographed the nation's antiquities, from the vast complexes of ruins freshly uncovered at the time to other symbols of the past like the famous Aztec Calendar Stone that was then on display at the National Museum in Mexico City.[54] Professional photographers and writers clamored to record these sites and symbols firsthand and to report back to audiences in the United States about the many ancient wonders that awaited the tourist. They treated native people in a similar fashion, erroneously reporting again and again that Indian people lived exactly as they always had in the "Land of the Montezumas," unchanged by the conditions of modernity.[55]

Travel discourse throughout the Porfiriato claimed that a journey to Mexico was a trip backward in time. One *Los Angeles Times* article claimed that

> had Jesus come to the west coast of Mexico a few years ago He would have seen people eating the same kind of bread, living in the same kinds of houses, and plowing with the same kind of plow as when He was on the earth before. There was contentment, certainly, but there was also ignorance of life as it is understood today, and the word "progress" meant nothing to them.[56]

Descriptions such as this abound in American travel writing from the Porfiriato. "It is like a dream, this passing from one civilization to another," noted Mrs. James Edwin Morris, "as if one had closed his eyes in the twentieth century and opened them in the fifteenth, everything is so different, even the blue jays are green, and there are honey bees that do not sting."[57] Another woman claimed at the end of the nineteenth century that "from the Anglo-Saxon civilization of to-day we pass, upon crossing the river, to the Spanish-American civilization of one hundred and fifty years ago."[58] Describing his stay in a rural posada in the 1880s, J. Hendrickson McCarty compared the antiques at the inn to the local people. "The furniture of my room were relics of another generation," he wrote. "The human beings around me, in their dress, manners, and customs, resembled more the embodied ghosts of a long-gone past, than the people of this advanced age of the world."[59] For each of these authors, Mexican people (and especially indigenous Mexicans) were living in the past, and part of the pleasure of going to Mexico resided, as it still does for some people, in taking a trip back in time. In this sense, Mexican travel functions like a time machine.

Travel discourse also constructed Mexico as a place where the past and the present (and even the future) confronted one another. Mexico had long been seen as a contact zone between cultures, and now it was the staging ground for encounters between times and temporalities. The *Los Angeles Times* article quoted above, for example, argued that the west coast of Mexico, where the word "progress" had meant nothing at the turn of the twentieth century, was rapidly transforming with the help of U.S. investment. The land that had not changed since Jesus's time looked increasingly like the United States—a welcome change for the Americans who hoped to capitalize on Mexican resources. The article claimed that the railroad had spurred "a new era in Western Mexico."

As tourism increased in the late nineteenth century, photos of busy factories, oil derricks, steaming locomotives, and other markers of modernity began to appear alongside ancient ruins and the native people who lived among them. By the turn of the twentieth century, travel writers and photographers began to see urban streets and coastal ports busy with commerce, the Gilded Age opulence of Porfirian architecture, and upper-class mestiza women dressed in Paris's latest fashions on the Paseo de la Reforma in Mexico City. These dual emphases on the "traditional" and the "progressive" proved most dynamic when they confronted one another, as they frequently did in travel discourse from that period. As one traveler in the late nineteenth century put it, Mexico came to represent "a marvelous conglomerate of the ancient and the modern—the pathetic and the ludicrous."[60]

Many travelers claimed that the encounter between the ancient and the modern was, in fact, what made Porfirian Mexico such a dynamic place to visit. W. E. Carson introduced his travelogue by declaring:

> The automobile, electric light, and promoter have come; the Indian with his *burro*, the *cargador* with his burden, and the old-fashioned village priest have remained. Thus it is that in Mexico the old and the new are everywhere side by side. It is this strange mixture of the ancient and modern that produces such queer phases of life as exist in Mexico to-day.[61]

For Carson and the countless travelers who saw Mexico as a meeting place between the past and the future, these "queer phases of life" made the nation quaint and picturesque, but also ripe for exploitation. Even the things that Americans had begun to take for granted as marvelous markers of modern life took on new meanings in Mexico. In 1888, one travelogue claimed that electric lights were "a thousand times more unnatural here, glittering above a people and a country as primitive as if the world were a thousand times younger."[62] The authors of this book (which, ironically, claimed in its title that Mexico was "picturesque, political, *progressive*"; emphasis mine), like so many others, found the

PEARSON'S MAGAZINE

VOL. XIX   MARCH, 1908   NO. 3

Photographed by Percy Cox, Mexico
THE MEETING OF TWO CIVILIZATIONS IN MEXICO TO-DAY

FIGURE 1.10. "The meeting of two civilizations." James Creelman, "President Diaz."

juxtaposition of modern convenience and primitive people both surprising and thrilling.

American photographers working in Mexico developed a series of visual tricks and tropes to capture the nation's supposed temporal difference in images that appeared in travelogues, newspapers and magazines, picture postcards, and a variety of other media. In one of the photographs by Percy F. Cox that illustrated both James Creelman's interview with Díaz in *Pearson's* and an article in *The World's Work* in 1907, an early Ford automobile faces a small line of burros bearing large loads on a dusty road (Figure 1.10).[63] The driver of the car appears to glance at the animals, which walk obediently forward but lack a driver of their own. They carry huge, neat loads, as they do in many representations of archaic Mexican transport. The gleaming auto represented the height of modernity in 1907 and 1908 when these articles appeared. It freed drivers from beasts of burden and from the train's oppressive timetables. Suddenly, the individual could see Mexican byways from behind the steering wheels of their own autos. The Ford product also connoted the highly rationalized means of production that began in Detroit and spread to disparate parts of the world in the first half of the twentieth century. Perhaps Cox was promoting in this image not only the Ford but also Ford*ism*, especially given the context of the articles illustrated by the photograph. Creelman joined the chorus of Americans promoting Díaz as the architect of Mexican modernity. The praise of this ethos was repeated in *The World's Work*. The overall aim of such promotional efforts was to replace traditional means of production with an economy that employed more modern means of production. The captions make this clear by describing the scene as "the meeting of two civilizations in Mexico to-day" and "the old and the new on Toluca road." Postcards turned similarly styled images with related messages into commodities that could cheaply circulate between friends and across international lines.

At the same time that the perceived backwardness of Indian people made them attractive and exploitable, as Waite's work suggested, it also implied that they were incapable of evolving into modern subjects. "The contact of these people with the outer world is so slight that they are not changed by it. Gazing at them one is carried back even beyond the times of the old Spanish kings and queens," wrote J. Hendrickson McCarty regarding native people in 1888. While for some (including, perhaps, Waite) this meant that Indians were quaint and picturesque, for others it raised serious concerns about the futures of Indian people and the Mexican state. "We are pointed by some historians to the glorious past of Mexico," McCarty continued, "but now we see only degeneracy, lack of ambition, and want of education."[64] This fallen state of Mexican Indianness, as still others saw it, meant that Indians were ripe for transformation.

The idea that Mexico was somehow in between the past and the future (but still not part of the present) reflected the ambivalence with which travelers viewed their southern neighbors. Placing them in this interstitial space helped to frame them within the politics of informal empire, since viewing them as *almost* but *not quite* modern worked to rationalize economic interventionism. Again and again, travel discourse suggested that capitalist development had a civilizing effect and would bring Mexico up to the present day. These representational practices also opened the spaces for American observers to think about Mexico's future—and their own nation's role in plotting that future. Alongside the stock images of Mexican backwardness (including the sleepy peon, who also appeared frequently in the photographic work of Waite and his peers) emerged an intense interest in markers of progress and the potential to transform Mexico into an economically and culturally modern nation. Such motifs served as an endorsement of the Díaz regime and attested to the positive influences of U.S. capitalist intervention. Waite contributed to this view by taking pictures of Mexicans engaged in more modern forms of work. While it is tempting to guess that images like these would have replaced the representational practices associated with "Old Mexico," they merely began to appear alongside images connoting backwardness.

While these representational systems add up to a dominant view of Mexico as a nation in flux, other travelers saw a trip across the border as a trip directly backward in time. This is perhaps unsurprising, as this trope persists wherever, in Gloria Anzaldúa's terms, the "Third World grates against the first and bleeds."[65] According to scholar Mary Pat Brady, national borders "utilize the fantasy that on one side of the border a nation exists in one phase of temporal development while the other side functions in a different stage of temporality."[66] Travelogue writer Phillips Russell captured this fantasy, still evident in travel guides and memoirs, by describing his relief upon returning to the United States from Mexico in 1929 because it meant a return to the twentieth century. Americans, according to Russell, were "sleek and comfort loving . . . unified, electric, and uniform. They are living in the present day, the present hour, the present moment. How odd to see this all again, on coming up from dusty Mexico, where in almost every man's soul the Spaniard fights the Indian . . . and medievalism wars with the shortcuts of the twentieth century."[67] Perhaps G. L. Morrill, the flamboyant American preacher whose career I examine more fully in Chapter Five, most succinctly captured the temporal differences between the countries when he claimed, upon returning from Mexico in 1917, "Civilization marches to America's time."[68]

WOMEN AS RUINS

With the question of Mexican temporality in mind, we return to the place of women in Waite's and other photographers' representations of Mexican backwardness. Over and over in the work of Waite and his peers, women, especially indigenous women, represented Mexico's transition to modernity and modern times. While travelers sometimes claimed that Mexican men, especially mestizo men, stood at the cusp of modernity and could be remade into good workers and capitalist subjects, Mexican women consistently stood for the nation's apparently tenuous grasp of modernity. This presumption was demonstrated in a

Photographed by Percy Cox, Mexico

HERE ARE OLD MEXICO AND NEW MEXICO FACE TO FACE

FIGURE 1.11. New technology and an "ancient race." James Creelman, "President Diaz."

second powerful image by Percy Cox from *Pearson's*, which appeared just a few pages after the picture of the burros and the Model T, depicting an Indian woman on a crumbling staircase (Figure 1.11).[69] The woman pauses on the stairs to look to her left; a small baby is tucked into her rebozo. From around a bend, a steaming locomotive barrels toward her, thick black smoke billowing into the sky. The engine and the woman mirror each other at the center of the image. Creelman, echoing perceptions of Mexico as a meeting place between the ancient and the modern, captioned the scene "Here are old Mexico and new Mexico face to face." Indeed, the woman's days seem numbered, as the coming of progress and modern development was, in Creelman's view, inevitable. This view was not merely the domain of imperialists or capitalists. Reformers also saw Mexico, being close to the United States but culturally backward, as an ideal testing ground for their principles. The spread of literacy, hygiene, compulsory education, and (in the case of the many missionaries who worked there during the Porfiriato) Protestantism would modernize the nation and make it closely resemble the "progressive" United States. However, women like the one descending the staircase in Cox's image belonged to the past. Reformers, like the capitalists and industrialists, were interested in the nation's future.

As feminist visual and film theory has established, women's bodies have long been used as synecdoches for both the nation and, more generally, for civilization. In the North American context, for example, Phillis Wheatley first personified the spirit of the United States as a female "Columbia" in a 1776 poem.[70] An abstract figure based on principles rather than a discrete landmass or political formation or real historical figure, Columbia has symbolized the nation ever since. In contrast, the women pictured in American travel discourse as belonging to the past were flesh-and-blood real women who were marked by photographers, writers, and editors as the embodiments of Mexico. Photographs were particularly useful in equating women with civilization, as they did in the nineteenth- and early-twentieth-century sentimental portraits described by Laura Wexler in *Tender Violence*. Photography, as Wexler argues, "was part of the master narrative that created and cemented new cultural and political inequalities of race and class by manipulating the sign 'woman' as an indicator of 'civilization.'"[71] White women were equated with civilization above all "Others." But in the Mexican context, brown women (meaning mestizas and *indígenas*) were the ones equated with the nation and its only tenuous grasp of civilization in American photographers' eyes.[72] It is telling, therefore, that these women embodied a culture looking at its own demise in images like the ones described above.

This does not mean, however, that relegating women to the past made them undesirable to their observers. Waite, for one, frequently posed women among ruins to suggest that they, like the ruins themselves, were a beautiful and ancient part of the landscape that demanded the viewer's attention. Likewise, the Indian women and girls that he more explicitly eroticized (those who were topless, naked, or posed in suggestive manners) almost always engaged in old-fashioned, even archaic-looking, activities, such as grinding corn on a stone metate or bathing in a river. No North American woman who considered herself living in modern, progressive times would take part in such activities (nor have their pictures taken while doing so), but positioning Indian women in this way was easier for photographers because they were not seen as living in the contemporary moment.[73]

In the context of my emphasis on economic conquest and the politics of representation, what does it mean to relegate women and girls to the past? One possible interpretation of images like Cox's is that women like the one pictured here were desirable because they posed no threat to American manhood, which many politicians and cultural workers understood to be threatened in the late nineteenth century. The "New Woman" emerged in the United States as a concept and social force around the same time that Americans began to travel to Mexico in large numbers. As Michael Rogin notes, the New Woman "appears everywhere at the end of the nineteenth century, in the work force and reform movements, in literature, art, social thought, and psychology."[74] The New Woman was also a staple in popular culture. Lantern slide shows and other forms of popular entertainment, for example, featured songs and images of wives and mothers who fled suburban comfort to pursue individuality in the city—and the faithful parents, husbands, and children who waited, hoping that they would return. In an interesting contrast, Ethel B. Tweedie illustrated her travelogue with an image of herself riding on the front of a train engine (Figure 1.12).[75] In body-hugging clothing and a jaunty cap, she returns the camera's gaze, seeming to embody the independent spirit of the New Woman. Unlike the woman on the stairs, she confronts and conquers the engine.

Perhaps the women whom photographers and writers positioned as "Old Mexico" represented an alternative to the New Woman. New Women, as many examples from U.S. popular culture at the time attest, posed a problem to traditional family and social structures. Popular songs and melodramas claimed that women's liberation from the home would mean the wide-scale abandonment of American husbands and children. This was, to be sure, a reactionary mode of representation. As Kristin L. Hoganson's work on manliness and U.S. political culture has shown, U.S. politicians like Theodore Roosevelt and Albert J. Beveridge also waged a counterattack on the New Woman by promoting Victorian sexual and gender mores in speeches and political tracts. It might have been their imagined backwardness that made indigenous women, framed as "traditional" and "old fashioned," attractive to American men, who saw them as charmingly shy, old-fashioned, and demure. The woman descending the stairs in Cox's image, for example, seems to passively accept her fate. Regardless of what attributes American view-

A ride on an engine.

FIGURE 1.12. Tweedie on an engine. Mrs. Alec (Ethel B.) Tweedie, *Mexico as I Saw It*.

ers saw in supposedly timeless Mexican women, it is clear that ideas about time, progress, and modernity intersect in images such as these.

CONCLUSION

The Mexico of Charles B. Waite and his contemporaries was filled with helpless girls and strong burden bearers, but Indian difference also posed some dangers to the expansion of U.S. capitalism and modernity to Mexico, as Chapter Three will describe. As for the man whose work has framed this analysis, C. B. Waite spent the last decade and a half of his life back in the United States, where he could only witness the chaos of the Mexican Revolution from a distance. He had lost in the war his land, his brother, and perhaps his love for Mexico, the nation that he obsessively photographed for almost two decades. When Waite and his daughter returned to Mexico City in 1925 for a brief visit, one newspaper wistfully described him as "another old-timer who has deserted us for other lands."[76] While I have focused on Waite, dozens of other foreign photographers who worked in Porfirian Mexico, including Abel Briquet and Winfield Scott, would also have served my purposes here (with only minor divergences in techniques, subjects, and artistry). The chapters that follow will revisit Waite's impressive body of work and put it in conversation with other media makers and the ways of seeing and knowing Mexico that they developed.

Even today, encounters with Indian people in Mexico still lend the illusion of credibility and authenticity to the touristic experience for non-Indian people (including, sometimes, me). Inheriting ways of seeing from Waite and Hamilton, Americans continue to fix their gazes upon Mexicans and to take pleasure in the act of looking. Any cursory glance at the human subjects found in travel and promotional materials produced in Mexico, the United States, and elsewhere finds that native people still serve as powerful signifiers of the pleasures that await them in Mexico, second only to images of white heterosexual couples enjoying the country's beaches. And when one travels to Mexico, whether as a scholar or a tourist (I travel to Mexico as both), one cannot escape the presence of North American and European tourists pulling out their cameras when they see particularly compelling indigenous people.

At the same time, the desire to photograph the Other is no longer unidirectional. When I visited Teotihuacan several years ago, I could not help but notice that several members of a mestizo Mexican family were snapping pictures of my friend Andrew, his fine red hair and pink skin barely visible from under the protection of a huge straw hat that he had bought for a few dozen pesos. Giggling, some of the teenagers in the family approached us and asked him to pose for a photo at the top of the Pyramid of the Sun. Andrew, perplexed but flattered, obliged. When I asked them, in Spanish, why they would make such a request, one young man looked at me blankly, as if the answer were obvious. "*Porque es muy extranjero,*" he said, explaining in just a few words that Andrew's foreignness made him a desirable photographic subject. I am reluctant, of course, to suggest that the politics of representation examined throughout this chapter have been reversed in any way, but I did take heart in the possibility that, almost one hundred years after Waite packed up his negatives and returned to California, the practice of looking at racial, social, and cultural difference could go both ways. If the camera is a gun, as Sontag famously claimed, perhaps more Mexicans have access to arms than ever before.

"THE GREATEST AND WISEST DESPOT OF MODERN TIMES": PORFIRIO DÍAZ, AMERICAN TRAVELERS, AND THE POLITICS OF LOGICAL PATERNALISM

Now, one president for twenty years. Some will say that this is not republican. Possibly not, but it is business.
CHARLES F. LUMMIS (1902)

THE HUMBLE BEGINNINGS OF José de la Cruz Porfirio Díaz Mori, who was raised by a downwardly mobile mother in remote Oaxaca, could not have foretold his enduring relevance to Mexican history. As one American reporter grandly put it, the "slender, dark-eyed Oaxacan boy, with the Spanish-Mixtec blood in his veins, who was to do these wonderful things for his country, and change Mexico from a weakness and a shame to an honor and a strength among the American nations, could not foresee the part he was to play in history."[1] Díaz's terms as President spanned 1876–1880 and the long period from 1884 to his 1911 exile. While he did officially cede the office to Manuel González from 1880 to 1884, Díaz continued to wield power during those years as the governor of Oaxaca and general commissioner of the Mexican delegation to the 1884 New Orleans World's Fair—no small task in an era in which the nation's elite desperately attempted to alter Mexico's international reputation.

Despite the undeniable fact that Mexico became more stable and prosperous under Díaz's rule, the century of historiography that followed the Porfiriato has not been kind to this president. As historians of Mexico have shown, Díaz's tactics became increasingly authoritarian and contradictory as the regime became untenable, especially after the economic crisis of 1907, which had shaken the faith of his circle of advisors that modernization was possible in Mexico. The material improvements that travelers spied from the comforts of their Pullman cars were increasingly concentrated in the hands of the country's elite. By 1910, just three thousand wealthy families owned fully half of Mexico's land, and seventeen of those families controlled one-fifth of the country, as historian Frank McLynn has shown.[2] Fully three-quarters of Díaz's subjects worked as farmhands. Most of these campesinos were caught in a brutal system of debt peonage that closely resembled slavery, despite the fact that the president was quick to boast that slavery had never been legal in the Republic of Mexico. The campesinos were also highly susceptible to fluctuations in the nation's economy, and many suffered greatly in the years following the 1907 crisis. Still, Díaz never gave up on his attempts to present Mexico as a modernizing state, even when the pomp and circumstance of his statecraft glaringly contradicted the everyday realities of the vast majority of the populace. McLynn claims that Díaz spent more on his eightieth birthday gala than was spent on Mexico's entire 1910 national education budget. In the years following the dictator's downfall, scholarly and popular attention to (and valorization of) the Mexican Revolution has relegated Díaz to the role of a historical supervillain on whom many future representations of the Latin American dictator would be based. But that should not divert attention from the symbolic power of Díaz for the American promoters of Mexican modernity.

This chapter focuses on the image of Porfirio Díaz in American popular culture from the 1880s until the first decade of the twentieth century. Showing that Díaz served as a marker of imperialist relations between the United States and Mexico, this chapter examines how he embodied in the American imagination both an idealized colonial leader (and father) who could facilitate their economic conquest and, crucially, the mestizo subject whose modernization would ensure the political stability of the nation. I am less concerned with the historical Díaz than with representational practices associated with him, especially the ways that Americans cast Díaz and his wife as the heads of a national family that was amenable to the cultural politics of economic conquest. Díaz serves, at least in my view, as another text, and a rich case study, that illuminates the imperialistic undertones of U.S.-Mexican relations during his rule.

HERO OF THE AMERICAS

For an elderly foreign dictator, Porfirio Díaz was tremendously popular with American travelers and observers by the end of his rule. Well-to-do Americans traveling to Mexico clamored to meet with him and his beautiful young wife, the former Carmen Romero Rubio, known popularly as "Carmelita." The presidential couple indulged a surprising number of these requests, and their lucky American guests described meeting them with an almost palpable sense of awe. "As you wait in the anteroom to meet the president," wrote one ardent American supporter at the end of the nineteenth century, "you are about to meet what is probably the greatest figure—and unquestionably the most romantic—in the world's politics this half century . . . and before you know it you are seated vis-à-vis with the creator of a new factor in American destiny."[3] Those who could not secure personal audiences with "the foremost man of the American hemisphere" sent home postcards featuring official-looking photographs or pasted *cartes de visite* of Díaz in their scrapbooks. Americans who wrote travelogues frequently credited him with single-handedly transforming the nation from a dangerous and unknown backwater into one that more closely resembled American ideas about order and progress. Newspapers like the *Los Angeles Times* and *New York Times* called the military veteran a "hero of peace" and the "lion-hearted son of Mexico." Díaz, to put it in contemporary terms, had star power.

One of the most remarkable elements of the positive media representations of Díaz that appeared throughout his rule is the almost complete lack of dissent from American observers of Mexico. In 1911, at the end of the Porfiriato, John Kenneth Turner, the first American to criticize the president to a mass audience, noted, "While the number of articles containing praise of Diaz which have been published in magazines—not to mention newspapers—during the past several years have undoubtedly run into the hundreds, I do not know of one prominent magazine that has prosecuted a criticism of the Mexican dictator."[4] It was Turner himself who would help persuade the American public of the regime's corruption, undoing the popular image of the president examined in this chapter. While Turner made no mention of travel discourse in his criticism of the media, his accusation also applied to the hundreds of travelogues that were published in the United States throughout the Porfiriato.

One only needs to glance at travelogues published during the Porfiriato to grasp how popular the president was with visitors from the United States. Díaz's portrait graced the frontispieces to scores of travelogues, from woodcuts presenting him as a dashing young soldier in the 1880s to later photographs depicting him as an old man, an august elder statesman in full military regalia. In 1897, at the apex of the Porfiriato, Marie Robinson Wright dedicated her *Picturesque Mexico* "to Señor General Don Porfirio Díaz, the illustrious President of Mexico, whose intrepid moral character, distinguished statesmanship, and devoted patriotism make him the pride and glory of his country," and claimed that Mexico's "importance as a nation is due to the patriot under whose administration Mexico now flourishes and holds its proud position among the republics of the world." The frontispiece featured a large photograph of Díaz clad in full military regalia and sporting huge whiskers, underscoring her vision of the man as a patriot, statesman, and creator of national stability (Figure 2.1, seen here as a postcard). Like many American proponents of the regime, Wright explicitly conflated Díaz and the nation. "Diaz's life," she wrote, "has been identified with the republic for the last forty years."[5] Fourteen years later, on the eve of the dictator's flight to France, Wright ironically claimed in another book that, "among the names of the wonder-workers of the world the name Porfirio Diaz will shine and remain imperishable."[6]

Charles F. Lummis, the founder of the Southwest Museum in Los Angeles (now part of the Autry National Center), was one of Díaz's most outspoken supporters in the United States by the late 1890s. Lummis, a Harvard graduate, had achieved fame by walking from Ohio to California to accept a position as the first city editor of the *Los Angeles Times* in 1884, the same year that U.S. and Mexican rail lines were linked in El Paso. Los Angeles had a population of just over twelve thousand at the time, but was experiencing a rapid growth in its Anglo population. Like many new arrivals, Lummis was entranced by the city's romanticized (and recent) Mexican past. Fewer than forty years prior, the city, like all of California, had been part of Mexico, but the cultural politics of Manifest Destiny and white nativism imagined Mexican California as a thing of the past. The city's boosters now saw its future in the ever-growing Anglo community. Though his job at the *Times* required him to promote white settlement, Lummis nonetheless became a proponent of Indian rights. In addition to travelogues and personal reflections on the conditions of native people in the U.S. Southwest, Lummis wrote fiction and poetry. Over the course of more than four decades in Los Angeles, Lummis remained a fixture among the Euro-American elite in the rapidly expanding city, eventually growing into the role of a highly eccentric elder statesman—a position that he relished.[7]

In *The Awakening of a Nation* (1898), Lummis praised Díaz in a chapter succinctly titled "The Man." The author, like many of the Ameri-

Géneral Porfirio Diaz, Presidente de México.

J. G. Hatton, Mexico.   No. 7976

FIGURE 2.1. Postcard depicting the official Díaz image. Author's collection.

cans who traveled to Mexico during this period, simultaneously championed and suspended his convictions about democracy in his homage to the president. Díaz infamously had the nation's constitution suspended to remove all restrictions on reelection and subsequently stayed in office through a combination of manipulation, violence, and savvy political maneuvering. Even so, travelogue writers, afraid to upset the delicate balance of friendly political and economic relations between the United States and Mexico or to loosen Mexico's seemingly tenuous grasp of modernity, found it extremely difficult to criticize the regime. Writing in 1899 in a magazine that he founded, Lummis described Díaz as "the autocrat of fifteen millions of people—and not merely autocrat but idol. The Czar has no more power; but no czar ever used his power so wisely and none was ever so beloved."[8] Despite the fact that Díaz faced constant criticism in his own country, Lummis even claimed that there was no opposition in Mexico, reinforcing the assumption common among American promoters and speculators that Mexico's stability was well worth the suspension of democracy and the squelching of dissent. It was not until the 1910 publication of *Barbarous Mexico* more than twenty years later, in fact, that Díaz would become associated with debt peonage, the endurance of the hacienda, the subjugation of the Yaqui and other indigenous groups, and countless wrongs against the people that he ruled. Throughout the Porfiriato, however, American observers proved themselves quite adept at idealizing his undemocratic regime at the same time that they promoted Mexico's move toward American political and economic systems.

Even the few observers who criticized the economic and governance systems that kept the regime afloat could not help but admire the transformation of Mexico under the "great soldier." John Rice, for example, wrote a scathing indictment of debt peonage within the hacienda system in *Mexico: Our Neighbor* (1888). An incensed Rice compared the hacienda to slavery decades before muckraking journalists turned their attention to President Díaz's role in perpetuating oppressive labor practices. "Peonage," Rice wrote, "is very nearly the equivalent of slavery, and exists, not by force of law, as formerly, but by the prescriptive claims of the landlord and the helpless ignorance and dependence of the peon."[9] But Rice was hesitant to write anything negative about Díaz, focusing instead on the president's military prowess and concluding that the "democratic oligarchy" that ruled the nation was the only stable form of power in a nation as racially diverse as Mexico. A careful observer of the nation's political economy, Rice would have known that Díaz allied himself with powerful *hacendados* and created policies that expanded the hacienda system despite the fact that the colonial hacienda seemed to contradict the modes of production associated with modern capitalism. Rice criticized the hacienda while celebrating the fabulous "progress" of the nation under Díaz. A heroic-looking etching of the president in his younger days served as the frontispiece to the book.

Ethel B. Tweedie was more blunt than most in her description of the Porfirian political system. "The fundamental laws of the country provide universal suffrage, it is true," she wrote, "but it has never been exercised, and the President is re-elected by his political following. The ordinary rancheros and cowboys know nothing about the election until they hear it is over, when they just nod and say nothing." Like most foreign observers, Tweedie understood democracy under Díaz to be a farce. Still, she championed Díaz, referring to him just a few lines later as the "greatest and wisest despot of modern times."[10] Tweedie's description demonstrates the fact that foreign travelers in Mexico found themselves willing to accept—and even promote—the contradictions of Porfirian modernity. Tweedie, like many of her contemporaries, perceived that a Mexican president could be great, wise, despotic, and modern all at once. Her insight is all the more fascinating because it came from a woman. Tweedie was, in fact, among dozens of women who published travelogues that lavished praise on the president, referring to him, in the Victorian sense of the term, as the most "romantic" figure in the Americas. Marie Robinson Wright, the woman who so extravagantly dedicated her travelogue to Díaz, concluded her chapter on the president by declaring that "history will place him among the nation-builders."[11] These women played a significant role in the project of convincing American readers that backing the regime would benefit both Mexico and the United States.

Newspapers and magazines also expressed deep affection for Díaz throughout the Porfiriato. The *Los Angeles Times* ran dozens of stories from the 1880s to 1911 that glorified the president as a modernizer, peacemaker, and striver who ascended, as one headline read, "from poverty to a palace."[12] The paper published three special sections between 1903 and 1909 dedicated to Mexico's development and the role of the United States in shaping the nation's future. Illustrated with dozens of photographs, each features articles and advertisements emphasizing the opportunities for pleasure and profit in Díaz's Mexico. Even following the president's exile, the *Times* and other papers held firm to the idea that the "Gray Eagle of Mexico" would return and restore order to his country. Coverage of his departure from Veracruz, for example, focused on his dignified appearance, the crowd's apparent love for their deposed leader, and Díaz's prophesy that he would return to and die in Mexico.[13] He never did make it back, but after his death in Paris in 1915, the *Times* eulogized him as "the creator of modern Mexico." Couching its praise in a criticism of the revolution then under way in Mexico, the paper wrote that "he was a dictator because it would have been folly to intrust the government to the wobbling masses; he was a great and good President for Mexico because only a spirit and will and a mastery like his could keep Mexico from falling where it has now fallen. . . . Another Diaz— that is what Mexico needs today! But is there another?"[14] All through these years, however, the *Times* neglected to note that its publisher, Harrison Gray Otis, owned more than a million acres in Mexico.

James Creelman's hagiographic interview with the president for *Pearson's Magazine*, published in February of 1908, late in the Porfiriato, endures as one of the most famous representations of Díaz to appear in the United States during the Porfiriato.[15] Titled "President Diaz: Hero of the Americas," Creelman's article created an instant sensation in both the United States and Mexico because it contained Díaz's announcement that he would not seek another term—a promise that might have been the result of pressure from U.S. diplomats and one that he later reversed. However, as Claudio Lomnitz has argued, scholars have considered the interview almost exclusively in terms of how it affected Mexican popular opinion about Díaz.[16] It is true that the Creelman interview is so iconic in Mexican history that some historians and critics mark the start of the Mexican Revolution with its publication. Víctor Agustín Casasola, for instance, the eminent practitioner and archivist of early photojournalism in Mexico, began his *Álbum histórico gráfico* of 1921, a pictorial history of the revolution drawn from his vast photo archives, with a reproduction of the Creelman interview.[17] Still, without underestimating its impact in Mexico, we must acknowledge that the interview made significant waves in the United States as well.

This should not imply that Creelman presented a boldly original view of Díaz and the Porfiriato. In fact, the reporter recycled the material established in American travelogues since the 1880s. However, Creelman reached a wider audience at a critical juncture in Mexican history in which it became clear that the regime could not last forever but unclear what would follow the Porfiriato. Like Marie Robinson Wright and Tweedie, Creelman presented the president to American readers as the human embodiment of a romantic and modernizing nation. "There is not a more romantic or heroic figure in the world," Creelman claimed,

> nor one more intensely watched by both the friends and foes of democracy, than the soldier-statesman, whose adventurous youth pales the pages of Dumas, and whose iron rule has converted the warring, ignorant, superstitious, and impoverished masses of Mexico . . . into a strong, steady, peaceful, debt-paying, and progressive nation.[18]

The words used to describe the nation in this description—"strong, steady, debt-paying, progressive"—might also apply to Díaz himself, especially given how eager the president's American boosters were to conflate Díaz with the nation. The great popularity of the article illustrates that Díaz interested readers on both sides of the U.S.-Mexico border, but even more telling is the fact that American businesses used the Creelman article to promote Mexico as a stable nation with which to conduct business. The American-owned Mexican National Packing Company, for instance, distributed free copies of the article in the United States.[19]

On the whole, the article succinctly captured the American zeal for the Porfiriato and its continuation. It praised him, for example, for assuaging Mexican suspicion of the United States by opening the rail connection between the two countries. "It had been proposed," wrote Creelman, "that no railroad should be permitted between Mexico and the United States. The country was to be saved from future invasion by an intervening wilderness. Against the bitterest opposition . . . Diaz welcomed the great trunk railways built by American capital, and had generous subsidies granted to them."[20] Creelman closed the piece with a statement from Elihu Root, a lawyer, statesman, public intellectual, and enthusiastic Díaz supporter who would go on to win a Nobel Peace Prize in 1912. Root's description underscored Díaz's popularity outside of Mexico: "It has seemed to me that of all the men now living, General Porfirio Diaz, of Mexico, was the best worth seeing." Root went on to describe Díaz's "commanding character" and "singularly attractive personality," concluding, "As I am neither poet, musician nor Mexican, but only an American who loves justice and liberty and hopes to see their reign among mankind progress and strengthen and become perpetual, I look to Porfirio Diaz, the President of Mexico, as one of the great men to be held up for the hero-worship of mankind."[21] Root helped improve relations with Latin America during his tenure as U.S.

Secretary of State, and like many elites on both sides of the border, saw Díaz as a stabilizing factor necessary for U.S. economic inroads in the resource-rich nation. According to Gilbert G. González, Díaz's receptiveness to foreign investment "presaged the 'globalization' schemes of the late twentieth century sponsored under the mantra of neoliberalism," and Root's hagiographic language probably reflected his interest in opening Mexico to American markets.[22] Creelman provided the necessary medium for these sentiments to reach a popular audience.

Mexico's modernization was a wide-scale social and economic project involving, over several decades, countless members of the nation's political elite—especially the *científicos*, a circle of technocratic advisors and ministers who adhered to positivist "scientific politics" and were deeply committed to modernizing the nation. Some historians argue, for example, that José Yves Limantour, Mexico's finance minister from 1893 to the fall of the regime, played a momentous role in the production of the modern Mexican economy. Even so, Creelman, Root, and countless foreign boosters stubbornly refused to see modernization as a group effort. "Under his stern rule," wrote traveler W. E. Carson, "the progress of Mexico has been marvellous [*sic*]. The old Mexican cities have suddenly become busy places, with new public buildings, fine shops, asphalted streets, electric lights, electric street cars, and other visible evidence of modern progress."[23] According to Carson and other makers of Mexican travel discourse, "modern progress" could be measured in architectural and infrastructural innovations. Carson called these improvements to the cities—along with new sewers, waterworks, and electrical plants—the "adjuncts to civilization" and credited such advancements to Díaz's collaboration with foreign investors. Thanks to Díaz, he claimed, "men with money are swarming into Mexico from all parts of the world to engage in business."[24]

As Carson's description suggests, it was not only infrastructural improvements that dazzled travelers and "men with money." Díaz himself was also an attraction. Many of the Americans who wrote about their adventures in Mexico, especially those carrying diplomatic papers, claimed to have personally met Díaz, creating a sense of the president as one spectacle among the many with which travelers could directly engage. It helped, of course, that Díaz always seemed to be willing to play along and that the president had cultivated such an air of aristocratic elegance. "On the part of prominent Americans traveling in Mexico," observed John Kenneth Turner, "it has become a custom, a sort of formality of the trip, to banquet at Chapultepec castle—the lesser lights at Chapultepec cafe—and to raise the after-dinner voice in most extravagant praise, loudly to attribute to Porfirio Diaz the virtues of a superman, even of a demi-god. . . . As prominent Catholics journeying to Rome seek an audience with the Pope, so Americans traveling to Mexico seek an audience with General Diaz; they usually get it and are flattered."[25] Wallace Gillpatrick, an American expatriate who wrote for the English-language *Mexican Herald* and published *The Man Who Likes Mexico* in 1911, represented his encounter with the president as a celebration of diplomatic relations between their two countries, a moment that echoed the author's frequent references to Mexico as a grateful younger sibling to the United States. A lunch shared with the president and some American friends, for example, provided an opportunity for the author to reflect upon Mexico's debt to the United States. Gillpatrick related Díaz's own claim that "it was our revolution and achievement that had heartened Mexico to cast off the yoke of Spain; that Mexico's government was modeled, so far as possible, after ours."[26] Díaz made a habit of flattering visiting Americans in this way, but it is ironic that in 1911 he should identify the revolutionary spirit of the United States as an inspiration.

Meeting with the president allowed already-impressed American visitors to express even deeper admiration for the man and his country. Despite the fact that Díaz spoke very little English, travelers found him to be polite and hospitable. They saw his formal and slightly aloof manner as an intrinsic and distinctly Mexican part of his personality. Travelers failed to note that this was a public persona that Díaz had carefully crafted over several decades as a politician and one that, it seems, his wife had played a significant role in developing. The lucky ones who attended formal occasions such as balls or state dinners saw that these traits extended to the nation's upper classes in general, since Mexican high society welcomed travelers with the right credentials.[27] However, like Díaz, the Mexican aristocracy practiced perfect manners at the same time that it guarded itself against intimacy with strangers.

Hospitality was important to how travelers presented the president, but above all they described Díaz as a man with an almost religious zeal for his country. "We felt that we were in the presence of a great and holy passion," Gillpatrick wrote, "the passion of a patriot for his country. . . . [H]is eyes filled with tears as he talked of his hopes for Mexico. But I saw the great compelling motive of his life, his love of country."[28] The trope of patriotism, reinforced by countless photographic illustrations of the president in military regalia, helped to rationalize the Porfirian regime's grip on the nation by suggesting that Mexico was in the hands of the man who loved it most. Díaz was known to be a despot, but his friendliness and patriotism helped to elide any questions about whether his rule was good for the country.

Travelers who lacked the social connections to meet with the president collected his image in the form of postcards, newspaper clippings, and *cartes de visite*. While it was common for heads of state to have their images commodified in these ways (postcards of Queen Victoria come to mind), the photographic image of Díaz, constructed to suggest that he embodied the nation at the intersection of the romantic past and the modern present, took on meanings that went beyond the ordinary. Photographic conventions emerged during the Porfiriato that underscored the politics of economic conquest by playing on the image of Díaz as a logical and much-needed patriarch for an underdeveloped nation. These representations of Díaz tell an important part of the story of the American fixation with Mexico during the Porfiriato, offering insight into the ways that the image of one man and his family could open the discursive space for some Americans to imagine that U.S. capitalist investment south of the border might facilitate Mexico's modernity. In particular, they illustrate how discourses of masculinity, paternalism, and proper subjecthood rationalized the Díaz regime for the producers and consumers of photographic images, an important step in justifying the politics of economic conquest.

Americans did not, of course, create the photographic conventions associated with Díaz. A number of photographers, including non-Mexican photographers like Guillermo Kahlo and C. B. Waite, worked closely with the regime to create what we might call Díaz's "official image." As mentioned above, the photograph was a key technology through which the regime disseminated its vision of modernity, and Díaz's picture served as the dominant signifier of the regime and, by extension, the nation. Díaz's image reinforced the "cult of personality" that helped to consolidate his power between 1884 and 1911. As Paul Garner has argued, "The cultivation of deference to the patriarchal figure of Porfirio Díaz was a central goal of the regime, and one of its defining characteristics. It was also an essential component of a deliberate strategy to establish Díaz as the uncontested (and incontestable) source of political legitimacy and authority."[29] As Garner and other historians have noted, organizations like the Society of Friends of the President and National Porfirian Circle promoted Díaz's official image across a variety of media, including *El Imparcial* and *El Mundo Ilus-*

trado, the leading *porfirista* newspaper and supplement.[30] The regime subsidized these publications, and photographs of the head of state appeared ad nauseam in their pages, demonstrating that Díaz and his advisors understood the power of images to reinforce the regime's control. Later in the Porfiriato, when it became clear that the president's adversaries were gaining momentum, Díaz's official image suggested that not only the president but, more broadly, his regime and the entire system that they represented were aging but stubbornly indelible. By presenting himself as a stern national father, Díaz expertly performed what we now call "image management."

Díaz's official image evolved over the course of his long rule. In official photographs that appeared early in his tenure as president, Díaz is usually dressed in a plain black suit with a stiff white collar and looks markedly humble and sober. In one such image, circulated widely in American scrapbooks and travelogues from the early Porfiriato, Díaz looks strikingly similar to Benito Juárez in his iconic portrait that now appears on Mexico's twenty-peso note (Figure 2.2). In later photographs, however, such as the ones examined more closely in this chapter, Díaz appears much more august with his white hair, large moustaches, formal clothing, and military decorations. While neither his demeanor nor his gaze changed very much over the years, later images are layered with symbols of power, nationhood, and masculinity, tropes that proved important to rationalizing and justifying the dictatorship in American eyes. These latter photos enthralled American travelers, who reproduced them again and again as representations of the "man who made Mexico," despite the fact that the elderly Díaz in no way embodied American ideals. However, Americans also adopted and adapted the official image of the president to suit their own purposes.

American cultural workers widely circulated the official Díaz image but also revised it in a number of important ways. Some visitors presented a friendlier, warmer president than the stern official image by offering glimpses of Díaz playing with his grandchildren or talking sweetly to his wife in their living quarters. They constructed Díaz as open, honest, and easy to talk to—despite the fact that he was, in reality, very closely guarded and deeply elusive about his personal thoughts (some political foes called him "The Sphinx"). Other American revisions to the official Díaz image included the portrayal of the president as a reluctant and humble dictator, an exalted head of state who loved democracy but knew that his country was not ready for it. However, it is those depictions of Díaz as a *masculine* head of state that

FIGURE 2.2. Díaz looking strikingly similar to Benito Juárez. Mexico: Nineteenth Century Views Photograph Album, Center for Southwest Research, University of New Mexico.

most powerfully illustrate American revisions of his official image. As we will see below, men and women who traveled to Mexico associated Díaz with American ideas regarding "political manhood," the term that Kevin P. Murphy uses to describe the masculinist approach to Progressive Era statecraft that prioritized manliness as both a driving force of the nation and the result of a well-run state. By focusing on his body and his behavior, travelers reimagined the potential for Mexican modernity through Díaz's performance of vigorous and virile manhood. These representations also contradicted dominant American views of Mexican masculinity in general. In magazines and travelogues, Díaz's image appeared alongside countless representations of nameless Mexican Indians and mestizo men, whom Rice, for one, described as "small of stature, uneducated, and poverty stricken, but docile, submissive, [and] polite."[31] (We will see more of this vision of Mexican Indianness in Chapter Three.) However, some American writers and photographers, especially those working later in the Porfiriato, began to present Porfirio Díaz as an alternative to "deteriorated" Indian and mestizo masculinities. In these newer representational patterns, the masculine Díaz served as both a model for his subjects and a metaphor for Mexico's changing relationship to the United States.

DÍAZ, MANLINESS, AND CIVILIZATION

Representations of Díaz's masculinity often began with surprisingly candid descriptions of his body and his ability to care for it. "His countenance was handsome and rather impassive, his dark complexion fresh and sanguine," Gillpatrick proclaimed in his description of meeting the president. "His hand-shake was firm and cordial and his hand warm and dry, denoting perfect circulation."[32] Many travelogues include language like this, even if every author was not so thorough as to consider the president's circulation. In a long description of Díaz's appearance, Creelman observed

a straight, powerful, broad, and somewhat fleshy nose, whose curved nostrils lift and undulate with every emotion; huge, virile jaw that sweeps from large, flat, fine, ears, set close to the head, to the tremendous, square, fighting chin; a wide, firm mouth shaded by a white mustache; a full, short, muscular neck; wide shoulders, deep chest; a curiously tense and rigid carriage that gives great distinction to a personality suggestive of a singular power and dignity—that is Porfirio Diaz in his seventy-eighth year.[33]

Creelman marks the president's body in distinctly masculine terms, using words like "virile," "rigid," and "muscular." His description is grandiose but typical, for many other writers saw Díaz's body as a reflection of his innate fitness to rule the nation. Here the term "fitness" has a double meaning, referring both to Díaz's capacities as a leader and to his corporeal strength. "There is something in his manner which at once wins confidence and commands respect," wrote Tweedie, "a certain quiet repose, and yet a healthy complexion and deep chest denote the man of action and exercise. He might be a smart English colonel, so well-preserved is he."[34] Ending with this comparison to an English colonel emphasized the view that he possessed a rugged but highly civilized body.

Scores of Americans like Gillpatrick and Creelman offered firsthand accounts of the president's physical strength and personal commitment to what Theodore Roosevelt famously called "the strenuous life" in his influential speech of 1899, upholding the image of Díaz as one of healthy and self-controlled Mexicanness. Even as Díaz neared eighty years of age toward the end of his rule (at least one historian has referred to this period as a "gerontocracy"), they continued to describe him as a physically strong stabilizer for Mexico, one whose vigor and "rugged endurance" could ensure the continued success of Americans in that nation. In Creelman's view, the aged body still maintains its "power and dignity," terms that once again refer to both his body and his presidency. "His astounding good health and strong constitution are . . . distinctive of this wonderful leader of men," wrote one Mexican biographer of the elderly Díaz in 1910, claiming that,

> at an age where most people would be incapacitated from work, either through disease or the impairment of some of their faculties, President Diaz attends to his business, takes violent exercise, goes out hunting, endures fatigue, and does a vast amount of work. Undoubtedly his regular and abstemious habits greatly contribute to . . . the result to which we refer.[35]

The author, José F. Godoy, went on to describe the president's daily ritual of rising at six, bathing, and beginning work at an early hour— all qualities that he hoped would convince readers that Mexicans were able to follow the rigors of modern life if properly trained. Godoy was an elite Mexican, but his book on Díaz was aimed at American readers. Some travelers read his biography with keen interest and parroted his descriptions of the president's personal habits. They reported on everything from Díaz's diet to his sleeping habits to his abstention from deleterious vices. "In his daily life President Diaz is a remarkable man," wrote Marie Robinson Wright in 1897. "He is a human dynamo, and infuses life and vigor into every department of his administration. Today, although in his sixties, he is as alert and active as he was at forty. Take him all in all, he is one of the greatest men of the century." This passage is typically hagiographic but also particularly revealing in how it blurs the lines between the "administration" of his office and of his own body. Wright, like many of her compatriots, presumes that Díaz's care for his body helps to qualify him to care for the country, with all of the paternalism that this implies. "He is a simple liver," she concluded, "preferring a soup and a plain roast to the most elaborate *menu*, drinking very sparingly. He cares little for tobacco, only occasionally indulging in the mildest cigars."[36]

But why, of all subjects, would Americans find themselves interested in the personal habits of a foreign president? Despite the intense interest in Mexican modernity that travelers espoused, many wondered whether the Mexican people were really ready for modern life. After all, Mexico looked rather backward to American travelers, and the Mexicans appeared to some to lack the proper discipline to prepare themselves for the "progress" that they hoped American capital would bring with it. Writers could not shake the old perceptions of Mexicans as too savage and too resistant to change to embrace modernity. The focus on his personal habits suggested that less civilized Mexicans had a model in Díaz. Unlike the stereotypical "greaser" or "dirty Mexican," he seemed to understand and to model the good habits that corresponded with proper subjecthood during the Progressive Era. For travelers during this period, a proper subject was the individual who took good care of him- or herself, who could plan for the future, and who understood and could work for the ethos of "progress."[37] Descriptions of Díaz's personal habits therefore served as much more than superficial praise; they made a powerful but submerged statement that Mexicans might possess the potential to become proper subjects. What is more, good personal habits suggested that the Porfirian regime would endure. "President Diaz should have a long life," Gillpatrick decided. In an interesting rhetorical turn, the author discussed the president's capacity for self-care in relation to his racial difference and status as a metonym for the nation: "He comes from a hardy race and his habits are conducive to longevity. . . . His identity is merged completely with the national life."[38] Indeed, Díaz would have a long life, but his last four years would be lived in exile.

Talk of the president's body and health not only offered hope for his continued rule but also connected him to popular discourse about the rugged new brand of politics at play in the United States. Theodore Roosevelt became president at age forty-two when William McKinley was assassinated in Buffalo in September of 1901. As illustrated by Gail Bederman, Kevin P. Murphy, and other historians of the Progressive Era, Roosevelt owed his early political success at least partly to his self-styling as a rugged frontiersman in the 1880s and his public image of hawkish manliness in the later years of the nineteenth century. Although reared in a privileged old-money Manhattan family, he had fled to the Dakota Territory to recover from the almost simultaneous deaths of his wife and mother in 1884. Refashioning himself as the "Cowboy of the Dakotas" upon his return to public life, Roosevelt constructed a persona that would influence American conceptions of masculinity and politics for the better part of the early twentieth century.

The Cowboy of the Dakotas was a powerful trope as America's frontier closed, but Roosevelt's presidential persona had its real roots in his actions during the Spanish-American War. He parlayed his history as an Indian hunter into fame as the leader of the Rough Riders in 1898. The photograph of Roosevelt with the cavalry unit following the battle of San Juan Hill became an icon of the war and launched him to national fame. In it he stands below a waving American flag at the center of a large battalion of young, virile white men. One of the soldiers, seated just to the right of Roosevelt, props up a rifle. This image represents a turning point for Roosevelt's public persona—and perhaps, more generally, for American conceptualizations of imperialism—because it is among the first and most famous instances in which the future president would transfer the cowboy image that he previously cultivated to a setting beyond the borders of the United States. As Roosevelt avowed in a propagandistic memoir, the unit's uniforms were purposefully contrived to evoke this cowboy image.[39] Once Roosevelt ascended to the presidency, the image of a rugged, globe-trotting American president undoubtedly played a powerful role in garnering popular support for the culture of U.S. imperialism.

As Bederman argues, Roosevelt's brand of masculinity was intimately linked to the culture of white supremacy that lay at the core of U.S. imperialist thought. In the Progressive Era, white masculinity was perceived to be endangered due, among other causes, to shifts in the means of production in the United States and the increasing call for white women's rights. Roosevelt understood how to parlay anxieties about white masculinity into political projects like the extension of American military control in disparate parts of the world. Roosevelt himself made his thoughts on whiteness and imperialism clear in his historical writings. "It is of incalculable importance," Roosevelt wrote in *The Winning of the West*, his four-volume history of expansionism and the frontier, "that America, Australia, and Siberia should pass out of the hands of their red, black, and yellow aboriginal owners, and become the heritage of the dominant world races."[40]

Díaz, as a mestizo with an aristocratic air, did not fit very neatly into the racial and political schemas around which Roosevelt's image was built. Mexico was not in the hands of a member of one of the "dominant world races" but a man who clearly had mixed indigenous blood, as noted by almost every American who wrote about him. This posed a serious conceptual problem for foreigners who hoped to play a role in the modern development of the nation. Despite the fact that Americans could have noted the fact that Díaz set in place antinative policies and practices (which none did until John Kenneth Turner, very late in the Porfiriato), complicating his relationship to his Indian ancestry, they instead presented Díaz as an Indian (or part Indian) president. How could Mexico modernize and prosper when, in the American imagination, modernity and progress were so intimately linked with whiteness? The answers lay in representations that directly addressed the question of *mestizaje*. While few authors would have used this term, many did use their descriptions of Díaz to express their ideas about the racial makeup of the nation.

In order to prop up a regime headed by a mestizo—especially to an audience that abhorred the very idea of race mixing—many writers attempted to convince their fellow Americans that Díaz manifested the best qualities of the Indian and the Spaniard. Consider, for example, Lummis's physical description of the president:

> A man of five feet eight, erect as the Indian he is disproportionately confounded with, quick as the Iberian that he far more nearly is, a fine agreement of unusual physical strength and still more unusual grace, with the true Indian trunk and muscular European limbs, Diaz

is physically one man in twenty thousand. The . . . infusion of Indian blood . . . is an inheritance much more visible in his figure than his face. The features and expressions are essentially of Spain; it is only in full repose that the face recalls that certain hauteur and inscrutableness of the first Americans. . . . This man seems to have taken the best from both types.[41]

With his Indian body and Spanish face and limbs, Díaz served as an ideal symbol of both Mexicanness and *mestizaje* in Lummis's view. As we will see in Chapter Four, this was part of a broader representational strategy through which some travelers and other observers of Mexico positioned the nation's mestizo population as a boon for the prospects of economic conquest.

Americans like Lummis both admired and denied Díaz's *mestizaje*. It is telling that Lummis downplayed Díaz's indigenous appearance, rendering his Indianness a mostly invisible aspect of his countenance and character, visible only when the man is seen "in full repose." Like many depictions of an admirable, even noble, *mestizaje*, such as Díaz's, indigeneity is a condition of the blood, not a threatening phenotype. "Although of Indian descent," wrote Tweedie, "he is also descended from the Spaniards who left their mother country in the early years of the conquest of Mexico by Cortés. On his father's side he has good ancestry, and his grandmother was an Indian woman of [the] Mizteca tribe, one of the finest people of Mexico."[42] Lummis's conclusion that Díaz could "take the best from both types," along with Tweedie's suggestion that he was descended from noble stock on both sides, exemplified hopes that the mestizo was not a tragic mulatto in the American style but rather represented a population advantageous to aggressively capitalist foreigners. As Thomas Benjamin and Marcial Ocasio-Meléndez have noted, "The mestizo was . . . the protagonist of Mexican progress, and the group's greatest representative was Porfirio Díaz."[43] To be sure, representations of Díaz's *mestizaje* went far beyond the individual depicted in them; they suggested the potential of mestizos to emerge as modern subjects.

Although most travelers celebrated Díaz's mixed heritage in this way, they were also discordant about his lineage, as the examples in the previous paragraph suggest. Travelers and other observers simply could not agree on exactly *how* Indian was Díaz. A British observer named Edward J. Howell told London's Society of Arts in 1893 that the "ancestry of Porfirio Diaz, on his father's side, were Spaniards, who left their native country in the first years of the conquest. On the mother's side he is descended from one of the most civilized of the original native races."[44] This was the most common way to frame Díaz's *mestizaje,* but other writers adjusted the amount of "Indian blood" contained in the president's veins in order to fit with their own agendas. The tireless Díaz booster Marie Robinson Wright, to cite just one, claimed repeatedly that Díaz was mostly European. She claimed that Díaz's mother's family "came from Asturias, whose strong and valiant sons are noted for their independent spirit and their ancient lineage, possessing the impetuosity of the Celts and the frankness and integrity of the Goths," and that the president's great-grandfather, "a Spaniard," had married a Mixtec woman. This would have made Díaz only minimally Indian— a claim that was contradicted by his appearance. Lest even this trace of Indian blood arouse suspicion, Wright assured her readers that "the Mixtecas were fully as advanced in civilization as the Aztecs.[45] Again, this is both a celebration and denial of *mestizaje,* for it acknowledges Díaz's racial difference while at the same time minimizing his Indianness by claiming heritage from one of the more "advanced" tribes of Mexico and, therefore, by definition, un-Indian.

Despite the fact of Díaz's *mestizaje* and its threat to Mexican modernity, travel writers nonetheless attempted to compare him with his American counterpart. One strategy was to pair the presidents' images to highlight resemblances between the styles and comportments of the men. In *The Maker of Modern Mexico* (1906), her second travelogue celebrating the Díaz regime, Tweedie juxtaposed strikingly similar signed and dated portraits of the presidents in her chapter on the daily life of Díaz (Figures 2.3 and 2.4). Each featured a mustachioed and formally dressed head of state.[46] The exposure of Díaz's photograph lightens him considerably, and its soft focus makes him appear closer in age to the American president. Though the photos closely resemble one another in composition, the men's faces underscore Tweedie's claim that they were politically similar but possessed opposite personalities. Díaz looks serious and aristocratic in profile, while Roosevelt appears heartier and more approachable. Tweedie claimed in the text that, despite their dissimilar personalities, each man told her that he greatly admired the other. Americans living in Mexico also paired the images of the presidents, as evidenced by an image of an office at the El Coco rubber plantation taken around 1904. Paired portraits of Roosevelt and Díaz loom over A. A. Morrell posing in his tidy office (Figure 2.5). This image captures the sense that prevailed among Americans doing busi-

The President of Mexico.

FIGURE 2.3. The president in elegant formalwear. Mrs. Alec (Ethel B.) Tweedie, *The Maker of Modern Mexico, Porfirio Díaz*.

Photo by BELL.]
The President of U.S.A.

FIGURE 2.4. Díaz's American counterpart, Theodore Roosevelt. Mrs. Alec (Ethel B.) Tweedie, *The Maker of Modern Mexico, Porfirio Díaz*.

ness in Porfirian Mexico that their efforts to develop Mexico's natural resources would benefit both nations.

In an interesting twist, Creelman even applied some of the tropes associated with Roosevelt's self-styled cowboy image to Díaz. In contrast to the highly formalized conventions of the official Díaz image, Creelman included a series of three casual-looking (though probably quite purposefully staged) snapshots, attributed to Díaz's son, that depicted the president on a hunting expedition in some mountainous terrain. The first depicts the elderly Díaz, with rifle, a dog at his side, and a few of his companions, in a clearing (Figure 2.6). The president clasps the tip of a long rifle placed between his legs, which underscores his masculine presence on the hunting grounds. The second image shows the larger hunting party in front of an open building in which the carcasses of slain deer are clearly visible.[47] In each of these images the president wears a Victorian hunting costume, complete with a cap and high boots. The third hunting scene reminds the viewer of Díaz's purportedly high level of personal taste and cultivation, for it depicts the president and his companions dining alfresco in the forest. Together, these images suggest that Díaz, like Roosevelt, was attuned to the lavish but strenuous life that was all but required for the practitioners of turn-of-the-twentieth-century political manhood. This lifestyle included the pursuit of manliness through rugged engagement with the outdoors and, as Kristin L. Hoganson has argued, war efforts.[48] Lummis, for one, described Díaz as "a real hunter—as frontiersmen count hunters, and

FIGURE 2.5. A. A. Morrell's office, El Coco Rubber Plantation. Tabasco Rubber Plantation Photo Collection, Nettie Lee Benson Latin American Collection, University of Texas Libraries, University of Texas at Austin.

PRESIDENT DIAZ HUNTING IN THE MOUNTAINS, AT THE AGE OF SEVENTY-FIVE YEARS   MARK THE ERECTNESS AND
VIGOR OF THE FIGURE, THE STRENGTH AND BEARING OF THE MAN, COMPARED WITH HIS YOUNGER COMPANIONS!
THIS SNAP-SHOT WAS MADE THROUGH THE CAMERA OF HIS SON

FIGURE 2.6. Díaz's hunting party. James Creelman, "President Diaz."

not by the category of tilted trigger-pullers who butcher tame, fenced game."[49] His sporting life, as depicted by travel writers, was simultaneously masculine (requiring physical exertion, phallic guns, and killing) and aristocratic. Despite offering a rare glimpse of Díaz as a man of leisure, Creelman was careful not to diverge too far from the dictator's official image; facing the page that includes the image of the hunting party at the table is a full-page photograph of "the master of Mexico in his official chair."[50] This photograph, much more in line with the official image of the president, underscored the idea that, above all, Díaz was a ruler.

The inclusion of these hunting photographs might be read as a response to the U.S. president's self-styling as a sturdy outdoorsman. As Hoganson has argued, the strenuous life that Roosevelt advocated for American men was related to his imperial aspirations and U.S. involvement in Cuba and the Philippines. Positioning Díaz as an adherent of the strenuous life aligned him with the American president.[51] Writing in another venue, Lummis made an even more explicit connection be-

tween the Mexican president's soldierly experience and hypermascu-
line American war heroes, including those who were famous for invigo-
rating masculine ideals in the United States from the Civil War to 1899.
"In battle," he wrote, "Díaz showed the directing power of a Grant, with
the crusading dash of a Custer, a Roosevelt, or a Funston."[52] Creelman
likewise used the images of the hunting party to position Díaz within
the American fascination with political manhood. In one caption, he
encouraged his readers to "mark the erectness and vigor of the figure
and bearing of the man, compared with his younger companions!" Apparently, despite Díaz's advanced age at this point, his body still bore
the markings of true manhood. His "erectness," remarked upon repeatedly in American travel writing, suggested that the president remained
a virile, even sexual, symbol of the regime.

Whether or not the styles and tropes employed in the hunting scenes
were conscious references to the American president on the parts of
Díaz and his advisors, we do know that Díaz publicly and emphatically
praised Roosevelt when addressing the controversy over a potential
third term for the American president. "I believe that he has thought
more of his country than of himself," Díaz told Creelman.

> He has done and is doing a great work for the United States, a work
> that will cause him . . . to be remembered in history as one of the great
> Presidents. . . . Mankind understands the meaning of his attitude and
> its bearing upon the future. He stands before the world as a statesman
> whose victories have been moral victories.[53]

This feeling was apparently mutual, as demonstrated in Creelman's 1911
book, *Diaz, Master of Mexico*, wherein the author went straight to the
source. "The opinion of responsible men everywhere was summed up
by President Roosevelt," Creelman claimed, "when he wrote from the
White House on March 7, 1908: 'President Diaz is the greatest statesman now living, and he has done for his country what no other living
man has done for any other country—which is the supreme test and
value of statesmanship.'"[54]

This mutual admiration forces us to reconsider the question of
Díaz's status as a mestizo. Although Roosevelt had built his reputation partly on his adventures as a killer of American Indians, Díaz, the
Indian-mestizo, was such a flexible public figure, and one who proved
necessary to American business interests in Mexico, that he could appropriate some of the tropes associated with Roosevelt's highly culti-

vated Anglo manliness without erasing his own Indian heritage. This fact helped rationalize the regime and distance Díaz from leaders in other former Spanish colonies, such as Emilio Aguinaldo in the Philippines, whom American newspapers frequently represented in childlike, feminized terms. But at the same time, the racialized Díaz did not pose a serious threat to American influence in Mexico. While he looked convincingly masculine and authoritarian in Victorian hunting garb, predominant ideas about race in the United States, as well as the supposed inferiority of Mexican culture and character, assumed that he would facilitate rather than prevent the economic conquest. Furthermore, until Turner, travelers never mentioned that Díaz had anti-Indian ideas and practices of his own. This ultimately nonthreatening persona allowed the makers of American travel discourse to champion the dictator instead of positioning him as an obstacle to U.S. empire building, as they might have done if he had been white. Accordingly, some observers turned their attention to his fitness as a patriarch for the Mexican nation.

"LOGICAL PATERNALISM": STAGING THE NATIONAL FAMILY

Like those of her husband, portraits and descriptions of Carmen Díaz, known throughout Mexico and in American travel discourse by her nickname, "Carmelita," proliferated in American travelogues and magazines that appeared during the Porfiriato. First ladies are frequently popular figures, but travel writers fawned over Carmelita and exaggerated her popularity to a surprising extent.[55] "Señora Doña Carmen Romero Rubio de Díaz, besides being one of the most beautiful women in Mexico, is the best loved," Wright claimed in *Picturesque Mexico*, where she depicted the first lady as a popular and glamorous celebrity who loved to receive American visitors.[56] Lummis, in *The Awakening of a Nation*, called her "Carmelita, the idol of Mexico," and included a picture of the first lady looking sober but pretty in high Victorian garb.[57] Neither Lummis nor any of the Americans who wrote about her mentioned that Carmen Romero Rubio wed Porfirio Díaz when she was seventeen and he fifty-one. Instead, authors focused on her role as a helpmate to her husband and the most popular woman in the nation. "Gracious and unspoiled, prominent in all benevolences, and a model in the exigent Spanish traditions of the homekeeper," Lummis wrote, "she has won love beyond any woman in Mexican history."[58] Though Creelman's famous article made no mention of her, it included a large portrait of Carmelita in which "the beautiful and stately young wife of President Diaz" appears in a diamond tiara, situated opposite "the powerful and suggestive profile of Mexico's great president" (Figure 2.7). Like her husband, Carmelita had her own official style of portraiture, and this photograph typifies how she appeared in hundreds of travelogues, picture postcards, magazine articles, and newspaper stories that circulated in the United States. These portraits present her as the embodiment of Mexican aristocracy and, as we will see, as a fitting and proper wife to a man who served as the harbinger of a new brand of Mexican subjecthood.

Official portraits of Carmelita also served as the frontispiece to a few travelogues, all written by women who exalted her as the ideal of Mexican womanhood. Harriott Wight Sherratt, from Rockford, Illinois, was one of the women who did so. The entire first page of Sherratt's 1899 travelogue *Mexican Vistas* was dedicated to her, clad in black and looking staid, while her husband's portrait is buried on page 115 of the book. Sherratt's description of Carmen Díaz was glowing, and she used an encounter with the first lady to paint relations between the United States and Mexico in simultaneously patronizing and *sisterly* terms:

> The most popular woman in the country is Señora Díaz, the sweet-faced wife of the president. . . . She received us with the most graceful courtesy, paying the greatest compliment possible to pay a stranger by addressing us in our own tongue, and I blushed as I responded to her elegant English, knowing that I could not speak fifty words in her language. Señora Díaz spoke in the kindliest manner of the United States, and I was glad to answer her honestly that we were proud of our young sister republic and anxious to be on sisterly terms with her.[59]

This encounter with Carmelita Díaz, like many others described in American travel writing from this period, serves as an opportunity to think about relations between the United States and Mexico. At the same time that Sherratt uses Carmen Díaz's hospitality as a metaphor for U.S.-Mexican relations, she does not claim that the "young sister republic" is as democratic as her own country. The author acknowledges that Mexico is a republic in name only and then, like so many other writers, gratefully credits the current regime for bringing progress to the United States' wayward younger sibling. "He has," she wrote in reference to Díaz, "given the country railroads, telegraphs, free schools, and libraries." As we have seen elsewhere, democracy is simultaneously

Photographed by Waite, Mexico

THE BEAUTIFUL AND STATELY YOUNG WIFE OF PRESIDENT DIAZ

FIGURE 2.7. "Carmelita, the idol of Mexico." James Creelman, "President Diaz."

a marker of the progressive United States and is constructed as unnecessary for the modernization of Mexico. This might say as much about the general populations of these nations as it does about their individual leaders: Americans, as rational subjects, were able to adopt democratic principles and practices; Mexicans needed the paternalistic Díaz and his "sweet faced wife" to stage modernity for them. Representations of the Díaz family stood in not only for Mexico's status as a nation on the cusp of modernity but also for Mexico's relationship to the United States. "One admires his delightful, lover-like behaviour to his wife, his fatherly goodness to his children, his boyishness with his grandchildren, and his extraordinary power of turning acquaintances into friends, and friends into staunch allies," Tweedie wrote in a passage that ostensibly described the president as a family man but also spoke to how he handled national and international politics.[60] Americans like Tweedie saw Díaz as a tender-hearted family man but also used this fatherly trope to construct him as a patriarch who would facilitate rather than defend American intervention in the life and well-being of the *national* family.

Representing Porfirio Díaz as a stern but loving father helped assuage American audiences concerned that Mexico was too unruly a place to conduct business, further extending the cultural politics of economic conquest. But what kind of father was he? Charles Lummis described Díaz as a benignly autocratic father, one perfectly in tune with both gender norms in the United States and the cultural politics of informal empire, which presumed that non-Western and nonwhite people needed guidance to reach maturity as modern subjects. Lummis described Díaz's grip on the nation as "logical paternalism—a scheme frightfully dangerous under a bad father, incalculably beneficial under a good one," he claimed. This phrase perfectly captures how Americans came to see Díaz over the more than three decades of his rule. His regime was intensely focused on a logical, scientific approach to governance (hence the term *científicos* was applied to his circle of advisors) but also relied on the image of Díaz as a dedicated, loving father to the nation. This latter aspect of his image among travelers, and Americans in general, partially accounts for why so few observers from the United States would criticize the regime or call for its end. If Díaz was driven more by the call of fatherly duty than by a lust for power, to call for his undoing would be unthinkable. It would not be until late in the Porfiriato that representations of Díaz would emerge in the United States that made him look more like Lummis's bad father than that author could have anticipated. Of course, to position Porfirio Díaz as a father to the nation also suggested something about his subjects. For Lummis, logical patriarchy was important for Mexico because the Mexicans required a "strong, heavy fist" to thrive:

> Mexico is . . . free . . . as we are, but less licensed; happy, safe, prosperous under precisely the same system as that by which we administer our own homes—for in the family we are not yet ready to turn our minors over to their own heads and the ward-heeler. And it is proud of the remarkable man who has done what no other ruler of modern times has even dreamed of being able to do, and who still keeps a quiet, steady fist in the waistband of the youngster he has taught to walk.[61]

In Lummis's view, following Darwinian views of culture that were widespread at the time, Díaz was the guardian and guide of a nation in its infancy. Positioning Díaz in a paternal role—after all, he taught the nation to walk, according to Lummis—meant safety, stability, and prosperity for the nation, just as the family's success was supposed to be guaranteed by a strong and rational father in the dominant worldview of the Progressive Era. It also meant that Díaz, as the nation's patriarch, could facilitate relations between Mexico and its more developed northern neighbor as part of his fatherly duties. This is typical neocolonialist logic, which presumes that outside influence will be heightened if a native leader (read: dictator) will mediate between the outside power and underdeveloped native populations.

It is tempting to presume that writers would frame Carmen Díaz in maternalistic terms, since she was the wife of such a clearly patriarchal figure, but Carmelita's youth and her childlessness complicated her fitness as a mother for the nation. Travelers frequently skirted around these matters, as well as the fact that she was the president's second wife. They almost never mentioned the thirty-four-year age difference between them, focusing instead on her skills as a hostess and linguist (they frequently commented on her perfect English).[62] Neither did they mention that many in Mexico saw the marriage as a strategic political alliance more than a love match. Carmen Romero Rubio was the daughter of a well-connected, old-money liberal lawyer and the goddaughter of Sebastián Lerdo de Tejada, the president whose office Díaz usurped. The marriage helped unite Díaz's and Lerdo's factions within the Liberal Party and cement Díaz's image as an aristocratic gentleman. Observers from all sides of the political spectrum credited Carmelita with the president's sense of ceremony and social protocol. Her family was also closely allied with John W. Foster, the U.S. minister to Mexico from 1869 to 1880 who continued to advocate for the capitalist development of Mexico well into the twentieth century.[63] In 1884, Díaz appointed Manuel Romero Rubio, his father-in-law, as Secretario de Gobernación, Mexico's secretary of state, a position he held until his death in 1895. However, instead of focusing on these extensive political connections, travelers imagined Carmelita as a morally upright debutante who functioned as a social tutor and secretary to the president.

Even so, they did not see her as a mother for the nation. By not framing her as such, travel writers were free to appreciate her in purely aesthetic terms. Travelers from disparate parts of the world praised her "sterling qualities of goodness, sweetness, and affability," as one British writer put it.[64] The same writer claimed that from Carmelita's "blameless life, her many charitable acts, and her great tact and amiability, General Diaz no doubt receives a considerable accession to his own popularity."[65] She might also have helped make Díaz even more palatable to Americans, since she spoke English and the newlywed couple honeymooned in the United States, upon which occasion Porfirio Díaz established contact with prominent American politicians and businessmen he hoped would invest in Mexico. American and other foreign women were especially drawn to Carmelita's glamor. Some American women framed a journey to Mexico as a nearby and inexpensive alternative to a trip to Europe, pointing to the many European elements of Mexican society and reminding their readers again and again that aristocratic Mexican women wore fashions from Paris and frequently spoke flawless French or English. "Madame Diaz, besides being handsome, is always beautifully dressed," wrote Tweedie in a typically fawning description. "In some ways she reminds me of Queen Alexandra in type and bearing."[66] In this way, Carmelita seemed to embody travelers' fantasies of Mexican high society as aristocratic and distinctly European in nature.

Although Carmen Díaz's looks and charms captured the imaginations of foreign travelers, they were nonetheless careful to avoid representing her as possessing any degree of political agency. Percy F. Martin, a British visitor to Porfirian Mexico and author of exceptionally dry travelogues according to the *New York Times' Saturday Review of Books*, did not let Carmelita's description interfere with the paternalistic underpinnings of Díaz's public image:

The President's wife is regarded as the power behind the throne, and as a matter of fact, she very often is. Not so, however, is or ever has been Madame Carmen Romero Rubio Diaz. Possessed of many natural charms and sterling virtues, not the least of these has been her rigid abstraction from interfering with or attempting to influence in any way the public actions of President Porfirio Diaz.[67]

Martin claimed that the nation's populace was dedicated to the first lady, but made it clear that one of her "sterling virtues" was to stay out of the political sphere, unlike the New Women and suffragists in the United States and Great Britain. Tweedie's chapter in *The Maker of Modern Mexico* about Carmen Díaz, titled "The Influence of a Woman," toes a similar line, careful to relegate the first lady's influence to familial relations. After establishing Carmen as the most educated woman in Mexico and her husband's social superior, the author suggests that her importance to the nation is as a support to her husband:

> "I never ask anything about politics or that sort of thing," she said to me one day. "If my husband tells me, I know he wants me to know, and if he does not, or seems tired or bothered when he comes in from the Palace, I feel instinctively that something has gone wrong, and the best medicine is change of thought, so we talk of other things." This shows the wisdom of the woman . . . and she heals as many family breaches in a year as he negotiates affairs of state.[68]

In Tweedie's view, Mrs. Díaz's influence was limited to her home and the social scene in Mexico City that so dazzled foreign visitors. Her domain is the family; her husband's is the state. While Porfirio Díaz represented a vigorous nation that welcomed the invasion of foreign capital(ists) while maintaining its masculine dignity, Carmen Rubio de Díaz stood in for a passive Mexico whose charms were exploitable but merely aesthetic. As a couple, they provided gendered models of not only subjecthood, but also of how men and women might differently but ideally acquiesce to economic intervention. Images of the elegant dictator and his charming wife represented for these travelers the articulation of state power whose autocratic self-styling was exotic to American democratic sensibilities but nonetheless appealing.

"AFTER DÍAZ, WHAT?"

This chapter has argued that many of the producers of American travel discourse turned to the image of Porfirio Díaz—an image that they imbued with their own conceptions of race, gender, and sexuality—as a powerful symbol of the nation's potential to modernize with the help of U.S. capitalist investment. It is not surprising, then, that many travelogue writers would wonder what would become of the nation when this U.S.-backed dictator died or, since he would probably never step down or acknowledge democratic defeat, was ousted by a revolution. With more than $1 billion invested in Mexico, Americans had every reason to worry about what would happen after the Porfiriato. Creelman, ever the booster of the Porfirian system, attempted to downplay any potential losses for investors. "Americans and other foreigners invested in mines, real estate, factories, railways and other enterprises have privately assured me, not once but many times, that, under Diaz, conditions for investment in Mexico are fairer and quite as reliable as the most highly developed European countries," he wrote. "The President declares that these conditions will continue after his death or retirement."[69] However, the famous article gives no further explanation as to *how* those conditions would continue.

Carson, for one, asked the question explicitly: "After Diaz, what?" The author did not worry that Mexicans would remove their leader, suggesting (rather ironically, in retrospect) that "no prolonged revolution will ever undo the good that Diaz has done." Carson even claimed that nearly all of the nation's revolutionists had died, leaving no opposition to the regime. But, in what is perhaps his most fascinating claim, he predicted that Mexico's ongoing stability would ultimately result from the threat of U.S. imperialism:

The people have learned the benefits of tranquillity, and they are alive to the most serious danger which would menace them were there to occur any grave civil strife. Under those circumstances it is practically certain that in the interest of American capital and American residents the United States would occupy and possibly ultimately annex Mexico. This forcible destruction of their national integrity patriotic Mexicans are resolved to prevent; and if for no other reason than this, they will bury the hatchet and continue to support the stable government which will be President Diaz's legacy to the country.[70]

Here, then, is another rationale for U.S. empire: American hegemony would be feared by weaker nations, who would choose stability to avoid annexation.

Some writers were less confident that the dictatorship had established a long-lasting precedent for Mexico's "peace and prosperity." "A common supposition," wrote Percy F. Martin in 1907, "is that with the disappearance of General Porfirio Diaz, either by reason of his voluntary retirement *or other cause*, the present condition of peace and prosperity must come to an end."[71] Unlike Carson, Martin seemed to anticipate the coming revolution and to suggest that, without Díaz at its heart, the nation would revert back to its pre-Porfirian state of chaos and poverty. In his interview with Creelman the following year, Díaz himself said that he had "defended the theory" of democracy but admitted that he had "adopted a patriarchal policy in the actual administration of the nation's affairs."[72] In a shocking reversal, he claimed that his nation was now ready for democracy. "I have waited patiently," Díaz told Creelman,

> for the day when the people of the Mexican Republic would be prepared to choose and change their government at every election without danger of armed revolutions and without injury to the national credit or interference with national progress. I believe that day has come.[73]

In what followed, Díaz and Creelman provided patronizing depictions of Mexican peoples and their capacities for democracy, reiterating themes of Indian backwardness while at the same time suggesting that the masses had thrived under Díaz's firm hand and modeling of proper subjecthood. Although Creelman continued to linger on the markers of Mexican pre- or antimodernity (he conjured images of their "monstrous hats" and childlike devotion to the Virgin of Guadalupe), it appeared on the surface that the dictator, satisfied that the nation's path to modernity had been secured by his own antidemocratic practices and fatherly guidance, was committed to democracy in practice as well as in theory. This added a new dimension to the question of what would come after Díaz. Were Mexicans ready to rule themselves? Was this the end of Díaz's logical paternalism?

The photographs that appeared in the article took up these questions by suggesting a burgeoning dynasty. On one page, Díaz appears in a photograph with his daughter and a tiny grandson.[74] The gray-haired dictator looks grandfatherly in a three-piece suit and bowler hat, his hands in his pockets in a rare relaxed moment. His daughter looks down serenely at the infant. On the opposite page, two more images suggested Díaz's legacy.[75] In the left column, Major Porfirio Díaz Jr. appeared in full military regalia. He sits regally in a chair, his sword upon his lap, and looks strikingly like his father, both in physical appearance and in the photographic conventions that frame him. Even more remarkable is the image of another of the president's grandsons that appeared in the right column. The young Porfirio Díaz III is pictured in military costume, complete with shiny knee-length boots and a Roman helmet and armor (Figure 2.8).[76] The images of the boy and his father suggest that each had the mettle to sustain the order that the eldest Díaz had established more than three decades previously. The young boy simply echoed the militaristic images that his father and grandfather had cultivated for themselves, but the effect of these three images is telling, for they conveyed the story of a retiring dictator with at least two generations of progeny to fill his very large shoes. Together, these images connote a sense of confidence that the Porfiriato could endure even without its originator.

The image of Díaz as a national stabilizer, patriarch, and unproblematic ally came to an abrupt end in the last years of the Porfiriato, as everyday Americans became increasingly aware of and concerned with the human cost of Mexico's apparent progress. In 1909, Carlo de Fornaro, a former journalist and caricaturist who worked in Mexico City's American colony, published a scathing English-language "arraignment" of the regime, indicting the president with evidence ranging from the outrageous behavior of his son-in-law (whom Fornaro calls "a well-known homosexual") to the assassinations of his political adversaries.[77] This book might have created a scandal but succeeded in creating only a minor stir, in large part because a New York judge found the author guilty of libel against a Mexican politician and sentenced him to one year in a hard labor camp.[78] Instead, it would take American activist journalists like John Kenneth Turner and John Reed to popularize the idea that Díaz was actually a tyrant, though their charges differed from Fornaro's. Their representations of the dictator dramatically contradicted the image of a benevolent patriarch that had dominated the American imagination for so long. After 1911, the representational practices associated with Díaz and his family examined in this chapter could no longer dominate travel discourse. But this situation was only

PORFIRIO DIAZ THE THIRD. HE IS THE SON OF THE
PRESIDENT'S SON

FIGURE 2.8. Porfirio Díaz III. James Creelman, "President Diaz."

temporary. Within just a few years, a new generation of travelers would enter Mexico and express a strong desire to *return* to the Porfiriato. They would look back on that era as a time when order prevailed and economic conquest was in full swing, facilitated by the patriarch at the head of the state. Díaz's death in exile in 1915 only heightened such feelings. As we will see in the final chapter of this book, Díaz's star power shone so brightly in the United States that not even death—or a revolution—could extinguish it.

CHAPTER 3

AMERICAN TRAVEL WRITING AND THE
PROBLEM OF INDIAN DIFFERENCE

*The people of Mexico are not Latins. They are Indians. And they
are Indians, only somewhat resembling the Indians of the United
States. They are not merely a different tribe. They are a different
race of Indians.* JACK LONDON

*All apologies for the Díaz system of economic slavery and political
autocracy have their roots in assertions of ethnological inferiority
on the part of the Mexican people . . .* JOHN KENNETH TURNER

*Americans who were setting out to make a new society could find a
place in it for the Indian only if he would become what they were —
settled, steady, civilized.* ROY HARVEY PEARCE

THE PORFIRIATO COINCIDED WITH a period in which savage but subdued native people populated travel books. From Kipling's British colonial adventure stories set in India to Boy Scout novels that transported
young American readers to the Philippines, colonized or semicolon-
ized native people played important roles in travel discourse during
the late nineteenth and early twentieth centuries.[1] As scholars of imperialism and the literary imagination have argued, the appearances of
native people in travel writing almost always reinforced white dominance over those that Kipling called "new-caught, sullen peoples/Half-
devil and half-child" in "The White Man's Burden," his famous paean
to turn-of-the-twentieth-century imperialism.[2] Even in Mexico, where
no formal empire existed and one could not accurately describe indigenous people as "new-caught," travelers saw indigenous people within
an imperialist frame.

Chapter One examined a large body of photographic evidence that suggests that Americans saw the Indian as a desirable, if endangered, part of Porfirian Mexico. Photographers like Charles Burlingame Waite developed visual tropes that constructed the Indian as hardworking and attractive but poor and needing rescue by, in words that appeared in an article in *Harper's*, a "higher and more progressive race."[3] These views of Mexican Indianness, which were sometimes erotically charged, helped underscore the view of Mexico as an attractive place for tourists and profit seekers alike. Travel writing followed suit, and a number of travel books focused on Indian people and themes, including ones with mysterious and compelling titles such as *Che! Wah! Wah!, or, the Modern Montezumas of Mexico* (1883), *Unknown Mexico* (1902), and *In Indian Mexico* (1908). These books and the many like them that were published in the Porfiriato opened up new ways to talk, write, and think about indigenous people in Mexico. Indians were no longer merely local color, as they had been in the eyes of American observers prior to the Díaz regime, but were now treated as a real force in Mexican life. This does not mean, however, that travelers necessarily championed Indian Mexico as a place to find opportunities for business and pleasure. Instead, an entirely new set of concerns emerged in American travel writing about Mexico's indigenous population and how it fit with the imperial adventures of the United States.

In 1894, as U.S. investment in Porfirian Mexico continued to grow, *Scribner's Magazine* published a travel article by John G. Bourke describing the Río Grande as "The American Congo." A West Point graduate and experienced Indian hunter, Bourke had fashioned himself as an eminent frontiersman, explorer, and amateur ethnologist of the Gilded Age by the time his travelogue appeared in *Scribner's*.[4] Like many white travelers from the United States who considered themselves experts on the places they visited (and the reader knows by now that there were many), Bourke used a trip to Mexico as an occasion to think about Mexican Indians' relation to race, civilization, and the growing power of the United States. His bleak vision of the indigenous people in the region of the Río Grande fit within a powerful counterdiscourse that emerged during the Porfiriato, for an equally large number of representations construed the Indian as an obstacle to bringing American progress to Mexico.

Referring to the Río Grande as the "American Congo" was a provocative comparison in the 1890s, as the Congo was then gaining infamy as an example of European colonialism's excesses (King Leopold of Belgium had established the Congo Free State as a private colony; atrocities perpetrated against the native people there caused an international sensation).[5] The Río Grande has little in common with the Congo, the deepest and one of the longest rivers in the world, but Bourke compares native people in Northern Mexico to the inhabitants of this infamous "Dark Belt." Bourke's description of the Indians of Northern Mexico drew upon racist presumptions surrounding Africans and other groups:

> Through the centre of this unknown region, fully as large as New England, courses the Rio Grande, which can more correctly be compared to the Congo than to the Nile. . . . [S]tress cannot be too pointedly laid upon the existence within this Dark Belt of thriving, intelligent communities, such as Brownsville, Matamoros, Corpus Christi, Laredo, San Diego, and others, in which are to be found people of as much refinement and good breeding as anywhere else in the world, but exerting about as much influence upon the *indigenès* [sic] around them as did the Saxon or Danish invaders upon the Celts of Ireland.[6]

Bourke points to "thriving, intelligent communities" (probably referring to mestizo population centers or communities of Anglo settlers) but constructs the Indian of Northern Mexico as hopelessly unable to be civilized. Interestingly, he uses a supposedly savage European group, the Celts, to drive home this point. (This would have resonated with American audiences who were already well accustomed to seeing anti-Irish, anti-immigrant words and images in American popular media.) Throughout "The American Congo," Bourke makes it clear that he saw Mexico's indigenous population as living on the wrong side of a seemingly rigid line separating the civilized from the uncivilized.

The Río Grande demarcated that line. Following the creation of overland routes across the river, American travel writers made a habit of framing the river (and, more generally, the border) as a hard line separating truly distinct—and, in Bourke's mind, irreconcilable—peoples. According to Marie Howland in 1902, "The moment one sets foot in Mexico one knows that he is in a foreign land." For Howland, like so many of her compatriots who ventured into Porfirian Mexico, the act of crossing the river was a confrontation with difference, for she found "the new and picturesque around every corner."[7] This included people. Other travelers painted a more dramatic picture of what, exactly, the Río Grande separated. "If one should go up in a balloon and drift away into space . . . and should then drop down on some distant planet," wrote seasoned traveler J. Hendrickson McCarty, "he would not likely find himself surrounded by more unaccustomed scenery or more strangely appearing people that he will meet in crossing the Rio Grande into Mexico."[8] This was perhaps among the first published comparisons between Mexicans and aliens, a trope that is still in use to construct undocumented Mexican immigrants as otherworldly Others. In any event, it was up to the makers of travel discourse to describe and define the people who populated this strange land near home.

This chapter unpacks how travelers made sense of the supposedly stark contrast between themselves and those "strangely appearing people." In contrast to Chapter One, which explored the ways in which travelers and photographers aestheticized indigenous people during the Porfiriato, this chapter deals with representational patterns that abjectified the Mexican Indian. With a few notable exceptions, travel discourse almost never positioned native Mexicans as abject because they were hostile or naturally violent. Travelers rarely expressed concern that native people threatened their safety or property. Instead, the Indians that appeared in travel discourse during the Porfiriato posed a problem because they were indolent, lazy, backward, and resistant to change. This marks a difference from the discourses that guided settlement and nation building in the United States, which imagined the Indian as savage, hostile, and unwilling to adapt to American visions of progress.

Though travelers to Porfirian Mexico constructed a somewhat less hostile view of the nation's Indians, their visions of Mexican Indian difference help us understand how writers and photographers framed the Indian as an obstacle to progress and how these views fit into the broader politics of economic conquest. As we have seen, several key tropes constructed indigenous people in Mexico as belonging to a vanishing race—an ethnoracial group that, confronted with steaming locomotives and other apparent signs of progress, began to see its own demise. However, we have also seen that travel discourse from the Porfiriato presented Mexican Indianness, despite its backwardness, as a source of scopic pleasure. It is imperative to ask about other ways in which travel discourse imagined Indian people as backward and as obstacles to the massive and wide-ranging project of expanding American capital and capitalism into Mexico. The Indian-as-obstacle narrative appeared in a variety of media, but I focus specifically on travel writing because it provides the richest accounts of Mexican Indianness and its perceived threat to the project of modernizing the nation through capitalist development. My point in this chapter is not simply to identify racist views of Indian people (which are ample and self-evident) but to situate the idea of Indian racial difference within the context of economic conquest. Accordingly, this chapter also explores travel writers' prescriptions for Indian transformation intended to make native people amenable to the importation of U.S.-style capitalism in Mexico.

MEXICAN INDIANS AND THE RACIAL LOGIC OF U.S. IMPERIALISM

Before turning to specific tropes related to Indian abjectification that appeared in American travel discourse, it is useful first to explore where Mexican Indians fit into the racial logic of U.S. empire building. As scholars in American studies and related fields have shown in recent decades, the idea of "race" shaped the course of U.S. imperialism in the late nineteenth and early twentieth centuries. The desirability of potential colonies—regardless of the course taken by the U.S. imperialist project, either formal annexation or economic conquest—was judged in the popular arena by the racial characters of their inhabitants. Despite the fact that we now know "race" to be a crude, contradictory, and often illogical shorthand to describe physical differences between large populations of human beings, stereotypical representations of racial difference consolidated and organized American anxieties over—and desires for—the feasibility of U.S. empire building.[9] Stereotypical portrayals of native people circulated widely in U.S. popular culture at this time, from the wily and savage Filipino *insurrecto* to the docile Mexican burden bearer, as a means to educate the American public about the suitability of the natives of colonized (or potentially colonized) territories as colonial subjects.

American observers sometimes attempted to assuage concerns in the United States that newly colonized spaces were too racially diverse and too divergent from American racial ideals to adhere to modern social and economic systems. This was part of the aim of Trumbull White, a war reporter and imperial propagandist who published a number of books and articles about Cuba, Puerto Rico, Hawaii, and the Philippines in the late 1890s. In *Our New Possessions*, a richly illustrated volume that deserves a full critical analysis of its own, White captioned one arresting image of an Afro-*boricana* as "A Colored Belle of Puerto Rico." The central figure of the photograph is a black woman standing against a wall on a busy street. She wears a necklace, hat, and a floor-length dress with huge puffy sleeves. Upon closer inspection, it becomes clear that certain details in the woman's clothing and jewelry have been stippled in to enhance detail and shading. Other women are busily engaged with the day's work on the cross street that is visible in the right half of the image, but the "colored belle" stops to pose, somewhat stiffly, for the camera. Remarkably, she returns the camera's gaze with what appears to be a sly smile. A barefoot white boy pauses on the street to look at her.

The picture's caption makes it clear that White meant this woman to exemplify a racial type on the island and, more broadly, the caste system that she represents:

A COLORED BELLE OF PUERTO RICO

The mixture of African and Spanish blood is not found in all of the people on the island. The higher classes of white people hold themselves as strictly to their own society as in any other country. This attractive colored girl is the higher type of that race.

This caption illuminates two facts related to the racialized views of U.S. imperialism. First, it preempts any concerns about race mixing in this "new possession." Laura Briggs's research has shown that the supposedly hyperfertile Puerto Rican woman, particularly the prostitute, served as a symbol of Puerto Ricanness among both imperialists and reformers who set their sights on the island during this period. In White's view, this woman did not threaten the racial system of empire because white Puerto Ricans segregated themselves sexually from other racial formations on this island. The wives of soldiers and speculators could, therefore, send their husbands to the island with at least a modicum of assurance that Puerto Rico was not a sexual free-for-all (as islands of the Caribbean were perceived to be).[10] To drive home this point, White assures the reader several pages after the image of the "Colored Belle" that Puerto Rico "is known as 'the whitest of the Antilles' because the population is less dominant than in any other of the West Indies."[11] This observation undergirds his prediction regarding the ease with which the United States could manage the island's population. "There is nothing about the people of this island," he wrote, "which makes the prospect of adapting them to American methods and manners a dubious one."[12] Second, the caption identifies a high caste of black locals, the descendents of African slaves who now, at the turn of the twentieth century, had adapted to and even facilitated the takeover of their island. As American fixation on Porfirio Díaz showed, the proponents of economic imperialism almost always depended on the presence of a native aristocracy that could serve as a model for the ideal colonized subject and help facilitate foreign dominance. In presenting this striking woman for the U.S. imperialist gaze, Trumbull White constructed Puerto Rico as a place that was already fully colonized by the time it reached U.S. hands and where U.S. conceptions of white supremacy were already fully entrenched in local cultures. This was, of course, a fiction, but it represents a necessary step in doing the cultural work of making the island an object of empire.

But travel writers found no "higher type" among the Indians in Mexico corresponding to the "Colored Belle of Puerto Rico." As we shall see below, most Americans who wrote about their journeys south of the border saw the native people there as primitive and as only marginally capable of assimilation into modern society. Neither could those writers easily claim that racial groups did not mix in Mexico. They did, however, taxonomize and name racial formations in Mexico in ways that rendered them legible to American readers. This practice repeated and updated forms of knowledge that date back to the *casta* paintings of the eighteenth century, which "intended to define, normalize, and differentiate the various elements of a heterogeneous society in constant mutation through multiple interracial exchanges."[13] Published in 1897, Marie Robinson Wright's *Picturesque Mexico* did not pretend that racial mixing did not occur in Mexico but nonetheless made it clear that the racial "castes" were rigidly upheld:

> There are supposed to be seven castes in Mexico, which are kept distinct. First, the Gachupino, or Spaniards born in Europe; second, the Creoles,—that is, whites of European families born in America; third, the Mestizos; fourth, the Mullattoes, descendents of whites and negroes, whom there are a few; fifth, the Zambos, descendents of negroes and Indians, the ugliest race in Mexico; sixth, the Indians; and seventh, the remains of African negroes.[14]

Wright was an extremely ardent proponent of the Porfirian regime, and this racial taxonomy, buried on page 380, is one of the few times in which she mentions the nation's rich cultural and racial diversity throughout her two massive travelogues about Mexico.[15] I reproduce this passage here because it typifies the American sense that Mexico could be both racially mixed and segregated at the same time. This was necessary to rationalize expansionism in a place where members of racial groups did not strictly mix with their own kind.

Not every author detailed Mexican racial formations quite as exhaustively as Wright did, but many gave the nation's distinctive racial system at least a passing glance. Most acknowledged just three extremely broad categories: whites, mestizos, and Indians. All of the Americans who published travelogues during the Porfiriato would have identified themselves as white, and going to Mexico offered an encounter with racial difference the likes of which most had never experienced. Mexico offered a field in which to think and write about the meanings of race from beyond the confines of the U.S. racial system, which many saw in terms of a black-white binary.[16] We might, in fact, read travel to Mexico as part of what Michael Omi and Howard Winant call a "racial project." According to Omi and Winant, a racial project "is simultaneously an interpretation, representation, or explanation of racial dynamics, and an effort to reorganize and redistribute resources along racial lines."[17] This is a rather useful framework, since the creation of travel discourse was an act through which certain Americans actively interpreted, represented, and explained racial dynamics, both within Mexico and between the United States and Mexico. Indian people, in particular, were also regularly integrated into an effort to "reorganize resources along racial lines." The popular burden-bearer trope suggested, for instance, that Indian labor represented one of the many harnessable resources that Mexico offered American investors.

Though a good number of travelers expressed sincere interest in and concern for Indian people, their knowledge about Indian Mexico was never "pure" in the sense that Edward Said uses the term. Said writes against the notion that any form of knowledge can be divorced from its broader political context. As he shows in *Orientalism*, to read cultural texts, even those that ostensibly have little or nothing to do with the politics of empire, apart from the colonial contexts out of which they emerged is fruitless. The same can be said for travelogues and other modes of travel writing dating from the Porfiriato. These texts were always what Said calls "political," meaning that they were always embedded in travelers' awareness of Mexico as a field for capitalist expansionism. It is in this context that travel writings must be read as political texts.[18] Omi and Winant also provide a useful framework for understanding travel writings as political texts. They argue that a racial project "can be defined as *racist* if and only if it creates or reproduces structures of domination based on essentialist categories of race."[19]

Travel writing about Indian people (and, as we will see in the following chapter, people categorized as mestizos) always presumed racial difference to be the innate, immutable reflection of a natural social order. The writers simply never entertained the notion that race and the hierarchies produced by race are social constructs. Rather, they asked how one might draw a profit from the racial "caste system" that was already in place.

Wright's placement of native people at the bottom of the social hierarchy not only reinforces structures of domination based on essentialist categories of race but reflects a conundrum, rooted in racial thought, faced by American promoters of the Porfirian state and the role of the United States in shaping Mexico's economic future: How could Mexico modernize with such a large population of native people who looked, at least to American eyes, like the antitheses of modern subjects? Popular opinion in the United States imagined that native people within the U.S. borders had been thoroughly subdued, especially as the latter Indian Wars drew to a close and the myth of North American Indians as belonging to a "vanishing race" took hold, but indigenous people remained a highly visible part of Mexican life. Though denied political power, native people accounted for approximately 40 percent of Mexico's total population in 1900, a presence that travel writers could hardly ignore.[20] Nor would travelers want to ignore the Indian, as native people had created such a picturesque backdrop to their Mexican adventures. Still, travelers had to develop a way of seeing the Indian that did not threaten the politics of economic conquest.

It is crucial to note that it was not only the proponents of economic empire who saw native people in Mexico as members of a fallen race or denizens of the past. Travelers and critics of all political stripes espoused racist views of Indian people and framed travel to Indian Mexico as a temporal encounter. These American observers simply could not think beyond the racial system in which they were immersed. As Edward Said has argued, "The whole question of imperialism, as it was debated in the late nineteenth century by pro-imperialists and anti-imperialists alike, carried forward the binary typology of the advanced and the backward . . . races, cultures, and societies."[21] Indeed, similar to abolitionists who could not escape dominant views of black people in the United States, writers from a wide variety of political stances regarding U.S. imperialism in Mexico, even those who advocated for Mexican political and economic sovereignty, saw indigenous people as racially inferior to themselves. Even John Kenneth Turner, an indefatigable proponent of social justice, could not escape the racial system of the late nineteenth and early twentieth century. Near the end of *Barbarous Mexico*, as Turner calls for the abolition of economic slavery and the ouster of Díaz, he makes a case against the notion of Indian inferiority—but then reiterates a social Darwinist view of race that presumes that the various races exist on a spectrum that runs from the savage to the civilized. "Biologically," he writes, "the aboriginal Mexican is not to be classed with any of the so-called lower races such as the negro, the South Sea Islander, the pure Filipino, or the American Indian. The Aztec has been a long time out of the forest. His facial angle is as good as our own."[22] Here he refers to the theory that the races' capacities for civilization was reflected in the angle of the face's profile, a popular view of race in the late nineteenth century and into the twentieth. Turner might have painted a more sympathetic (if equally racist) view of Mexican Indianness, but it is clear that he was among the countless Americans who looked to Indian difference as a way to explain U.S. imperialism south of the border. The sections that follow address the political underpinnings of American desires to look at Mexican Indians and trace several of the key tropes through which dominant perceptions of Indianness emerged. An examination of how travel writers sought to assure their readers that Indian difference could be surmounted through key "civilizing" practices will expose how these representations coincided with and served the politics of economic conquest. First, however, it is important to address how and why Americans abroad looked at Mexico's native people.

LOOKING AT MEXICO'S INDIANS

Americans were already used to looking at Indians by the start of the Porfiriato. Beginning in the second half of the nineteenth century, even as the so-called Indian Wars continued to be fought, travelers from the Eastern and Midwestern United States began to tour the U.S. Southwest, tramping through "Indian country" and looking for the supposedly last vestiges of Indianness within the borders of the United States. As with travel to Mexico, the railways created an interest in—and market for—travel into Indian country. Travel narratives and visual ephemera framed a trip into the Southwest as a benignly nostalgic trip back in time, as we have seen.

Native Americana became an increasingly important motif in the United States around the turn of the twentieth century, reaching far beyond tourism and the modes of popular ethnology described in Chapter One. Elizabeth Hutchinson has identified, for example, an "Indian craze" in American art from 1890 to 1915. According to Hutchinson, certain Native American artists skillfully skirted the boundaries between primitivism and modernism to gain critical and popular praise. Far more prevalent, however, were representations of Indians and Indianness created by nonnative people for popular consumption. This mode of cultural production romanticized Indian people despite the fact (or perhaps *because* of the fact) that it constructed them as belonging to a vanishing race. It is from this line of representational practices that we get the gauzy, hyperromantic view of Indianness that persists even today. We might consider Longfellow's *Song of Hiawatha* an early example of this mode of cultural production.

Edward S. Curtis was the individual most responsible for popularizing this view of Indians. Originally from Minnesota, Curtis was a professional photographer living in Seattle by the late 1890s. He first became interested in photographing Native Americans after he met and photographed the famed Princess Angeline, a daughter of Chief Seattle who was then a local celebrity. (She lived in a wooden cabin in downtown Seattle, in violation of the 1855 Treaty of Point Elliott, until her death in the year that Curtis took her picture.) In 1906, J. P. Morgan commissioned Curtis to undertake a large-scale project photographing Native Americans west of the Mississippi and Missouri Rivers. The following year, Curtis published the first volume of *The North American Indian*, his magnum opus that would eventually consist of twenty volumes of photographs, along with exceedingly popular lectures and articles in some of the most popular magazines in the United States.[23] The final volume of this massive undertaking would not be published until 1930. Taken as a whole, *The North American Indian* both valorized native people and advanced the idea that they had been left behind in the march of time and progress across the United States.

Curtis actively staged white fantasies of Indianness in making his photographs, a fact lost on most viewers at the time but which now seems to exemplify the nonnative gaze as it was fixed upon Indian people. In the darkroom, he sometimes rubbed out clocks and other markers of modernity from his images. In making others, he prompted his Native American subjects to perform dances or religious rituals out of context. Many of the resulting images suggest that Native American peoples and cultures had remained unchanged over the three hundred years since contact with Europeans. Erasing the signs of Indian modernity both celebrated native tradition and implied that native modernity, or even adaptation to modern life, remained an impossibility. Within the contexts of expansionism and the rise of U.S. global power, to lack modernity or potential as modern subjects meant to be excluded from the national body politic. Such was the view of the North American Indian popularized by Edward S. Curtis and other purveyors of the Indian image in the late nineteenth and early twentieth centuries.

Not surprisingly, travelers took these views with them to Mexico. Dean Harris, who traveled throughout the U.S. Southwest and Mexico around 1905, opened his *Travel-Talks* with a message about Indians, modernity, and extinction. "The march of civilization is a benediction for the future," he wrote,

> but it is also a devastation before which savage nature and savage man must go down. Unable or unwilling to adapt himself to new conditions and to the demands of a life foreign to his nature and his experience the original man of North America is doomed, like the wild beast he hunted, to extinction. . . . The lonely regions of our great continent, over which there brooded for unnumbered ages the silence which was before creation, are disappearing with the vanishing Indian; a new vegetable and a new animal life are supplanting the old now on the road to obliteration. The ruin is pathetic, but inevitable.[24]

Harris uses this grim view of Indian disappearance to rationalize the need for his book, a travelogue through Indian country on both sides of the U.S.-Mexico border. But this opening passage also reflects how Americans saw Indians in the borderlands and in both countries. Indians are doomed in Harris's view, but, like so many of his compatriots, the author gives no sense of the oppression and genocide that preceded native peoples' supposed disappearance in the United States and in the borderlands. Instead, he describes Indian extinction as a neutral and natural result of progress, one in which the unprogressive is simply replaced by "a new vegetable and a new animal life." In racial terms, this meant that white settlers had successfully and inevitably replaced "the original man of North America" in the United States, a process that, for Harris and other writers, was heading southward.

Many other observers applied American ideas about Indian extinction to Mexico. Nonetheless, the ways in which U.S. travelers looked at native people in Mexico differed from how they looked at native North Americans in a number of significant ways. First, as mentioned above, native people in Mexico constituted a much higher percentage of the nation's total population—roughly 40 percent, according to the 1900 census. Part of the appeal of looking at native people in the United States was the sense that Americans were seeing something fleeting and rare. In sharp contrast, travel writers consistently referred to the ubiquity of Indians in Mexico, even though some writers did claim that their numbers were dwindling. American perceptions of Indian fertility, as we will see, reflected anxieties that indigenous people might even be too numerous (and might have anticipated contemporary views of hyperfertility among Mexican migrants in the United States). Instead of *vanishing*, it seemed to some that Mexico's Indian population was too rapidly multiplying.

So while the myth of the vanishing Indian justified and confirmed white nativism in the United States, imagining that the United States had been emptied of people with rightful claims to the land, no such myth was possible in the Mexican context. After all, the population of people who qualified as white in Mexico was extremely small (though politically and economically powerful), so white nativism would never serve as a key theme in American travel discourse. The Díaz regime did encourage immigration from the United States and Europe in an attempt to engineer the racial makeup of the nation, but white colonists never became numerous enough to constitute a formidable force in Mexican life. As Robert McCaa has noted, 99.5% of Mexico's population in 1900 had been born in the country, signaling that the administration's attempts to attract foreign immigrants was a failure.[25] Instead of nativism, travel writers couched representations of Indianness within a more general view of white supremacy. Instead of claiming that Mexico belonged to white people because of destiny or God-given rights to the land, as the proponents of Manifest Destiny would have framed it, they claimed that white people (including white Americans) should exercise influence in Mexico because Indian people—and to some extent mestizos—were incapable of caring for the nation themselves.

Second, Curtis idealized Indianness through the content and techniques of his photographs. Unlike a wide array of Waite's images and other travel discourse depicting native people in Mexico, Curtis's images do not focus on Indian "squalor" or poverty, as these themes would have jeopardized his vision of Indian people in the United States as noble but doomed. Nor do his photos suggest that the Indian was an active threat to the U.S. body politic, as some who looked at Mexican Indians did during the Porfiriato. Curtis's pictorialist sensibilities (most apparent when he employed the soft-focus and chiaroscuro lighting techniques favored by other art photographers of the era) heightened his romantic view of native people, for pictorialism frequently elevated its subject matter into the sublime. In contrast, the dominant view of Mexican Indians was split between romantic views and those that framed Indian poverty as an endemic and pervasive problem in Mexican society. At times, poverty and desire went hand in hand, a representational practice that Americans used for depictions of native people outside of the United States but that does not appear to have been a major trope in representations of North American Indians.

Finally, as we have also seen, explicit and implicit modes of desire appeared in some representations of Indian Mexico during the Porfiriato. Curtis's images frequently presented a romantic view of Native Americans and their lifestyles, but rarely positioned indigenous people as the objects of erotic desire. American photographers like C. B. Waite and others mentioned in the previous chapters consistently made images that either showed native women and children in stages of undress or otherwise suggested that Indian women and girls were backward but desirable, or perhaps desirable because of their backwardness. While North American Indians still seemed dangerous to many viewers in the United States—which, according to many Curtis scholars, is why Curtis's photographs of the "vanishing race" became popular—the foreignness of Mexican Indians might have made them more pleasurable to look at. Because American observers claimed that native people in Mexico posed no threat to the politics of economic conquest (with the exceptions of the Yaqui and a few other "hostile" tribes in the north), photographers could present them as merely picturesque.

I refer to Curtis's work here to remind the reader that Indian-themed photography inhabited an important place in American visual culture throughout the Porfiriato. I do so to reiterate that travelers brought with them into Mexico an American way of looking at native people. It seems, in fact, that foreigners were always looking at Mexican Indians, so much so that buying and making photographs of native people increasingly became a regular part of the touristic experience during the Porfiriato. As mentioned above, foreign and Mexican photographers immediately began to tap the market for pictures of Mexico when tourists arrived on the trains in the 1880s, selling pictures at stations and in souvenir shops all over the country. These *cartes de visite* inherited representational practices developed by photographers during the French Intervention, mostly focusing on Mexican Indian *tipos*.

Starting around the turn of the twentieth century, professional photographers also began to create picture postcards illustrated with pictures of Indians. These could be cheaply bought and sent back home.[26]

Also around this time, Americans in Mexico began to use newly available automatic cameras like the Kodak Brownie to take their own pictures of Indians. Photographing Indian people became such standard practice, in fact, that travelogues and guidebooks began to advise their readers about the best ways to photograph Indian subjects. They warned that Mexico's Indians were serious and sullen people who had to be enticed to have their pictures taken. Some guidebooks claimed that a way to get around this fact was to pay photogenic Indians for their time. *Terry's Guide to Mexico*, the famous guidebook first published in 1909, advised tourists against overtipping, noting that "in photographing native types, it is well to remember that a ragged urchin will stand just as still for 25 cents as he will for a peso."[27] Many other writers claimed that Indians were among the most picturesque sights in the nation and offered tips for how to best coerce a pose out of reluctant or suspicious natives. Directly following a claim about Indian people that "in ignorance they are primeval," Grace Brown goes on to declare that "Mexico is a paradise for the camera fiend[.] . . . I go snapping around like a Spitz dog! If only the camera could reproduce the wealth of color in the outlandish costumes, in the soft eyes and olive skin of the people."[28]

An encounter described in an American travelogue fleshes out Terry's advice a bit more fully and underscores Brown's rapturous declaration that Indian people served as ideal photo subjects. In *A Tour in Mexico*, Mrs. James Edwin Morris described the delight that she took in making pictures of a particularly charismatic Indian boy—and his savvy in knowing the price of his image:

> Jose was a bright little fellow, a veritable clown, a perfect mimic, a delightful companion, a very king Chico among his playmates. . . . Yes indeed, Jose was a bright youngster, a financier, for when we proposed that he stand for his photograph he stipulated that he should receive ten centavos instead of the five that we had offered, but Jose made his bargain in such a delightfully winsome manner that we poured out centavos, all we possessed and added some American coins also.[29]

Morris writes that she and her husband found José near a rubbish heap outside Zacatecas and that the boy followed them all over the city, dancing and entertaining them along the way. All parties involved accept that the act of taking a photograph can be an economic exchange (meaning that traveling white people will pay to take pictures of people like José). In the end, José's image appears on page 310 of Morris's travelogue.

Amateurs and professionals alike amassed a huge corpus of images of native people throughout the Díaz regime, from highly stylized studio portraits to casual snapshots that increased in number as cameras became simpler and cheaper in the early twentieth century. Perhaps "staring" is the better term for how Americans looked at Indians in Porfirian Mexico. In a provocative inquiry into the politics and meanings of looking at physical difference, Rosemarie Garland-Thomson argues that staring marks social difference in modern life. "Staring," she writes, "offers an occasion to rethink the status quo. Who we are can shift into focus by staring at who we think we are not."[30] What happens if we consider how the practice of staring at Indian people helped Americans rethink (and sometimes reinforce) the status quo in Mexico? And what happens if we include travel writing in this analysis? Can writing about looking be a form of staring? Photographs serve as powerful evidence that travelers looked endlessly at Indians in Mexico, but equally compelling is the fact that many travel writers also described in writing the pleasures and perils of staring at Indian people. Ethel Tweedie, an Englishwoman whose travelogues were published in New York for American audiences, rang in the turn of the twentieth century in Mexico City's Catedral Metropolitana, where a small group of Indian people caught her attention:

> There for an hour they prayed—that ring of five women, two babies and a dog, illumed by a single candle. What a group! What a picture! How delightful to witness their honest faith. Yet there was another side to it all, for my friend had a beautiful pearl pin stolen from her scarf while we stood there watching that group.[31]

Tweedie finds herself enthralled by the praying Indian women in a scene that illustrates the pleasures that travelers found in looking at Indian people. The women become an object of fascination. They become a *picture*. Tweedie and her companion were, however, so focused on looking at the Indian women that they became (so the author claims) the victims of a theft. It never occurred to them that the Indians could be looking back.

Tweedie's impulse to stare is best exemplified by one of the many images that illustrate the 1901 edition of *Mexico as I Saw It*. Many of the illustrations depict the author at play in Mexico, and this photograph finds her seated atop a freight car (Figure 3.1). According to the caption, Tweedie was watching "the sham-fight at Monterey [*sic*] in honour of General Diaz being re-elected President for the sixth time." In the rather stark image, Tweedie looms above whatever action is taking place below. Seated and in high Victorian dress, her face is not discernible but she looks toward the foreground (and perhaps toward the camera). The photograph is a strange one but nonetheless speaks to what it meant for American travelers to look at Mexico. This is because, like many of the foreigners looking at and in Mexico, Tweedie is present but removed. She seems to draw power—or at least narrative authority—from the fact that she looks from a distance. Once again, Tweedie's arrangement of images is most telling. Next to this image appears a solemn photograph of "a Mexican beggar" standing near an open doorway. A woman shrouded by her rebozo peers out from the building's interior. For Tweedie and so many other travelers during this period, especially those who were women, it was necessary to properly distance oneself from the natives in order to experience Mexico.

Despite this distancing, Indians served as a rich source of scopic pleasure for travelers from the United States and Europe. Tweedie pauses to look at Indians throughout *Mexico as I Saw It*. Even the book's title tells us that looking and seeing were the key frameworks through which the author and her readers would come to know Mexico. Following the midnight Mass in the capital, she ventures into the tropics where, like many American travelers, she watches Indian women washing clothes in a stream. "It was all very picturesque, charming, and quaint," she observes. "The dark olive skin of the people, the bright coloring of their clothes, the nakedness of the children, and the gorgeous tropical vegetation, were all so different to anything ever seen in Britain."[32] Again, Tweedie describes the pleasure of looking at difference, a theme that appears throughout Porfirian travel discourse and which continues to shape how travelers see Mexico. Tweedie positions herself as a sympathetic observer by refusing to judge these seemingly uncivilized natives against their western counterparts. "We were in the tropics," she reminds the reader, "and one must not measure the half-clad ladies and gentlemen of those regions, the naked children scampering about or riding on pigs, with the cold-blooded inhabitants of northern climes."[33]

It is tempting to presume that all travel involves looking at the locals, but Tweedie suggests that there are different ways of seeing based on

The writer viewing the sham-fight at Monterey in honour of General Diaz being re-elected President for the sixth time.

FIGURE 3.1. Tweedie watching a Mexican "sham-fight." Mrs. Alec (Ethel B.) Tweedie, *Mexico as I Saw It*.

the social standings of both the looker and the looked at. In *Mexico as I Saw It*, her encounters with Indian and non-Indian people contrast sharply. This was partly regional. "High civilisation, great refinement, beauty and talent can be found in the Capital itself," she writes, "yet great barbarism exists outside."[34] As an upper-class Briton, Tweedie was socially interested in Mexican high society. Throughout the book she attempts to engage with "Mexicans of the better classes," as she calls them, offering detailed descriptions of her social triumphs among the nation's social elite (all the way up to the president and Mrs. Díaz). For Tweedie and other travelers, *la clase alta* was not only an economic or social category but a racial one as well. Mexicans of obvious European descent were included in this charmed circle, as were members of sizable communities of Europeans and Americans who lived in Mexico during the Porfiriato. These groups appealed greatly to Tweedie, who details her movement among them in a chapter titled "Mexican Society." More than half of the individuals mentioned in this chapter are European and American foreigners living in Mexico, such as upper-level management in American firms and members of the diplomatic circle that socialized with one another. It is telling that Tweedie, who claimed to be an astute observer of Mexico, would refer to this tiny sliver of the population as "Mexican Society." At the same time, it is not surprising, since many travel writers lobbied for more of their compatriots to populate the thriving "American Colony" in Mexico City. Tweedie seems to assume, at various points in *Mexico as I Saw It*, that white Americans who relocated to Mexico could take part in high society. Like the Indians and mestizos discussed in this chapter and the next, white settlers in Mexico might even be remade through the process of economic conquest. Travel writing helped frame Mexico as a logical destination not only for the tourist but also for longer-term settlers.

However, despite this tendency to celebrate the Americans and other foreigners who lived in Mexico, well-connected mestizos with political power were also a significant part of the high society that so fascinated Tweedie and other travelers. Accordingly, writers looked for ways to discuss *mestizaje* without abandoning their deeply held anxieties about racial admixture. One general strategy for representing the Mexican elite was to Europeanize Mexican high culture. Tweedie, for example, writes:

> The sons of most of the best families have been educated in England—
> they have been sent to Stoneyhurst or Beaumont between the ages
> of twelve and eighteen; some have even been to our Universities. . . .
> [I]ndeed several men looked, dressed, and spoke so much in accordance
> with English ideas, that it seemed impossible to believe they were
> Spanish Mexicans.[35]

This is one of many examples of writers' visions of elite Mexicans as a European gentry and is a far cry from the ways that Tweedie and other observers wrote about Indian people in Mexico. Referring to Anglophile elites as "Spanish Mexicans" might have reflected their status as descendents of the powerful criollo class, or might have simply been an attempt to Europeanize those at the top of Mexican society—including upper-class mestizos. Foreign accounts of Mexican society frequently emphasized the Spanish heritage of "highly cultivated" mestizos.

Although Tweedie finds commonalities with *la clase alta*, she looks at Indians, who are "so different from anything ever seen in Britain," only from a distance. This does not mean, however, that she had little to say about Indianness. "They cannot read or write, they do not know how to think; all they want is food and shelter, and so their animal existence continues year in, year out," she writes.[36] These examples from *Mexico as I Saw It* remind us that travel inspires different ways of looking at people based on their social standings. Some people, such as indigenous people at New Year's Mass, become objects while others are granted full humanity and citizenship. Mexicans of the higher classes, whose attentions were sought by Tweedie and other travelers, certainly fall into this latter category. Mestizos fit somewhere in between.

With the disparities in Tweedie's views of Indians and non-Indians in mind, it is important to note that travel discourse served as more than just entertainment. I have attempted in this book to treat travel discourse as a serious mode of knowledge production, and Tweedie's vision of Mexican Indianness is no exception. Tweedie and her peers, while seeming to proffer images of the Indian for aesthetic reasons, also offered a way for Americans to understand who the Mexican Indians were and how they fit into the epistemology of "civilization" that so concerned American readers during this period. As Chris Jenks has claimed, "looking, seeing, and knowing have become perilously intertwined" in the modern West.[37]

The relationship between looking and knowledge is exemplified in a variety of media but was especially evident in early anthropological works. In his preface to *In Indian Mexico*, for example, Frederick Starr outlines the methodology for his previous book, *Indians of Southern Mexico*, published almost a decade earlier, in this plan of work:

1. The measurement of one hundred men and twenty-five women in each population [each tribe], fourteen measurements taken upon each subject; 2. The making of pictures,—portraits, dress, occupations, cus-

toms, buildings, and landscapes; 3. The making of plaster busts of five individuals in each tribe. To do such work, of course, involved difficulty, as the Indians of Mexico are ignorant, timid, and suspicious.[38]

In this brief passage, Starr makes it clear that his mission is to look at Indian bodies—and to prompt the reader to take part in the act of looking. Each of the tools mentioned here (measuring instruments, a camera, plaster casts) is a visual method designed to record Indian difference, a way of producing what Michel Foucault calls the "clinical gaze." Foucault writes that doctors developed ways of seeing the human body to understand its normal and abnormal functions. For Foucault, this practice reflected modernity's emphasis on looking as a means of finding truth.[39] Similarly, Starr's tools attempt to find an objective truth about what made Indian bodies different from white bodies. Although the *campo* barely resembles the clinic, Starr's way of looking at Indian bodies articulated systems of knowledge and power developed in Europe and the United States throughout the nineteenth century. Even so, despite Starr's scientific aspirations, his project reflected his view of native Mexicans as "ignorant, timid, and suspicious." In other words, Starr could measure Indians, but he could not escape his own view of what Indianness meant, a view that owed a debt to phrenology and eugenics, pseudosciences that, at the time, still shaped how people made sense of physical differences between individuals and racial groups.

One of the most remarkable elements of *In Indian Mexico* is the extent to which Starr suspends his scientific principles to produce a book that would appeal to a wider audience than the more esoteric *Indians of Southern Mexico*. It is clear that Starr wrote for a popular audience interested in learning more about Mexico through his observations. Charles Lummis, the writer, editor, impresario, and promoter of Porfirian Mexico in the United States, implored Starr to lecture in Los Angeles, convinced that the public would be interested in the prominent scholar's stories of travel among the Mexican Indians.[40] The author details his own journey, with its hardships, rewards, and minor irritations. The lines separating serious ethnological inquiry from popular travel writing were blurry at the start of the twentieth century, the era of the intrepid ethnologist toiling alone in the field, and Starr's account barely diverges from other travelogues written by well-educated non-anthropologists. Little distinguishes *In Indian Mexico* from the conventional travelogue, in fact, except for the author's scientific credentials and the fact that he includes the names and tribal affiliations of many of the native people depicted in its photographic illustrations. This latter action is notable, as it results in a travel narrative in which Indian people are granted individual identities and personalities rather than serving as generic "Indian types." Still, Starr's attitudes about indigenous people were deeply immersed in the racist ideologies of the early twentieth century. "Mexico has a serious problem in its Indians," Starr surmised. "The solution of the problem has been attempted in varying ways, according to whether the population dealt with was Totonac, Yaqui, Maya: it is no small task, to build a nation out of an indian population."[41] In the end, in a rhetorical move that echoed colonialist views of native people, Starr decided that there were indigenous groups that could be reformed through capitalist development and state intervention and those who were hopelessly savage, closing his book with the claim that "there are indians, and indians, in Mexico."[42]

Despite the fact that they wrote from very different subject positions, both Tweedie and Starr exemplify the impulse to look at Mexican Indians. Both casual travelers and serious scholars looked closely at Indian people and relished the act of looking in the narratives that they disseminated to the public. But travelers from a wide variety of backgrounds and political standpoints also saw Indian difference as an impediment to Mexican nation building. What Starr failed to mention was that Mexico's Indian "problem" also belonged to the United States. If it was no small task to build a nation out of an Indian population, as Starr claimed, many travel writers also saw the difficulties in building a potential economic colony out of an Indian population perceived as too unruly, deficient, and savage. Several key tropes emerged in American travel writing during the Porfiriato that explicitly and implicitly positioned the Indian as a barrier to capitalist development and modernization. It is to these representational patterns that I now turn.

DEFICIENT BODIES

The act of looking—and staring—at Mexico's indigenous people always involved bodies. As described above, writers and photographers took great interest in the Indian body, frequently presenting it as an object of fascination and desire. The most famous Mexican body that travelers looked at, wrote about, and photographed was that of Porfirio Díaz, whose physical presence underscored his status as a logical patriarch for the nation. Americans projected onto him their desires for a Mexico that was self-disciplined, forward thinking, and attuned to the manly pursuit of nation building, finding interesting ways to champion the president despite the fact that they also described him as a dark-skinned mestizo raised by a "full-blooded" Zapotec mother. The makers of American travel discourse advanced a similarly charged view of Indian women, sometimes framing Indian women as desirable. Given the presence of these somewhat positive representations of Díaz and Indian women on the American cultural scene, it might appear that travelers had learned to suppress the views of Indian inferiority that predominated in the United States.

To the contrary, Indian bodies also served as the sources of anxiety and derision in many representations of travel to Mexico, as travelers frequently claimed that Indian corporeal difference posed a problem for the interwoven projects of Mexican cultural and economic transformation. Although their supposed *cultural* backwardness posed the biggest problem for assimilating native people into U.S. capitalist systems, writers and photographers also employed a number of representational strategies that advanced the idea that Indians were physically inferior to people of European descent, including mestizos. As we shall see, these descriptions of the Indian body reflected broader anxieties about Indians' capacities to be assimilated into a more modern Mexico.

As any student of American history well knows, the colonization of North America was based in part on the idea that European newcomers to the continent were physically superior to indigenous people. Native people's lack of immunity to European diseases was just one piece of evidence in the eyes of some colonists that their bodies were superior to Indian bodies—and that they, Americans of European descent, were destined to populate the landmass that would become the United States. Slavery was, of course, another social and economic system that depended on corporeal difference and the idea of white supremacy. By the time of the Porfiriato, black slaves had been emancipated, but whiteness remained a prerequisite for full enfranchisement in the United States. American race science emerged to catalogue human differences and to identify the corporeal standards for whiteness. Even so, the boundaries of whiteness were strictly enforced in legal and popular spheres as well.[43]

Americans took the idea of whiteness—and its relationship to the body—with them to Mexico. As mentioned above, Frederick Starr, as one of a handful of American ethnologists interested in Mexican Indians, measured and recorded bodily difference among native people. Starr attempted to identify and quantify Indianness, a project that was in tune with the era's positivist approach to human difference. But even writers who had little to do with the emerging field of physical anthropology shared their thoughts on the Indian body and, by extension, the superiority of their own bodies. Most frequently, they did so by rearticulating the long-standing theory that the Mexican Indian body had degenerated through Spanish colonialism, that a once strong and noble race had been compromised physically and culturally as a result of contact with the most brutal form of European imperialism. (This is but one part of the so-called Black Legend of Spanish colonialism). This vision of Indianness explained both the past achievements of native cultures—with the nation's many archaeological sites serving as physical reminders of these past glories—and the contemporary inferiority of native people.[44]

The Indian body made other appearances in American travel discourse as well. Some writers worried, for example, that Indian people's preference for folk cures over Western medicine reflected unbridgeable cultural divides that would make it impossible to assimilate native people into the modernizing nation. "It is difficult for any of these people to consent to a vaccination," wrote John G. Bourke in the aforementioned *Scribner's* article. "Most of them are fatalists. . . . If a hapless child dies, the parents will say 'Dios lo quiere.'"[45] Bourke, like many of his peers, lamented Mexicans' trust in folk ways over scientific rationalism, and went on to describe what he saw as the "foolishness" of folk cures and *curanderas* (native healers). Doing so reflected American concerns that Indians' backward ideas about health and medicine precluded their formation as modern subjects. As scholar Nayan Shah has put it in regard to Chinese migrants in the United States, "What was crucial to the formation of the modern self was the capacity to reason 'correctly' and follow 'civilized' codes of conduct"—especially in relation to the body.[46] Shah's important historical and theoretical work on San Francisco's Chinatown illustrates how ethnic communities in the United States were constructed in the popular imagination and public health discourses as the sites of contagion. Shah shows that health reformers and the makers of popular culture saw the healthy body as the result of a subject who practiced proper "self care" and constructed the unhealthy body as deviant. Along with more general ideas about race, whiteness, and the body, travelers would have taken these ideas about health and sickness with them to Mexico.

These travelers were immersed in a culture that promoted the idea of the healthy body as a reflection of one's modernity. Some therefore saw disease and other health problems in Mexico as the results of the inhabitants' inability or refusal to adhere to civilized conduct, as we have seen with Bourke's disgust regarding Indians' adherence to folk medicine over science. Travel discourse repeatedly claimed that Indian people could not care for their bodies like white Americans could. Travelers read the markers of disease, poverty, and malnutrition as racial failings. Such a view ignored the systems of structural violence that kept native people at the bottom of social and economic hierarchies in Mexico, suggesting that Indians' care (or lack of care) for the self reflected their inherent backwardness rather than their economic and social oppression.

Within this representational schema, dirt loomed large as a marker of Indianness. Scholars in postcolonial studies have shown that popular culture of the late nineteenth and early twentieth centuries explored the lines separating "dirty" and "clean" subjects, as in the infamous Pears' soap advertisements, which claimed that "the first step towards lightening the white man's burden is through teaching the virtues of cleanliness."[47] Calling an Indian dirty, as many travelers did, was not only a description of that person but also an attack on Indians' relationship to modern subjecthood. The idea that Indians took an "annual bath" became a stock joke for American observers of Mexico, for example. "In the highlands, where the water courses are dry for the greater part of the year," wrote W. E. Carson near the end of the Porfiriato, "the Indians never take a bath; and you will often see them by the roadside picking vermin from one another as monkeys do. The peons of the temperate zone seem, in fact, to have a deep-rooted horror of soap and water."[48] This view was supported by photographs depicting Indian grooming habits, including a somewhat notorious image made by C. B. Waite of pretty Indian girls apparently delousing one another.[49] At the same time that Americans like Carson ridiculed native Mexicans for being dirty, others took great interest in the sight of men, women, and children bathing in public places like streams and lakes. Waite, too, was no stranger to this subject matter.

At times, travelers connected indigenous ways of eating to specific social problems. Tweedie blamed Indians' poor diet for their high infant mortality rates. "Tortillas and pulque are hardly proper food and drink for a baby," she writes, "yet on such diet they are nourished by their ignorant parents, the resulting infant mortality being appalling. . . . It is not want of proper medicine or surgery, it is ignorance of nature's teaching that produces this enormous death-rate among native children."[50] Tweedie does not clarify how native people would have accessed "proper medicine or surgery," claiming instead that it was Indians' refusals to properly care for themselves that led to their physical unfitness for modernity.

It is clear that white travelers from the United States saw Indian bodies as inferior to their own. What, then, were the results of representing Indianness in this way? Why does it matter that a good number of travelers saw the Indian body as deficient? Some writers attempted to relate intrinsically inferior Indian bodies to Mexico's fitness as a field for U.S. economic expansionism. In 1883, traveler Howard Conkling, like many writers, directly compared the Indian body to the white body. "In physique," Conkling wrote, "the peons are far inferior to the laboring men of the United States, but their deficiency of muscular power is somewhat counterbalanced by their power of endurance and ability to bear exposure to the elements."[51] Conkling argues that a white working class is superior to an Indian one, but does concede that Indians were a hearty race. Several chapters later, Conkling marvels at burden bearers on the highway between Mexico City and Cuernavaca.[52] This was a common representational strategy, for writers like Conkling felt a certain ambivalence about indigenous people: at the same time that they racialized the Indian as corporeally inferior, they knew that Indian labor would be an essential part of the nation's new economy.

GENDER PROBLEMS AND SEXUAL THREATS

Travel writers frequently couched the problem of Indian difference within their troubled views of gender in Indian Mexico. The Porfiriato spanned an era in the United States in which Victorian gender norms collided with the New Woman and other markers of gender's shifting meanings around the turn of the twentieth century. Accordingly, travelers to Porfirian Mexico brought ambivalent ideas about proper behaviors for men and women with them south of the border. They constantly compared and contrasted gender norms in the United States to those in Mexico, whether to suggest that American women were more liberated than their Mexican counterparts (which American women frequently claimed, especially when they compared themselves to aristocratic and "old-fashioned" women that they glimpsed behind veils or barred windows) or to comment on what they saw as Indians' inability to adhere to gender norms. On a deeper level, ideas about gender in Mexico helped American observers think through such thorny issues as civilization, savagery, and the politics of economic conquest. Indian people, especially Indian women, served as particularly powerful symbols of Mexico's inability to adhere to what many Americans saw as proper ways of performing gender.

Historian Gail Bederman has argued that differences between men and women served as an important framework through which Americans in the late nineteenth and early twentieth centuries understood and aspired to civilization. According to Bederman, the Victorians

> could identify advanced civilizations by the degree of their sexual differentiation. Savage (that is, nonwhite) men and women were believed to be almost identical, but men and women of the civilized races had evolved pronounced sexual differences. . . . In short, the pronounced sexual differences celebrated in the middle class doctrine of separate spheres were assumed to be absent in savagery, but to be an intrinsic and necessary aspect of civilization.[53]

Bederman's argument illumines much of the travel writing examined here. Americans who went to Mexico frequently commented on their impressions of Indian men and women as inadequately differentiated from one another. This is true despite the fact that many American women distanced themselves from Indian women by claiming that the native women were bound to the metate and their babies and were thus "victims" of their highly gendered but primitive society.

Sexual differentiation required men and women to perform different forms of labor, and travelers from the United States frequently stood aghast at the sight of Indian women engaged in "men's work." Photographers underscored this way of seeing Mexican gender in representations of the burden bearer, which sometimes included images of women carrying huge loads. François Aubert's studio photograph of an old woman carrying a large bundle of sticks or grasses, to name one analyzed above, captured not only the hardships endured by this particular woman but also a whole constellation of concerns that Indian people did not properly differentiate between men's and women's roles (see Figure 1.8). A frequently reprinted photograph by Abel Briquet, to cite another example, depicted barefoot Indian *carboneros* (charcoal vendors) carrying huge loads of coal wrapped in straw (see Figure 1.9). The woman casts a downward gaze while her male companion looks into the camera with a pained expression, his hat in hand. In stark contrast to the public images of Porfirio and Carmen Díaz as well as to those of other mestizo and white elites in Mexico, the man and woman in this image seem to illustrate Bederman's argument that "savage . . . men and women were believed to be almost identical." In fact, the man and woman in this image seem to mirror one another. They are both bare-foot and carry loads that look equally huge for their slender frames. Put simply, this man and woman are not different enough to be considered civilized. This, along with other visual cues in the image (bare feet, pained expressions) would have helped viewers in the late nineteenth and early twentieth centuries see them as savages rather than simply as native people struggling to perform a day's work.

The idea that Indians lacked proper gender differentiation extended to, or perhaps stemmed from, anxieties regarding Indian sexuality that appeared in American travel writing. To approach the question of Indian sexuality and the threat that it supposedly posed to both trav-elers and to Mexico, let us begin with the question of Indian beauty. We have seen by now that photographers and writers sometimes framed Indian women as the objects of desire. The women of the Isthmus of Tehuantepec were especially valued as Indian beauties, as countless travelogues, magazine articles, and widely circulated photographs at-test. Images of dark-skinned Tehuanas in their exotic lace headdresses in fact became the most ubiquitous and recognizable symbol of Indian beauty in the Porfiriato. As one *Los Angeles Times* article put it in 1909, Tehuantepec was "famed up and down the Pacific Coast from Panama to California as the abode of the most beautiful Indian women."[54] Even in Frederick Starr's more scientific writing, the anthropologist could not help but remark upon their beauty. "For personal beauty the Tehuantepec women are famous: all travelers emphasize the fact and some assert that they are the most beautiful women in the world. Much of this favorable impression is due to their fine forms, their free and graceful movement, and their straightforward and fearless man-ner."[55] This "fearless manner" compelled travelers to frequently repeat the claim that the culture of the isthmus was matriarchal in nature. "Strange to say," Tweedie wrote, "in this very un-up-to-date, far-away spot, 'women's rights' are undisputed. Ninety per cent. of the trade is done by women, and a woman has to vouch for her husband before he can even get credit. . . . Not only do the women predominate in busi-ness, but they prove beyond all doubt, that because a woman can earn a livelihood, it is not necessary for her to be either ugly or mis-shapen."[56] According to travelers like Tweedie, the women of Tehuantepec pos-sessed both beauty and social power. This vision of Tehuana matriarchy might be read as an exception to the rule of Indian backwardness or as yet another throwback to premodern social relations.

Though none compared to the Tehuanas in the popular imaginations of foreigners, other Indian women garnered the attention of travelers. Writing in a book published by an American-owned railway, one author claimed, for example, that "Jalapa is famed for its beautiful women, and the proverb '*las jalapeñas son halaguiñas*,' truthfully applies. Bewitching, alluring are the women of Jalapa is the meaning, though not its literal translation. The truth of the saying can be vouched for by many a beauty-loving *Americano*."[57] Interestingly, the pictures of Mexican women that illustrate this guidebook, titled *Mexico: Tours through the Egypt of the New World*, are all found in the section dedicated to hotels. These materials might suggest that Indian women represented another resource from which sexual pleasure could be drawn. This was certainly the case in other imperialist contexts, as scholars in postcolonial feminist studies have established. Edward Said argues in *Orientalism* that representations of native women's sexuality helped rationalize and justify imperialist endeavors. Within colonial representations, Said posits, "women are usually creatures of a male power fantasy," in which they "express unlimited sensuality, they are more or less stupid, and above all they are willing."[58] This imagined "willingness" certainly colored representations of travel to Porfirian Mexico and the view of that nation as a conquerable domain.

But we must also contend with the fact that representational practices like these ran counter to the dominant view of Indian women as less beautiful than their North American or mestiza counterparts. In an article about Indian poverty, the *Los Angeles Times* forthrightly asked "Are the women pretty?" and then answered with, "No; taken as a whole, they are not, unless one looks into the very depths of [their] eyes—there one reads much of a nature untamed, uncontrolled."[59] The last few words of this quote are particularly compelling, as they illustrate the search for Indian beauty and the qualities associated with Indian womanhood. Despite the fact that the *Times* author seemed willing to gaze deeply into Indian women's eyes, he concludes that, in the end, Indian women were not beautiful. Travel writers often repeated the myth that Indian women could be appealing in their youth but quickly lost their looks. This tendency poses the inverse of the question posed in Chapter One, where I considered the cultural politics at work in photographic representations of Indian desirability. How do we make sense here of Indian women's supposed ugliness? Is there a politics of presenting particular groups of women as less beautiful than others? Put simply, we must ask how and why American and other foreign travelers framed native Mexican women as ugly.

Descriptions of feminine Indian ugliness constitute one more way in which writers constructed Indian bodies as deficient. Take, for example, W. E. Carson's description of Indian women written in 1909. Carson, who presented indigenous people as a threat to Mexican modernity throughout his travel memoir, reserved his harshest criticisms for Indian women:

> The Indian man has a fitting mate in the Indian woman, who is not a wholesome-looking person. Nearly all of the women are small, plump, and slatternly, with tousled hair, their dresses torn and dirty, their general appearance being reminiscent of gypsies. Some of the girls are handsome enough; but the hardness of and monotony of their lives make them old before their time, and an Indian maiden of thirty is often simply a bent and wrinkled hag. . . . Like their husbands, the women are invariably dull-witted and unprogressive.[60]

Indian abjection is clearly gendered in Carson's view. Carson saw the Indian woman's ugly appearance as a reflection of her moral and intellectual failings, related in turn to her unprogressive attitudes. Ugliness, in other words, served as an outward reflection of internal backwardness. Like poverty and sickliness, ugliness reflected deeper racial failings in the eyes of foreign travelers. Countless images of bedraggled Indian women, some of the same ones used by Waite to connote Mexico's desirability, supported Carson's gendered view of Indian inferiority. While I am reluctant to create a tidy link between ugliness and backwardness, the archival evidence does suggest that these two discourses of Indian difference went hand in hand. However, admiring the beauty of the Tehuanas did not compromise the dominant view of Indian women, as attested by an earlier *Los Angeles Times* article. "Beautiful and graceful of figure, with faces always attractive, if not pleasingly pretty," the article claimed about the native Tehuanas, "they are so much in contrast to the Indian women that one sees in other parts of Mexico as to make the visitor to their native sections admire them as he has almost forgotten to admire women of other races than his own."[61] Many other representations of Tehuanas included subtle and sometimes quite explicit reminders that these women were the exceptions among indigenous people and, even then, were not proper objects of desire for white men.

In addition to the supposed ugliness of the Indian body, travel discourse suggested that Indians posed *sexual* threats to themselves and to anyone foolish enough to consider the possibility of sexual or romantic intercourse with the native population. While many travelogue writers who visited Porfirian Mexico found upper-class courtship rituals there charming (referred to as "playing the bear"), Mexicans' failures to adhere to marriage and family practices like those sanctioned in the United States alarmed American observers throughout the Porfiriato.[62] As a result, travelers frequently contrasted Indian women with women of the "better classes," constructing them as sexually threatening to Victorian mores. As one traveler put it in the 1880s, "Personally speaking, I saw no laxity of morals among the better classes, although among certain Indian tribes women of easy virtue are the rule rather than the exception."[63] Two main sources of tension were Indians' reluctance to be legally married and the sizes of their families.

Matrimony was a complicated endeavor in Porfirian Mexico, as it required both a civil and an expensive church ceremony. As a result, many Indian people sidestepped these formalities altogether and formed families outside of official church or state sanctioning. According to one observer in 1910, "the enormous fees exacted by the priests . . . ha[ve] brought on the shameful condition of thousands and thousands of families over the country, in which the father and mother are living together unmarried, not being able to pay the necessary fee, and having been taught that the civil marriage is a farce."[64] Not surprisingly, this horrified Victorian Era travelers, who assumed that Indian people could not adhere to their own standards regarding courtship, love, and sex. Whereas mestizo and middle-class marital practices such as "playing the bear" fascinated and delighted them, Indian marriage became a source of tension in the travelogues and magazine writing they produced. Authors reported with disgust that Indian women rarely bothered with a legal or church marriage and that, as a result, domestic arrangements among indigenous women and their partners were marked by a certain casualness.

Family size functioned a bit differently than marriage in depictions of Indian Mexico, as travelers found large Mexican families both funny and abject. Postcards and the pictures found in travelogues and other travel writing frequently played up the strange and apparently comical

Una Familia, Méxicana.

J. G. Hatton, Mexico. No. 8042

FIGURE 3.2. Postcard of Indian family. Author's collection.

sight of Indian families lined up in front of their homes. One example of this motif is a photograph made by C. B. Waite in the first decade of the twentieth century and which circulated as souvenir cards, illustrations in travelogues, and hand-colored picture postcards (Figure 3.2).[65] Like other postcards of this genre, it features members of a large indigenous family posing with one another. What makes the image abject, funny, or titillating, depending on one's point of view, is the nakedness or near nakedness of eight of the twelve children in the family. In particular, five boys stand at the left of the picture looking alternately amused and annoyed at having their picture taken. The boys are no longer babies, so their nakedness suggests that the parents cannot afford to clothe all of their children, since only the four at the center of the frame wear the simple white clothing of the peon. The caption of the colored postcard, "Una Familia, Méxicana," implies that this is a typical Mexican family, but this is a family out of control in the eyes of American observers.

Family size spoke to American perceptions of Indian people, especially Indian women, as hyperfertile—a theme that continues to haunt American impressions of Mexicans and Mexican immigrants. In 1911, one guidebook claimed that Indian women were "much addicted to maternity," a stereotype illustrated by the twelve children that appear in the postcard described above.[66] Writers routinely framed Indian women in maternal terms, often as little more than baby-making machines.

They seem to have agreed with Harriott Wight Sherratt's claim that "Mexicans are sinfully prolific."[67] In the eyes of some American writers, hyperfertility was both a positive and a negative aspect of Indian sexuality. On one hand, it meant more workers could become part of the new modern economic system. But on the other, it reflected existing beliefs that Indian people could not practice sexual self-control or implement, or even imagine, what Americans would come to call "family planning." The small nuclear family was increasingly the model for American families but never caught on in Indian Mexico. As one travelogue from 1917 claimed, "It doesn't induce cleanliness or morality for a whole family of ten or fifteen to live in one room and bring up children like a litter of puppies."[68] This brutal but typical description of Indian reproductive practices once again dehumanized native people by comparing them to animals. It placed them outside of modernity by suggesting that Indian women and men were no better able to control themselves or plan ahead than the ubiquitous dogs that roamed Mexican cities and towns.

Indian sexuality was particularly threatening to Americans, however, because it represented a potential sexual contact zone, a site of potential contagion between the abject Indian and the American visitor. As mentioned above, American observers could not ignore the fact that to discuss race in Mexico meant to discuss racial admixture and its human results, as it had meant since the Spanish colonial era. So it is logical that some visiting Americans would wonder about the boundaries between themselves and native people. "Miscegenation" was a newly coined term at the start of the Porfiriato, having first been used in a pamphlet intending to discredit American abolitionists in 1864.[69] The word itself probably never appeared in any Mexican travelogues, but we can nonetheless infer from them subtle questions about whether desire between white people and Mexican Indians was appropriate. On the spectrum that guided most travelers' views of race, Indians were closer to whiteness than were African Americans. Although some did negatively compare native people with black people, they generally understood Indians as somewhere between the poles of blackness and whiteness that supposedly rested at opposite ends of the spectrum. Thus, the racial lines separating white travelers from Indian people in Mexico were more ambiguous than the black-white racial divide in the United States, making the possibility of desire a particularly vexing problem for the travelers who broached the subject. While black bodies could not overtly serve as the objects of white desire in mainstream publications during the late nineteenth and early twentieth centuries, it was less clear whether white Americans could openly desire the Indian (or mestizo) body when describing their journeys south of the border.[70]

As such, the makers of travel discourse toed a delicate line between avowing and disavowing erotic interest in Indian bodies. In countless images, like many of those produced by C. B. Waite, beautiful Indian women and girls appeared in various states of undress. It is fair to say that American photographers demonstrated ample interest in Indian women, as discussed in Chapter One. But, at the same time, writers like Carson attempted to convince their readers that Indian women were undesirable. Perhaps both of these representational moves reflect ambivalent American attitudes about the relationship of miscegenation to the politics of economic conquest. On one hand, the desirable Indian women and girls looked to some Americans like another of Mexico's alluring natural resources, practically demanding U.S. development. Consider, for example, Frank Hamilton's message to Porfirio Díaz that he was *particularly* interested in a girl standing among the ruins at Mitla if she was from a poor family. On the other hand, however, descriptions like Carson's reminded readers that Indian women were unsuitable companions for lonely American tourists or workers in Mexico. Unlike the "Colored Belle" in Puerto Rico, who, according to Trumbull White, knew to commingle only with her own racial group, visions of abject Indian women suggested that it was the Americans who must steer clear of Indian people as potential sexual partners.

At least one writer played Indian women's supposed degeneracy against dominant ideas regarding black masculinity that circulated in the United States in the era of Jim Crow. J. R. Flippin, who lived and worked in Chihuahua in the 1870s, published his letters home as *Sketches from the Mountains of Mexico* (1889). In this piece of reportage from the early Porfiriato, Flippin noted a small population of "negros" living in Mexico but summarily dismissed them as "exotics" who could not thrive in the mountainous environment. Still, he could not resist using black men as a way to highlight the depths of Indian women's depravity.

> Some of them intermarry with the *peon*, and, as it ever is, he soon descends to her level, for the husband seldom lifts up the wife; but the wife drags the husband down to her social scale. The negro is courted by this class of the Mexican population. And by the rest of her associates, fortunate is she considered who can bind in matrimonial chains

this sable son of Adam. She is considered as marrying *up*, and not *down*, as some would suppose.[71]

The question of interracial marriage was a significant part of the national dialogue in the decade following emancipation, when Flippin traveled in Mexico, and he provided an unusual twist on U.S. racial logic. The author knew that his reader would subscribe to the opinion that the people with the darkest skin inhabited the bottom of the social ladder, and he used black men's sexual and matrimonial desirability to abjectify Indian womanhood. Harriott Wight Sherratt espoused a similar logic in *Mexican Vistas* when she noted that "it would seem that the Indian strain is less vigorous, as well as less joyous, than the negro, [but] I was struck with the sloping shoulders, narrow chests, and awkward carriage of both sexes [of Indians]."[72] Unlike Marie Robinson Wright, who placed Indians above "the remains of African negroes" in her racial taxonomy (and the offspring of black-Indian unions even higher), Flippin and Sherratt claimed that Indians—and seemingly Indian women in particular—inhabited the lowest place in the Mexican racial system. Flippin posited that, in time, the black man would realize as much. "When his head is cool, and his heart is colder," he wrote, "[the negro] rightly calculates, 'that she is not fit for any gentleman of color.' These paint colors don't mix well, and nature rebels against the blending of such colors."[73] While Flippin never clarified how nature rebelled against black-Indian intermarriage, it is clear that he meant to extend into Mexico, but to markedly revise, American anxieties about miscegenation.

Something larger than sex and marriage was at stake in Flippin's description of black-Indian relations, for he used the supposed degeneracy of Indian women to tackle a topic that haunted countless travelers to Mexico who harbored hopes for economic conquest: the potential for civilizing the native population. He claimed:

In intelligence, progressiveness, and moral status, [the black man] is far her superior. . . . To some of my readers this will appear incredible; but it is nevertheless the truth. He is capable of improvement, and putting himself upon a higher plane of civilization, of better business capacities, and even comprehending the theory of government. Of such things neither she nor her forebears have ever heard or dreamed; but cemented in her abject stupidity and superstition, she will live and die.[74]

Flippin took for granted that his readers adhered to a racial system that placed black people, and especially black men, at its bottom and reached a shocking conclusion: black people could assimilate into modern forms of work and government—which boded well for his own nation, with its population of newly emancipated people of color—but Indian people could not. Again, this grim description reflects the ethos of economic conquest, for a nation populated by racial types incapable of assimilation nearly demanded intervention. Without intervention, it seemed that native people, who could not grasp modernity or even the idea of government, were doomed to extinction. The supposed degeneracy and ugliness of natives underscored and rationalized this sentiment. In this sense, Flippin's book is as much a political tract as it is a description of his experiences south of the border. What is more, after describing Indian inferiority, *Sketches from the Mountains of Mexico* goes on to describe the profits that could be wrestled from the underdeveloped territories of the nation; subsequent chapters focus on mining, manufacturing, and other opportunities for U.S. capitalist development south of the border.

INDIANS AND DEMOCRACY

Porfirio Díaz's grip on the presidency depended in part on the widely held belief that native people in Mexico could not yet comprehend what democracy meant. In his 1908 interview with James Creelman, Díaz claimed that Mexico was ready for democracy because he had created a middle class, "the active, hard-working, self-improving middle class, [upon which] a democracy must depend for its improvement."[75] But what of Indians, who were rarely seen as capable of assimilation into the ascendant middle class? Were they also ready for democracy? "The Indians, who are more than half of our population, care little for politics," Díaz said. "They are accustomed to look to those in authority instead of thinking for themselves. This is a tendency they inherited from the Spaniards, who taught them to refrain from meddling in public affairs and rely on the Government for guidance."[76] Claiming that native people avoided politics because of a deeply ingrained docility before governmental power was a convenient way to write them out of Mexican democracy.

The idea that Indian people were unfit for democracy was much older than the Creelman interview. In 1844, an American diplomat to Mexico named Brantz Mayer published a travelogue and memoir recollecting his two years in Mexico. Mayer wrote very little about Indian people, treating them mostly as servants and as local color, but he did briefly reflect on Indian poverty and what it meant for Mexico's system of government. "What can be the benefit of a Republican form of government to masses of such a population?" he asked. About the Indians themselves he wrote that

> they have no qualifications for self-government and they can have no *hope*, when a life of such toil avails not to avoid such misery. It appears to me that the life of a negro, under a good master, in our country, is far better than the beastly degradation of the Indian here. With us, he is at least a man; but in Mexico, even the instincts of his human nature are scarcely preserved. . . . Shall such men be expected to govern themselves?[77]

Many other writers would come to join Mayer in claiming that the black slave lived better than the Mexican Indian and in framing native people as no more able to govern themselves than the slaves—the ultimate embodiment of the rightless subject. The racial justification for Mexico's lack of democracy would persist for decades and serve as a rationale for Díaz's undemocratic practices. Recall, for example, Lummis's claim, after twenty years of Díaz's presidency, "Some will say that this is not republican. Possibly not, but it is business."[78]

Even after the Mexican Revolution began to unfold, James Creelman continued to advocate for Díaz's rule by arguing that Indian people were completely unfit to rule themselves. This was, to be sure, a well-established view of Indianness for Americans by 1910. According to Creelman in an article published in the *North American Review*, the underlying cause of the revolution was the fact that the framers of the Constitution of 1824, which was modeled after the Constitution of the United States, failed to take into account the racial makeup of the nation. In other words, Creelman claimed on the eve of his exile that Mexico needed Díaz because its population could not govern itself due to racial factors. This argument by a leading American apologist for Díaz's undemocratic practices rearticulated and confirmed the white supremacist thought evident in Creelman's more famous interview with Díaz, which constructed Indians as children in the national family.

In his article, Creelman went on to claim that because of its racial configuration Mexico never should have been declared a republic.

"There was no Hamilton, Jefferson, Madison, Franklin, or Adams among them to point out the racial unfitness of an Orientally derived people for the free institutions won through a thousand years of Anglo-Saxon growth and struggle," Creelman wrote. In a passage that echoes Mayer's description of Indians and democracy, Creelman claimed:

> When they declared Mexico to be a democratic republic and fashioned their Constitution after the Constitution of the United States [in 1824] they were mere imitators of a nation whose institutions were wholly alien to their followers. The frightful consequences of that blunder run all the way through Mexican history up to the time of Porfirio Diaz[.] . . . The Mexican Indians and part Indians have shown through all their history since Mexican independence was won that they are devoid of the sense of individual responsibility that must exist in a self-governing people. They are easily roused to fight and have shown through hundreds of battles that they can shed their blood or die or suffer years of persecution or starvation for the sake of liberty. But there is a tremendous difference between the man who is merely willing to fight for his rights and the man who is always ready to discharge his obligations as a citizen.[79]

Creelman goes on this way for twelve pages, describing Indians and their "hybrids" as people without "the democratic instincts, without the self-restraint and individual initiative that are the foundations of free popular government, without even an approximate idea of the hard, slow work and the unfailing respect for the rights of others that are imposed upon the people by absolute political democracy."[80] According to the very man to whom the dictator had announced that he would not stand for reelection in 1910, Mexico *needed* Díaz because it was racially unfit for democracy. Creelman saw the revolution, then in its infancy, as a reflection of a racial problem and already longed for a return to the Porfirian social order. After pointing out several material examples of the stability and prosperity that the dictator had brought to Mexico—now potentially lost—Creelman prescribed a Jim Crow-style version of suffrage, claiming that the "nearest possible approach to popular self-government consistent with peace and material progress would be a system in which the right to vote was restricted by educational and property qualifications."[81] Díaz fled to France a month after the article appeared.

THE PROSPECTS FOR INDIAN TRANSFORMATION

The idea that Indians were unfit for self-rule rationalized the Díaz administration and colored the mode of representing revolutionary Mexico that I call "Porfirian Nostalgia" in the final chapter of this book. As we will see, this idea also served as a rationale for U.S. interventionism in the second decade of the 1900s. But even as the specter of Indian abjectification loomed large in representations of travel, some writers began to publish their views on the prospects for Indian transformation during the Porfiriato. They wondered whether native people could be assimilated into Mexican economic and political systems, as many early Americans had hoped would happen within the United States, most notably Thomas Jefferson, who advocated for the Europeanization of native North Americans but who also set the stage for Indian removal in his presidential policies. The Europeanization of the national population came to pass in the United States, as early-nineteenth-century nation building increasingly pushed native people toward America's geographical and cultural margins. The Indian Removal Act of 1830, which relocated tens of thousands of native people (and their slaves) from the eastern United States to the newly organized Indian Territory, cemented the popular view that Indians could not be absorbed into the U.S. body politic. In the second half of the century, American popular culture, academic works, and public policy represented the Indian as vanishing or vanquished by the turn of the twentieth century. But representations of Mexico during that time could in no way suggest that Mexican Indians had been similarly removed or eradicated. Travelers knew that Indians could be excluded from self-government and the benefits of full citizenship, but they grappled with where Indians fit into the modernizing state and how the significant presence of native people in Mexico would affect the expansion of U.S. capitalism.[82]

One possible solution to the problem of Indian difference was to suggest that native people could be transformed into subjects who were better aligned with the values of that "progress" espoused by the United States. Writers revisited the idea of Indian transformation again and again throughout the Porfiriato but never reached consensus. John G. Bourke, for one, was pessimistic about the prospects for Indian transformation. He offered the disparities in development on the north and south sides of the Río Grande as an argument that Indian people could not assimilate. "With the coming of the American element," he wrote, "and especially the various lines of transcontinental communication, the wild tribes at the head of the Rio Grande were subdued and placed upon reservations, and the mineral and arable wealth of a great empire made available to the commerce of the world." In contrast, he sourly reported that "no such good fortune smiled upon the lower part of the Rio Grande valley, which remains to-day, as it has been for more than forty years, a sealed book, a *terra incognita* to the rest of the United States."[83] According to Bourke, placing Indian people on reservations and Americanizing their former territories were the best strategies for making Mexico modern and making Mexican goods available to the world.

The vast majority of writers took a more moderate approach than Bourke, admitting that Indian people were intrinsically inferior to other racial groups in Mexico—and, of course, white Americans—but naturally docile. According to some, this docility meant that Indian people accepted their place at the bottom of the social hierarchy in their nation but could also be transformed through foreign intervention. "Notwithstanding his dirt, his tattered clothes, his battered sombrero and his filthy blanket," wrote Carson, a traveler who did not shy away from detailing the Indian's deficiencies, "the Mexican Indian is one of nature's true gentlemen, if only he is properly treated."[84] Another traveler, Frederick Ober, wrote, "Humble and obedient, their self-abasement is such that they accept and apply to themselves the reproach of the whites, a term that implies that they have no understanding. A white man is to them a *gente de razon*,—a man of intelligence,—while the Indian is called a *gente sin razon*, or a man without reason,—of no understanding."[85]

This imagined acceptance of white superiority constructed native people as potential workers. First, however, a caveat. It is important to note that writers who shared this view never claimed that they saw Indian people as potential citizens. To frame them as workers in the new economy, writers and photographers relied on long-standing views of Indians as docile and hardworking but revised these older tropes in a number of significant ways, a few of which are detailed below. The burden bearer—the most powerful symbol of Indian docility and capacity for work—did not, however, disappear in American travel discourse. Rather, the burden bearer began to appear alongside representations of a new kind of Indian worker, one who more closely resembled American ideals for labor, self-control, and self-care, among other tenets of American modernity in the late nineteenth and early twentieth centuries. Through a variety of representational strategies and reversals,

Indians began to look more like proper subjects to American observers. In Pearce's terms, which appear as an epigraph for this chapter, they seemed to be more settled, steady, and civilized. Still, with some rare exceptions, writers almost always avoided the subject of whether the Indian could become a citizen.

Despite this perceived unfitness of Indians for citizenship, the creators of travel discourse frequently contemplated the question of whether the Indian possessed any redeemable qualities. John H. Rice, who advocated for the abolition of debt peonage two decades before John Reed took up the cause, characterized Indians as a fallen race but also claimed that they retained some serviceable qualities. He wrote that Indians "had greatly deteriorated through generations and centuries . . . from the many high and manly qualities possessed by their ancestors at the time of Spanish conquest; . . . [t]hey are now small of stature, uneducated, and poverty stricken, but docile, polite, industrious when work is attainable, and, as a rule, reliable and honest."[86] This schema seems to have applied to women as well, for Rice avoids the abject vision of native women that other writers reported. Like Rice, even Carson, whose description of Indian women's appearances was unflattering, suggested that the Indian woman might be saved through work and craft. "They have few virtues save their devotion to their husbands and children," Carson wrote, "but many of them are not unskilful [sic] in fancy work, being able to follow the most elaborate designs, doing also really delicate and pretty work on handkerchiefs and linens."[87] Rice and Carson, like many of their compatriots, did acknowledge some redeemable qualities in Mexican Indians bur never claimed that the Mexican Indian was ready to participate in industrial capitalism or democracy.[88] Instead, American writers painted native people as a raw material alongside the other natural resources that made Mexico such a desirable field for economic investment. And like other resources, Indians needed refining. What Indians really needed, many travel writers seemed to claim, was an external hand to intervene and make them better workers and better devotees to Western-style capitalism. "If it be conceded that the native races of Mexico are capable of development," wrote Susan Hale in 1890, "it is evident that what is needed for their elevation from their present low estate, is good religion, good government, and good education."[89] We have already seen that many Americans hoped to help Díaz maintain what they saw as "good government." The following sections turn to two other modes of Indian transformation frequently championed in American travel writing.

BUILDING BETTER WORKERS

While Americans swooned over the nation's natural resources and championed the Díaz regime's efforts to modernize its way of doing business, they also wondered whether Americans could find and properly manage good workers. The question of whether Porfirian Mexico possessed an adequate labor pool plagued American representations of Mexico. As F. E. Prendergast, the *Harper's* writer, put it, progress in Mexico required capital investment "in large enough amounts to develop her natural resources by the aid of the native races."[90] The nature of the Mexican Indian loomed large within such concerns, especially considering that native people in the United States had been largely written out of capitalist expansion. Despite the many deficits that many foreign observers perceived in Indian cultural and corporeal difference, most writers did concede that the native people in Mexico were a hardworking lot with a few qualities that hinted that they could be gainfully engaged with modern labor systems. Accordingly, some travel writing attempted to convince readers in the United States that native labor could help facilitate American profits.

A first step in doing so was to suggest that native Mexicans were in fact good workers, despite the enduring stereotype of Indian laziness. Writing at the end of the Porfiriato, C. Reginald Enock claimed that native people were naturally better workers because of Mexico's mild climate. Many other writers made similar claims regarding agricultural work, but Enock painted a particularly optimistic picture of Indians working in American-owned mines. "Unless under grave oppression," he wrote, "the native miner . . . has been a zealous worker. His picturesque surroundings, simple mode of life, and easy-going disposition, together with the pervading sentimental attributes which his religion lent, and the sunny skies under which he toiled, took from mining much of the material brutality and grey atmosphere which enshrouded it in Anglo-Saxon communities."[91] In Enock's view, the Indian was such a good worker that he could even make mining seem less gloomy. Other visitors from the United States agreed, claiming that Indian workers lacked ambition but took orders well and, as the image of the Indian burden bearer communicates, were naturally inclined toward hard labor.

Constructing Indians as docile and hardworking did not, however, answer the question of whether they could be transformed into *mod-*

ern workers. Mexico's political and business elite grappled with this question all throughout the Porfiriato, as their efforts to transform their nation into a modern state depended in part on the presence of workers who could build a new infrastructure and take part in an industrial capitalist economy. Many of the workers on the railroad, for example, came from the United States until Díaz and his *científicos* led the effort to gain controlling interests in the railroads after the turn of the twentieth century. But the regime operated with a dismal view of Indians and their potential, best evidenced in its infamous policies regarding the Yaqui, the indigenous group seen by the Díaz regime and some writers and policy makers in the United States as the most hostile and least capable of assimilation into the national body politic.[92] At the same time that Díaz and other leaders actively marginalized Indian people, however, the ruling elite desperately sought foreign investment. Mexico had much to gain if Americans saw the potential in Indian labor, and it appears that the regime actively strove to spread the message that Indians could become better and more modern workers.

American travelers doubted whether Mexican Indians could become modern people, but many did take up the Porfirian party line that native people had potential as capitalist subjects. "They work with what might be called passion, so intense is their application to any assigned task," wrote Mary Elizabeth Blake about Indian labor practices in 1888. "But that over, the relapse into stolid indifference is as complete as before. Good or bad, the gentle, trusting, superstitious, timid, easily yielding nature of their ancestors is continued in the descendents."[93] In other words, Indian workers needed management or else they would fall into their inborn bad habits. Blake hoped to convey the idea, then taking hold among American travelers and other observers of Porfirian Mexico, that Indian laborers could be managed—and remade into something better through this management. Another American woman, writing fourteen years later, noted another benefit of Indian labor and its manageability. Despite the fact that she mentions Indian laziness several times throughout her travelogue, Mrs. James Edwin Morris also claimed, "One good thing may be said of the peon. He is not a populist, and there are no strikes in Mexico."[94] This view of Mexican labor is especially ironic when one considers that the Mexican Revolution—the world's first socialist rebellion—would commence in earnest just eight years following the publication of this travelogue.

W. E. Carson waged a particularly forceful argument that native people required proper management, claiming, despite the fact that he was docile and polite—"nature's gentleman," according to the author—that the Indian

is essential to agriculture, yet his tropical surroundings and his mental characteristics unfit him for energetic work of the adoption of modern improvements. As a farmer the Indian is a rank failure. He brings no intelligence to his work. His ancestors hundreds of years ago scratched the soil with a wooden hoe, and he is content with the same implement. . . . His wants being easily supplied, there is really no incentive for him to be progressive. He cannot read or write, is unable to think, and his mode of life is primeval in its simplicity.[95]

This passage appears in a chapter titled "The White Man's Burden Bearer," in which Carson reiterates hundreds of stereotypes associated with Mexican Indians but finds the cheapness of their labor, along with the rigidity of the social hierarchy of the country, irresistible. Carson conveys that the white man's burden in Mexico was not imperial administration but industrial and agricultural management. As Carson would have his readers believe, this form of conquest was made easier by the fact that the native Mexican knew his place in the order of things: "Even if he is not naturally cleanly or naturally honest," Carson writes, "there is a charm all its own in the simple, whole-hearted way in which he accepts his subordinate position."[96]

Many writers supported their claims that Indians could be transformed into a modern workforce with images. Magazines, newspapers, and travelogue writing that focused on the touristic experience in Mexico began to include images of natives (and sometimes mestizos) engaged in rationalized modes of labor. These are the antitheses to the burden-bearer images, which pictured the Indian as naturally, and even comically, hardworking but hopelessly antimodern. Instead of showing Indians carrying huge loads or doing things the "Mexican Way," meaning the outmoded and overly labor-intensive way, these photographs portrayed the Indian worker as part of large-scale industrial and agricultural efforts. These images replaced the long-standing trope of the dazed and ragged impoverished Indian with ones that featured neatly dressed indigenous people, arranged in orderly configurations, engaged in rational forms of labor. N. H. Darton's *National Geographic* article includes ten illustrations of Indian people engaged in work, including photographs of water carriers in Guanajuato, a man climbing a tree to

FIGURE 3.3. Coffee hacienda, Veracruz. Braun Research Library, Autry National Center, Los Angeles.

harvest coconuts, and the image of the *carboneros* described above. All told, images of working Indians account for half of the twenty images that illustrate Darton's article.

Captioned by Darton as "Drying Coffee on a Large Mexican Plantation," one frequently reproduced image shows fieldworkers raking an orderly plot of the harvested beans (Figure 3.3). Other than the plot itself, which looks remarkably like a Zen garden with its perfectly raked contents, the focal point of the photograph is a campesino in white clothing. The worker stands barefoot among the beans, holding a shovel. In the middle distance, five more workers appear busy at various tasks. At the extreme left of the frame, a boy stands near an outbuilding holding an empty basket. Though Darton fails to credit a photographer, this image was made by the French photographer Abel Briquet on a trip to the Rancho de San Marcial in the state of Veracruz in the 1880s and reproduced widely in American travel discourse.[97] This rather mundane photograph was reproduced in a wide variety of places. In addition to Darton's article, it illustrated several travelogues published between the mid-1880s and 1910. It was also included in Briquet's "Vistas Mexicanas" series and for decades sold as a postcard with captions in both English and Spanish. A personal album at the Braun Research Library in Los Angeles shows that travelers would take the time to paste this image into scrapbooks commemorating their own trips to Mexico.

Why would such a mundane image garner such sustained interest over several decades? By reprinting the image again and again, the makers of travel discourse implied that this was a general view of Indian labor rather than a depiction of a particular place where Indians performed labor. It shows that native labor, rendered comical or sentimental in the trope of the burden bearer, could be harnessed into something rational and productive. The only thing that Indian labor needed, according to many travelogues and images like this one, was good management. This was especially pertinent in a publication like *National Geographic*, which habitually represented Mexico throughout the Porfiriato as an untapped labor and consumer market in its articles and photographs. The magazine served as a primary locus for the ongoing discussion about how Mexico might modernize and what role American capital—and, when it came to the natives, capitalist discipline—might play in that process. Darton, for one, struck a hopeful chord in his article, reporting, like other writers, that the "native labor force is increasing in effectiveness, for many of the laboring people are showing considerable capability as workmen and artisans when properly trained."[98] Briquet's photograph underscored this sentiment.

A related image from another *National Geographic* article reinforced this sentiment and hints at the rationalization of Indian labor.[99] The image accompanied John W. Foster's article titled "The New Mexico," which exclaimed, "Our countrymen, our capital, and enterprise are welcomed by the government and the people, and there is a wide field for the exercise of our surplus capital and energy."[100] Captioned "Coffee Pickers" by the *National Geographic*, this photograph depicts four native women sorting coffee beans (Figure 3.4). C. B. Waite photographed these women at Coatepec, on the rail line between Veracruz and Mexico City, but, like Darton, Foster fails to credit a photographer. In fact, the author or his *National Geographic* editors purposefully cropped Waite's copyright information out of the picture, perhaps to imply that the author had taken the photograph himself. Without this information, the image strongly resembles the photograph of the men drying coffee. Though made at least a decade apart and presenting differently gendered visions of Indian labor, each image presents an orderly, symmetrical vision of a modernizing labor force that includes native people.

FIGURE 3.4. Coffee pickers. Photo by C. B. Waite. DeGolyer Library, Southern Methodist University, Dallas, Texas.

The women in this later photograph wear matching skirts and blouses, and each has her hair neatly parted and plaited. Their appearances diverge from those of other native women who appear in American travel discourse, with their ragged clothing and ubiquitous rebozos. These women, in contrast, look markedly more Western in dress, particularly the woman at the center of the frame, whose high collar and ruffled shirt give her a Victorian look. Each of the women stands alertly around a large table with mounds of coffee beans and baskets for sorting. Two men, one in an American-style fedora, overlook their work. This fedora strikes me as a symbol that the Indian could participate as both a producer and a consumer of American capitalism. The fedora, as a replacement for either the Indian's or the *charro*'s sombrero, subtly suggests that the Indian could grasp the concept of management and could develop a taste for American styles of dress and consumerism. This last detail was crucial, since disciplining the Indian meant turning him into a consumer citizen. Proponents of economic conquest hoped that native people would not only increase production in Mexico but would also serve as new markets for consumer goods.

Travelers and other observers had long complained that indigenous people in Mexico lacked self-discipline, but the workers presented in these images made a case for the kind of Indian who inhabited Foster's "New Mexico." First and foremost, they are removed from a domestic setting. Photographers had long depicted Indian women engaged in home labor. Pictures of Indian women grinding corn at the metate to make tortillas had, in fact, become a master signifier of Indian womanhood by the start of the Porfiriato. Such images adorned countless picture postcards, stereoscopes, and magic lantern slides, depicting Indian women as backward but hardworking and alluring. But this photograph of the coffee pickers and others like it revise the notion that Indian women could only perform domestic labor or other traditional forms of work, such as lacework or other handicrafts, that could be done in the home. Instead, they could become part of the industrial workforce. This particular image also signaled the rationalization of the female Indian worker. Each of the Indian women in this image performs the same work. Even their appearances are rationalized, as they look strikingly similar to one another.

Rationalization is a mode of discipline, and each of these images suggests the Mexican Indian, long imagined by North American observers as alternately savage and laconic, could qualify as what Foucault calls a "docile body." According to Foucault, "A body is docile that may be subjected, used, transformed and improved."[101] The term "docile" is perhaps a bit confusing here, since Americans had long presented Mexican Indians as servile, laconic, and decidedly less fierce than their North American counterparts (with the exceptions of the Yaqui and a few other "hostile" tribes). Facility in the Foucauldian sense, however, is a different mode of docility, one that allows native people in Mexico to be "subjected, used, transformed and improved" in the service of capitalist modernity. The North American Indian, as represented by dominant modes of popular culture in the United States, had proved unable to be assimilated into American capitalism, with some notable exceptions, including perhaps those Indian children that had been subjected to the boarding school experience, but Mexican Indians, at least in the eyes of those who made and disseminated images like that of the coffee pickers, showed greater potential as docile bodies.

It is important to note, however, that when travelers published images like these they almost always appeared alongside photographs of Indian people engaged in "primitive" modes of labor. In Darton's article, just one example of this tendency, the seemingly primitive *carboneros* appear alongside the men drying coffee beans. One might at first presume that these types of images would, when placed along-side one another, cancel each other out as signifiers of Mexican Indian-ness because they present such contradictory views of Indian labor. But something else is at work in articles such as Darton's. Instead of canceling one another, these images work together to illustrate what is gained when one engages the native worker in a more rational mode of labor. This juxtaposition is, in other words, a call for intervention, one that is heightened when the primitive Indian comes face-to-face with the disciplined Indian.

According to many travel writers, disciplining the Indian benefited both the prospects for U.S. capitalism in Mexico and the Indians them-selves. If Americans saw the indigenous body as intrinsically inferior to the white body, work provided one route toward improving the "fallen race." Trumbull White, the war reporter turned imperial booster, sug-gested that Puerto Ricans would be physically improved by the intro-duction of U.S. labor systems. "Their constitution, like that of inhabi-tants of most hot countries, is frail and subject to sickness," White claimed, "yet there are many individuals, *especially those engaged in physical labor*, who are strong, agile, and robust."[102]

This win-win argument was an organizing principle of U.S. im-perialist thought, and many proponents of economic expansionism in Mexico argued that the natives of that nation would be similarly improved if disciplined into better laboring subjects. One American promoter of economic expansion into Mexico succinctly described the power of U.S. business to transform the peon in the *Los Angeles Times*:

A great many laborers were employed on construction. These, with the first money earned, bought shoes, which, to that time, had never been worn. They bought better clothes and better food. The manner of working and the machinery were an education to them. Today they are better workers and more intelligent.[103]

In a narrative common to many representations of capitalism and in-dustry in Mexico and elsewhere, the improvement of native people is a desirable by-product of economic expansionism. American observers identified a number of strategies to further improve Mexican Indians.

"COMMERCE FOLLOWS THE MISSIONARY"

Right in the very heart of old Romanism, almost under the eaves
of the old church that Cortez is said to have helped to build, a
Protestant Seminary and Protestant church with a Protestant spire
and a Protestant Bell and a Protestant Bible and a Protestant
organ and a Protestant choir of Protestant young men who
are in training to go out and do valiant service for Christ and
Protestantism. MRS. D. B. WELLS (1902)

While rationalized labor served as the dominant trope of Indian transformation, a smaller number of writers saw Protestant conversion as a way to assuage American concerns that Indian difference posed a threat to economic expansionism. American views of Catholicism colored many travelers' descriptions of Mexican customs and social life. The dominant view of Catholicism in the United States associated that religion with devotion to the Vatican and framed it as a threat to American democracy.[104] Very few Americans who wrote about their travels to Mexico identified themselves as Catholics, so Mexican Catholicism found almost no defenders in travel discourse. Although just about every traveler admired the country's beautiful churches, most stood aghast that Mexicans so strictly adhered to "papism," painting a picture of Mexican religious practices that stood in sharp contrast to WASP behaviors and practices. What is more, Mexican Catholicism fused pre-Columbian religious forms with Christianity. "The prevailing religion of the Mexicans is Roman Catholic," wrote Kate Durham in *The Home Missionary*, "into which have been adopted many of the heathen forms of worship practiced by the ancient Indian tribes."[105] This syncretism shocked and fascinated foreign observers, for it seemed to make Mexican Catholicism doubly barbarous.

Travel discourse frequently vilified Indian people as the most fervent adherents to a backward faith. "I do not want them any longer to be doing the things I saw them doing as acts of worship in some of the Roman Catholic churches," wrote one dismayed American woman in reference to Indian religious practices in 1902. The woman, one Mrs. D. B. Wells, reported that she observed Indian women "falling on their faces and kissing the dirty mud floor of the churches . . . ; going up long flights of steps on their knees; worshipping life-sized dolls; bowing before the image of the dog that barked and thus warned Cortez of the approach of his enemies."[106] According to Wells and other Protestant travelers, the Catholic zealotry of the Indians prevented them from reaching their full potential, including their potential to become full citizens. James Pascoe, an Englishman who worked for the Presbyterian Church in Toluca in the 1870s, informed readers of the *Missionary Journal* that "the Mexican Indian is essentially religious; his whole life seems devoted to the service of the priests and saints; his earnings are all devoted to wax-candles and rockets to be burned on feast days, and he seems to think of nothing but processions and pilgrimages to some distant shrine."[107] Such representations framed native Catholicism as one more dimension of Indian backwardness and as one more barrier to Indian modernization.

One photograph that frequently illustrated travelogues and magazine articles depicts an Indian woman in Amecameca paying penance on her knees, a living embodiment of overzealous Indian religiosity (Figure 3.5). She wears a crown of thorns on her head and is closely crowded by other native people, some of whom physically support her through this arduous act of atonement. This C. B. Waite image illustrated scores of books and articles written by Americans. It is so ubiquitous, in fact, that it appears to have served as the default image to illustrate Mexican Catholicism for several decades, slowly growing into an icon of Mexican Catholicism for travel writers, who clearly intended to shock their readers with this bald display of religious fervor. The photograph stood as a testament to the notion that native Mexicans' religious practices ran starkly counter to WASP values. It also suggested that Indians, as overzealous adherents of a corrupt faith, were ripe for conversion. Even as early as 1875, when a Protestant minister named Gilbert Haven published a travelogue about his previous winter in Mexico, travelers predicted a religious shift in Mexico. According to Haven, the "Bible will replace the Jesuit, and the trick by which he has held their souls captive these three centuries and a half will cease to possess them more. Christ the Liberator is coming. He is nigh—even at their doors."[108] This sentiment lasted for decades. Even though Protestantism never gained a foothold during the Porfiriato, writers continued to claim that Mexico was right at the cusp of a great awakening.

John Kenneth Turner proposed that there was another reason for American distaste for Indian Catholicism. According to the muckraking socialist, Indian religious practices frustrated foreign business owners and managers because, in addition to their already supposedly indolent attitudes, the Indians observed too many feast days. "Profits are lost on those *fiesta* days," he wrote, "hence the anguish of the Ameri-

1343. Doing Penance on her knees with crown of thorns up the Sacro Monte. Amecameca. Mex.

Waite. Photo.

FIGURE 3.5. A penitent, Amecameca. Dorothy Woodward Photograph Collection, Center for Southwest Research, University of New Mexico.

can promoter." Many travelers who preceded Turner to Mexico had already noted this as a liability in employing Mexican Indians. Turner, who was no fan of the Catholic Church, saw this as an injustice, admitting that the Church "alleviates [the Mexican's] misery somewhat by providing him with some extra holidays. And it feeds his hunger for sights of beauty and sounds of sweetness, which for the poor Mexican are usually impossible of attainment outside of a church."[109]

The Porfirian regime proved surprisingly friendly to Protestant missionaries, probably as a strategy for ensuring the confidence of foreign investors and to encourage as much foreign settlement from the United States as possible. As we have seen above, some writers praised Díaz for keeping quiet about his personal viewpoints on religion—even though, as Frank McLynn put it, the nation's Catholic hierarchy "enjoyed a halcyon period" during the Porfiriato because of his hands-off approach to the Church.[110] These writers may or may not have been aware that the strict separation of church and state was a hallmark of Mexican liberalism since Benito Juárez and that it was customary since Juárez for a Mexican president not to enter a church. Despite this fact, Protestant travelers preferred to credit Díaz personally for religious freedom in Mexico. They might also have been unaware or might have willfully ignored the fact that Díaz took his Catholic faith rather seriously, especially following his marriage to Carmen Romero Rubio in 1881, and that he consistently avoided conflict with the Church in his policies and actions as president.

Other Americans gratefully noted that the president granted private audiences to representatives from Protestant denominations and encouraged their efforts to establish missionary churches in Mexico.[111] According to Paul Garner's biography of Díaz, "by 1892, at the height of the expansion of Protestant societies in Mexico, there were approximately 469 Protestant societies in Mexico, with in excess of 100,000 members, including railroad and textile workers, schoolteachers, and rancheros."[112] These Protestant enclaves not only served their American expatriate parishioners; they also attempted to lure local natives away from Catholicism. The proponents of this mission saw themselves as improving Indian welfare by working against a corrupt and too-powerful Church. "Until the Protestants came and made their influence felt the Roman church seemed to care little and do less for the upbuilding of [downtrodden Indian] people," wrote Kate Durham. "Many now fully realize they must look to the Protestant Americans for example and help, rather than to the French priests who have so long kept them in subjection, superstition, and ignorance."[113] Like many of her compatriots who championed conversion, Durham saw Protestantism as a way to civilize Mexico's Indians and to undo the excesses of Catholicism. Other observers noted that the conversion of the Indians also served a broader political purpose: it was part of the ongoing project of bringing "progress" to Mexico. As Susan Hale put it, "There is . . . a wide open field in Mexico for teaching the impressionable native of Anahuac the simple tenets of the religion of Christ. Purity, honesty, charity, the love of his neighbor, duty to himself, the knowledge of God,—these sure foundations of life are only needed by him as his first foothold in upward progress."[114] Hale's representation of Mexico as a growth opportunity, repeated in dozens of other travelogues and memoirs written by Protestant missionaries, closely echoes the economic narrative of Mexico as a field for expansion.

One of the most ardently anti-Catholic missionaries who worked in Porfirian Mexico was James G. Dale. In Dale's view, Catholicism was a "religion without spirituality," an "enemy of the Bible," and a "Christless religion" that had contributed to the downfall of Mexico's Indian population. Along with his wife, Katherine, a medical doctor, he lived and worked in Mexico for a number of years, attempting to convert Mexican Catholics—especially native Mexicans, whom Dale saw as particularly slavish "Romanists"—to Protestantism. By the end of the Porfiriato, he and his followers had established three main mission centers in Mexico: Veracruz, Tamaulipas, and San Luis Potosí. His book *Mexico and Our Mission* (1910) detailed these efforts. Like his fellow missionaries, Dale saw Protestantism as a way to transform the Indian into a new kind of subject that more closely resembled WASP values of the so-called Progressive Era. Although Dale expressed sympathy for the plights of Indian people, he clearly also saw his work as a way to improve a spiritually and materially impoverished people. In addition to glaring need, there are two key political and cultural reasons why these missionaries would devote themselves to converting indigenous people rather than mestizos or middle-class Mexicans. As mentioned above, one reason is that Americans perceived Indians as particularly devout Catholics, practicing a barbarous and pagan form of the religion. Native people like the woman paying penance in a crown of thorns publicly performed the most shocking aspects of Mexican Catholicism. What is more, they frequently did so en masse. While some travelers did find Catholic religious festivals charming or picturesque, others noted the Catholic ceremonies in horror, using terms like "monstrous" to describe the Catholic Indian spectacles that they encountered on their journeys.

Second, ministering to native people did not disrupt the cordial relations that American writers and other visitors reportedly shared with the nation's more elite Catholics, including the president and his devout wife. Carmen Díaz's Catholic faith was a source of interest for many of her champions—and, as we saw in Chapter Two, she had many champions—but none dared to challenge her demure religiosity. Instead, they usually positioned her as a rational Catholic, nowhere near as fervent (or idolatrous) in her devotion as the Indian women of the country. Travel writers approached other elite Mexican Catholics with a similar sense of restraint and respect, in part because doing otherwise would have challenged the established narrative that those elite were highly rational facilitators of economic expansionism. The social class and political standing of Catholic believers played a key role in whether their faith would be vilified in travelers' accounts, and those at the top of Mexican society remained insulated from ardent anti-Catholic sentiment. Not surprisingly, Indians did not fare as well in travelers' depictions of Catholic Mexico.

The photographs that illustrate *Mexico and Our Mission* show two kinds of native people: the ragged, superstitious Indians that had always populated travelogues, and Protestant converts who more closely resembled the white missionaries in dress and comportment. The result is a before-and-after testimonial for Protestant conversion. This was a common representational strategy among the handful of American Protestants who wrote about religion in Mexico, and it reflected the commonly held assumption that outward appearances reflected spiritual rightness. This was also common in depictions of Filipinos, native Hawaiians, and other groups with which Americans now shared imperialistic relations. The Mexican context was somewhat different, as we have seen in other arenas, since the United States had only economic claims on Mexico, but writers and religious workers nonetheless presented the converted Indian as a more civilized (and civilizable) subject.

Many of the Western-looking indigenous people who appeared in *Mexico and Our Mission* also served Dale's church as ministers, aides, or parishioners. These were men whom Dale had trained to bring their friends and relations, as well as their wider communities, into the Protestant fold. Native ministers were crucial to Dale's mission, for he believed that "the heathen world can best be reached by its native sons," and several pages of his memoir and a photographic plate are dedicated to the indigenous men that Dale recruited to spread the Protestant gospel.[115] In their official church portraits, all seven of the native pastors featured appear in formal American-style suits. The younger men wear their hair elegantly styled, and one wears a pair of spectacles. While Dale consistently marks them as native in the caption and throughout the book, the pastors' appearances all suggest that they had adopted the missionaries' styles and standards of appearance as well as their religious views. They closely resemble images of reformed natives that circulated to affirm the civilizing power of European and U.S. imperialism.

Other photographic illustrations in *Mexico and Our Mission* support this theme of Indian transformation. On one page, two remarkably similar photographs of Mexican preachers and their families appear side by side (Figure 3.6). The picture on the left depicts Cresencio Cruz with his wife and two children, all dressed in Western clothing. The minister sports a dark suit with bow tie. His wife wears a lacy but modest dress, her hair pinned neatly into a bun at the top of her head. She holds their small daughter, who is dressed like a Victorian doll. Their son, lovingly embraced by his seated father, holds—of all things—a toy locomotive. The entire family stands on a floral rug in front of a painted backdrop that features elegant curtains and furniture. Professional studio portraits like this one signaled class ascendance for mestizos and indigenous people during the Porfiriato, especially when they emphasized Europeanness through clothing and decoration.[116] The Cruz family portrait closely resembles a picture of the Dale family that appears elsewhere in *Mexico and Our Mission*. In that family portrait, Dale, his wife, and their three children pose placidly for the camera. Overall, the Dale family portrait seems to serve as a model for Indian converts and their families. In the image that appears just to the right of the Cruz family portrait, Tomás Sánchez, his wife, and their daughter pose in almost the exact same manner as the Cruz family. However, the Sánchez family looks more indigenous, especially given their clothing. Sr. Sánchez lacks a tie and wears sandals instead of the sober black shoes worn by Cresencio Cruz. Sra. Sánchez, who does not quite return the camera's gaze, wears a native-style dress, including a rebozo that is wrapped around her shoulders and a cross on a long necklace that looks like a rosary.

This last detail is especially compelling, given Dale's comment that Tomás Sánchez had converted to Presbyterianism despite the stubborn "Romanism" of his wife. "The bitterest enemies [to his new faith] were

REV. C. CRUZ AND FAMILY.   REV. TOMAS SANCHEZ AND FAMILY, IN NATIVE COSTUME.

FIGURE 3.6. Churchgoing Mexican families. James G. Dale, *Mexico and Our Mission*.

those in his own household," Dale wrote. "His wife made life well nigh unbearable for him, but he stood bravely for the truth, and bore beautiful testimony for his Lord."[117] Sra. Sánchez eventually relented and became a Protestant herself, but the crucifix in this image serves as a reminder of the persistence of Mexican Catholicism, and perhaps the quiet resistance of Sra. Sánchez to her husband and the American missionaries with whom he collaborated.

If the Sánchez and Cruz families could be transformed through Protestant conversion, as Dale suggested in his descriptions of these native ministers, what kind of subjects would they become? What did the Protestant Indian mean for Americans interested in expanding their economy and influence into Mexico? The answers to these questions lie not only in Protestantism's evangelical mission but also in the politics of economic conquest. Writing near the end of the Porfiriato, German sociologist and political economist Max Weber was the first to note the connections between Protestantism and capitalism, arguing that the rise of capitalism was intimately linked to the spread of Protestantism. According to Weber, Protestant values helped shape how modern people conceptualized work, money, finance, and trade. The so-called Weber Thesis presumes that the growth of Protestantism and capitalism were social phenomena that depended on one another to reshape the social order in the "developed" world. We might read Protestant missionary work in Mexico (as well as missionary work then— and still—under way in other Catholic settings like the Philippines) as an unwitting extension of this thesis, for many of the missionaries and their proponents saw an explicit connection between Protestant conversion and the creation of new markets. To remake Catholic Indians into Protestants was to make them into capitalist producers and consumers. Reverend Josiah Strong, a vociferous and best-selling evangelist who blended evangelism and nationalism in his message, surmised near the start of the Porfiriato that "the world is to be Christianized and civilized, and what is the process of civilizing but the creation of more and higher wants. Commerce follows the missionary."[118]

CONCLUSION

Rationalized labor and religious conversion represented only two of the ways Americans suggested that Mexican Indians could be remade into subjects more amenable to the politics of economic conquest. Another key method was education, and many travelers marveled at the presence of schoolhouses in tiny native villages, crediting Díaz for uplifting his fellow Indians. In general, Americans saw any effort to "civilize" Mexico's Indian population as a positive step toward making the nation a safer investment. Elite Mexicans seem to have agreed, including those who published promotional materials for American audiences. As Matías Romero wrote, the "great task of the Mexican government is to educate our Indians and make them active citizens, consumers, and producers. Before we think of spending money to encourage European immigration to Mexico, we ought to promote the education of our Indians, which I consider the principal public need of the country."[119] Romero's end results—Indians who were better producers and consumers—would have appealed to Americans who feared that no labor or consumer markets existed in Mexico, a lament that frequently appeared in American travel discourse. While Indian difference posed serious sets of problems for those interested in U.S. capitalist expansion in Mexico, observers from both sides of the U.S.-Mexico border looked for solutions.

One more important method of Indian transformation is missing from this chapter. Rational labor, religious conversion, education, and foreign management could all diminish the problem of Indian difference to a certain degree, but some Americans called for the transformation of Mexico's indigenous population on a deeper level. Although none called for Indian removal like that which had taken place in the United States during the early part of the nineteenth century, a significant number of American observers began to see the mestizo as, in the words of one traveler, "the most promising element in Mexican society." Decades before José Vasconcelos called for the fusion of races into *la raza cósmica*—the "cosmic race" that would usher in a new era in human history—some travelers from the United States began to frame *mestizaje* as the solution to Mexico's Indian problem.

"THE MOST PROMISING ELEMENT IN MEXICAN SOCIETY": IDEALIZED *MESTIZAJE* AND THE ERADICATION OF INDIAN DIFFERENCE

We in America shall arrive, before any other part of the world, at the creation of a new race fashioned out of the treasures of all the previous ones: The final race, the cosmic race.
JOSÉ VASCONCELOS (1925)

THE PORT CITY OF VERACRUZ shocked an American traveler named Helen Sanborn when she arrived there in 1886. Like many who traveled through that port city before and after her, she was less than pleased with the locals. Hot and fatigued by the time she disembarked from the steamer that brought her to Veracruz, she regarded the city's infamous buzzards and the *veracruzanos* with equal suspicion. "The population is rather mixed, and impressed us most unfavorably," she later recalled. "All the bad that has been said about Mexicans and Spaniards we could easily believe when we walked on the street and looked into the villainous faces of those we met—faces enough to make one shudder, whereupon the word desperado was plainly written."[1] This author's view of the much-maligned port city was nothing new, but Sanborn's impression of the *veracruzanos* is somewhat ambiguous when it comes to race. Do Sanborn's comments about a "mixed population" express concern that people from different racial groups lived in close proximity to one another or that individual *veracruzanos* tended toward racial ambiguity? Did *mestizaje* lend a villainous countenance to the locals?

Sanborn lived in a country that explicitly condemned, but also often quietly condoned, sex and marriage across racial lines. The dominant trope associated with racial admixture in the United States was the "mulatto," a cultural figure that emerged before the Civil War and lasted well into the twentieth century, reaching its apex during the Porfiriato in sentimental plays and popular novels.[2] As several scholars have shown, the tragic mulatto—or, more accurately, mulatta, since this cultural figure was typically gendered as a woman—stood as a warning against crossing social and cultural boundaries. This warning was particularly aimed at women, as representations of women driven to tragedy because of their racial in-between-ness proliferated in American popular culture. According to the racial logic of the era, the mulatta could never find happiness because she was trapped in limbo between two seemingly discrete racial groups. She usually met a bitter end through suicide or exile from the community of people who adhered to rules for law and society. For the relatively wealthy and exclusively white Americans who created the vast majority of travel discourse, the mulatta resonated because their society was built around explicitly segregationist laws and customs (even though racial admixture had been a historical reality for Americans since the colonial era).[3]

Mexico, in sharp contrast, had long traced its racial and cultural origins through the mixture of different bodies and cultures. This is not to say that the racial system in Mexico lacked a racist framework, but that Mexicans simply have not been able to deny the fact of interracial and interethnic sexuality as Americans have throughout our history. Mexico, it should be noted, still uses the term *mulatto* to refer to people of mixed African heritage, a category of Mexicans that has also been constructed as a threat to the social order.[4] But at the same time, the self-consciously mixed mestizo class has numerically and politically dominated Mexico since the middle of the nineteenth century.

Enter travelers from the United States, many of whom arrived in Mexico with ideas like those of Helen Sanborn but eventually revised their visions of how race should work in a nation with Mexico's population dynamics. Despite their deep suspicion of interracial love, sex, and marriage, many American observers of Porfirian Mexico came to write about *mestizaje* as the best hope for Mexico's economic and social transformation. In a reversal of American representations of tragic mulattoes, and drawing on the explicit tactics of the Díaz regime, they framed mestizos as the potential solution to the problem of Indian difference. In 1888, an American named J. Hendrickson McCarty even declared that "the cultivated Mestizo is the most promising element in Mexican society."[5] This chapter asks how these competing notions about race in Mexico came to appear alongside one another over the course of the Porfiriato. It examines the uses and meanings of *mestizaje* in American travel writing by exploring the tensions at play when travelers looked closely at what it meant for indigenous, white, and mestizo

Mexicans to mix with one another. (Again, travelers mostly ignored the possibility of any other racial stock in Mexico, including any African presence.) My point is not to reinforce the supposed realness of these categories but to ask once again how travel discourse served as a site of racialized knowledge production. In the end, this chapter shows that Helen Sanborn's description of the people of Veracruz is remarkable partly because of the fact that, by the end of the Porfiriato, it would look antiquated to travelers who, influenced in part by eugenic theory and by the exigencies of economic conquest, had come to see the mestizo as the most promising element in Mexican society. Travel writing is the key framework for my analysis in this chapter, but, as in the previous chapters, I will also examine some of the rich visual representations that helped travelers to promote *mestizaje*.

INDIAN DECLINE AND *MESTIZAJE*

American interest in Mexican *mestizaje* is especially surprising when we consider that white supremacists in the United States had long made a habit of holding up Mexico's racial state as a model that illustrated the disastrous results of racial admixture. In his famous 1858 debates with Abraham Lincoln, for example, Stephen A. Douglas "counted the existence of the Mexican people as proof of the deleterious effects of 'the amalgamation of white men, Indians, and negroes.'"[6] Douglas's argument is baldly racist and anti-Mexican, but it is useful here because it reflects the fact that, just prior to the Porfiriato and the blossoming of economic conquest, Americans had not yet noticed an alternative view of Mexican *mestizaje*, one that positioned it as a boon for American prospectors rather than as the worst possible result of a society that does not properly police its racial boundaries. Just a couple of decades after the Lincoln-Douglas debates, Americans would begin to idealize the amalgamation that Douglas found abhorrent.

This was a period in which prominent thinkers in North America and Europe began to apply positivism to age-old questions regarding cultural and physical differences, as well as social inequalities, in the human population. Just before the start of the Porfiriato, Charles Darwin applied his new theory of evolution to human racial and cultural differences. Darwin, like many who came after, offered a dire prediction regarding the future of human civilization. "At some future period," he wrote, "the civilised races of man will almost certainly exterminate and replace throughout the world the savage races."[7] American thinkers applied "social Darwinism" to their country's so-called race problem. In the United States, the culture of white supremacy far outlasted slavery, leading some to invoke Darwin to proclaim the dominance of white people as a natural and inevitable part of the social order.

A few decades after Darwin published his theories, at the end of the Porfiriato, his half-cousin Sir Francis Galton warned readers that lower elements in the gene pool threatened British civilization. He coined the term "eugenics" to refer to a system of racial purification through selective reproduction.[8] Eugenicist thought quickly caught on in the United States, and its proponents applied the pseudoscience to American government, public health policy, academic pursuits, and popular culture.[9] Some proponents of social Darwinism and eugenics claimed, for example, that the African American population would slowly die out or be absorbed into the dominant white population, as the Native American population supposedly had. With these ideas circulating in the United States, travelers looked to the Mexican racial system to better understand the future of race in their own country.

As several historians of science and race have shown, eugenics influenced mainstream views of race, so travelers to Mexico would have brought with them the idea that society and nation could be improved if people would be selective about whom they reproduced with. In the eyes of some American travel writers, the mestizo represented social Darwinism at work. *Mestizaje*, as we have seen, represented the blending of indigenous and European origins into something distinctly Mexican, but the mestizo also represented the whitening of the nation. Contrary to long-standing fears in the United States that race mixing darkened the progeny of the lighter race, travel writers began to report that the children of Indian women and mestizo, European, or criollo men were lighter than their mothers and their ancestors "on the Indian side of their family." They also took this idea to an extreme by arguing that the instinct to improve the lot of one's children inspired native people and mestizos to seek out unions with people with lighter complexions (and more modern behaviors) than themselves. To put it bluntly, travel writers began to see and write about *mestizaje* as the means by which Indian difference would be erased.

This idea first appeared in the United States in a book by Mexican geographer, ethnologist, and writer Antonio García Cubas. In *The Republic of Mexico in 1876*, published in its titular year and translated from the Spanish for an American audience, García Cubas presented a statistical and ethnological case that the Indian population of Mexico

was in the process of being slowly absorbed into the mestizo population. "If we make a careful examination of the state of the population
in different parts of the republic," he wrote, "we shall find the fact confirmed and our assertions corroborated, when stating that the indigenous race is gradually approaching extinction."[10] Some of the causes of
this decline were apparently endemic to indigenous people. According
to García Cubas,

> The indolence of the Indians, their attachment to their ancient cus-
> toms, their bad nourishment, their little shelter against the inclem-
> ency of the weather, their wretched attendance in their sicknesses, and
> other adverse causes . . . have contributed towards the degeneration
> and decline of the race. . . . *[T]he Indian race has decreased and con-
> tinues on the road to its decline.*[11]

Considering that the author couches his argument in supposedly empirical data and language, this is anti-Indian propaganda—a trope at
which the Porfirian elite excelled—masquerading as population dynamics. Still, it is clear that García Cubas means to imply that Indian
"degeneration and decline" is the result of the innate inferiority of indigenous people. The term "decline" is particularly noteworthy here.
For García Cubas, decline did not simply mean cultural or physical degeneracy. It meant extinction.

Another example of this line of thinking, culled from a popular
guidebook published in 1911, ends with an equally chilling prediction:

> Of the mixed Indian races only a small portion can be regarded as civi-
> lized. They are slowly but surely merging their identity with that of
> their neighbors; their national life is almost gone, child mortality is
> distressingly high . . . and their customs—which are not distinguished
> for pulchritude—aid in their obliteration.[12]

This is one of many examples of travel discourse in which American
writers adapted elite Mexicans' views that native people faced extinction because of their personal and cultural degeneracy. But the timing
of this example is important because it appeared so late in Díaz's rule.
While García Cubas's pseudoscientific description of Indian decline appeared at the very start of the Porfiriato, this one, which goes on to describe where readers might find the best Indian handicrafts and how to
best photograph native people, appeared at the very end of the era. De-

spite the fact that so much had changed in American visions of Mexico over the course of the Porfiriato, the idea of Indian decline and extinction endured.

Indian "obliteration" is in itself an alarming prediction, but more important here is the link between descriptions of Indian decline and the rise of *mestizaje*. After all, the guidebook claimed that Indians were "merging" with their "neighbors"—a reference to *mestizaje*. According to García Cubas's statistics, the European population nearly doubled and the mestizo population had tripled between 1810 and 1875, while the Indian population had decreased at a rate of .058 percent per year.[13] A few years following the publication of García Cubas's book, Ober published *Travels in Mexico*, which quoted heavily from and expanded upon the Mexican author's racial views. Ober also claimed that Indian and dark-skinned mestizo people strove to join a rising mestizo class through marriage and reproduction. He claimed that the forming of new mestizo families would mean "the gradual extinction of the Indian race, by gradual absorption into the more powerful mixed class."[14] A brief examination of how travelers interpreted the origins of *mestizaje* will illuminate how they came to conclusions like these.

ORIGINS OF *MESTIZAJE*

At the heart of the national narrative of *mestizaje* in Mexico is the much older historical pairing of Hernán Cortés and Malintzin, his Nahua slave, interpreter, and concubine. Malintzin is commonly known as "la Malinche," and her story of betraying indigenous people by forging an alliance with the colonizer has achieved mythological status among Mexicans and Chicanos. Even today, to call someone a "Malinche" is to call them a sellout or a traitor for preferring foreign ways to his or her "real" or "authentic" culture." But the story of Malintzin is also crucially important as a racial origins story. Many consider—and either celebrate or lament—the birth of Cortés and Malintzin's son Martín around 1523 to be the origin of *mestizaje*, an event that looms large in the Mexican national psyche, particularly because of the power relations that led to the birth of the child. Perhaps most famously, Octavio Paz referred to Mexicans in general as the *hijos de la chingada*: the sons of the fucked one, the children of Malinche. Following Paz, Mexican and Chicana feminist thinkers, including Cordelia Candelaria, began to revise the Malinche story in the 1970s and 1980s by focusing on Malintzin's agency as the progenitor of *mestizaje*.[15]

By the late nineteenth century, American travel writers repeated the Cortés-Malintzin story to explain how race worked in Mexico. Perhaps unsurprisingly, travelers used the same metaphors for racial amalgamation that predominated in the United States, including horticultural ones that described what happened when you mixed different kinds of "stock." One traveler in the 1880s succinctly claimed that over "three centuries the priest and the monk, the soldier and the young creole, have continued to engraft the Caucasian stock on the wild trunk. Thus arose the numerous Mestizo population, which has inherited in part the brown hue of the mother, but also the greater energy and more vigorous mind of the father."[16] This is a typical vision of Mexican *mestizaje*, one that simplifies and repeats the dominant narrative concerning *mestizaje*'s continuation and refinement after Cortés and Malintzin, namely that white men ("the priest and the monk, the soldier and the young creole") continued the process of domination and racial amalgamation instigated by Cortés.

One of the functions of this narrative of *mestizaje* was to differentiate racial admixture in Mexico from that which occurred in the United States. Sanctioned sex and marriage between white men and native women is one of the many ways in which Spanish colonialism differed from European colonization farther north, where natives and newcomers rarely formed families with one another. Chattel slavery complicated these matters, of course, but also led to new social and legal sanctions against sex and marriage across racial lines. The fictional interracial "love story" of Captain John Smith and Pocahontas, imagined to have transpired one hundred years after the pairing of Cortés and Malintzin, is an important part of the mythology of early America, but the Pocahontas story does not translate into a racial origin myth for the nation in the manner of Cortés-Malintzin.[17] Historians of New Spain have documented well how the Spanish colonial system provided much more flexibility as to who might partner with whom for sex and marriage. The famous *casta* paintings, the best visual signifier of this flexibility, provided a vocabulary for defining the offspring of various racial combinations. This, of course, does not imply that New Spain was any less hierarchical in its racial system but that, unlike their Anglo counterparts, the architects of the Spanish colonial order *acknowledged* the reality of race mixing.

Before going further into the uses of *mestizaje*, I want to return briefly to the imagined parentage of the mestizo body politic. What does it mean to frame the mestizo as the offspring of a white father and an Indian mother—and what does this say about interracial sex? Referring to mestizos in this way might have placed the possibility of interracial sex firmly in the past. Writers might not have meant that mestizos like the ones who appeared in *National Geographic* were literally the children of white fathers and Indian mothers. Rather, they might have used the words "father" and "mother" in an ancestral sense. Such a characterization would have alluded to the mythical pairing of Cortés and Malintzin and subsequent generations of Spaniards, criollos, and mestizos fathering Indian women's children. In this sense, the racial origins of the nation really were in a white father and an Indian mother. It is, however, important to note that such characterizations might have had sexual underpinnings that related to the politics of race and sexuality in the late nineteenth and early twentieth centuries. As we have seen, the visual culture of travel to Mexico was sometimes fraught with unexpressed desire for Indian women. Framing mestizo parentage in the manner of Ober and Darton would have advanced the idea that indigenous and mestiza women were proper objects for the sexual gaze of white men, for it reminded readers that sex took place between Indian women and non-Indian men.

This sounds like a dangerous proposition, but the framing of Indian women as sexual partners was legitimized through narratives of motherhood. Through popular travel discourse, mestizas and Indian women became valued as the mothers to a growing and increasingly white mestizo population. Take, for example, the mother of Porfirio Díaz, María Petrona Mori Cortés, whose Indianness was noted by most travelers who wrote about the president. Travelers marveled over the fact that the president could overcome his humble beginnings, which apparently included the bad luck of having been born to an Indian mother. This was, to be sure, a part of the Horatio Alger–like mythology surrounding Díaz, discussed in Chapter Two, that proved to be a popular motif in American travel writing. But surprisingly, writers never questioned Díaz's parentage or insinuated that his *mestizaje* reflected his parents' degeneracy, as representations of miscegenation in the United States usually did. In other words, authors took for granted that his indigenous mother was a proper partner for his father, whom they frequently described as Spanish. No writer ever questioned the sexual union between the president's parents. Instead, they portrayed Díaz's mother as a poor but hardworking Indian. Representing her in this way underscored the idea that Indian women could properly raise mestizo children. For this reason, they were deemed acceptable partners for mestizo and criollo Mexicans because they had the ability to make more mestizo babies.

In 1908, James Creelman claimed that Porfirio Díaz, inarguably the most famous mestizo person in the nation, "was the descendant of Spaniards who married women of the Mixtec race, an industrious, intelligent, and honest people whose history is lost in the myths of aboriginal America."[18] Other travel writers seem to have agreed with this alchemy for *mestizaje*, for they repeated the white father–Indian mother paradigm ad nauseam throughout the Porfiriato. In one sense, we might read this construction of *mestizaje* as evidence that the creators of travel discourse were aware of the sexual dimensions of colonization. They might have seen that Spanish colonialism viewed Indian women as native commodities and used sex as a tool to exert colonial power. Contemporary postcolonial scholarship has certainly come to understand the colonial project in sexual terms, so this formulation of mestizo roots might ring familiar. But it is also a gross oversimplification of *mestizaje*. It ignores, for example, the fact that Mexican *mestizaje* reflects a complex history. In addition to contact between indigenous people and Europeans through colonialism, *mestizaje* in Mexico reflected other forms of interracial contact, including African slavery, trans-Pacific trade and the migration of people from Asia, immigration from the United States and Europe, and, later, the Jewish diaspora.[19] Strangely, this formulaic view of *mestizaje* also suggests that mestizos result from parents who are racially pure: either "white" or "Indian." Thus, the same writers who sought to capture the complexities of race in Mexico and to champion *mestizaje* also subtly reinforced the concept of racial purity.

Claiming that *mestizaje* was the result of sex between white men and Indian women served another purpose in travel discourse: it insulated white women from the possibility of sex with indigenous or mestizo men.[20] Many travelogues, brochures, guides, and other ephemera from the late nineteenth and early twentieth centuries included special sections dedicated to assuring American women that they could travel to Mexico without jeopardizing their sexual propriety. Unlike the swarthy brigands that populated representations of the country in previous generations or the "greaser" and "*insurrecto*" that would come to dominate later representations of Mexican masculinity, Mexican men during the Porfiriato were seen as nonthreatening to white women. A few travelogues were written by women who traveled alone or in small groups, painting a view of Mexico as a destination where New Women might exercise their freedom without endangering themselves. To fully realize this view of Mexico as a sexually nonthreatening space, male and female travelers alike typically represented mestizo men as either extraordinarily chivalrous caballeros, alluring because of their social class but too bound to tradition to go near women travelers, or as harmless peons under giant sombreros.[21]

It is important to stress that American visions of *mestizaje* served a broader political project. Darton, Ober, and the other writers mentioned here were deeply committed to promoting Mexico as a field for capitalist expansion. As we have seen, the idea that Indian difference served as an obstacle to expansionism posed a serious threat to spreading the gospel of economic conquest. But the idea that mestizos were this civilized (or civilizable) helped to promote the nation as a field for investment. The mestizo did not represent a perfect subject but was always preferable to the Indians, whom many saw as intrinsically resistant to capitalist modernity. Seemingly positive representations of mestizos and *mestizaje* were never innocent. Rather, like all of the representational patterns examined in this book, they performed cultural work specific to the politics of economic conquest.

IDEALIZED *MESTIZAJE*

American proponents of capitalist expansionism in Mexico knew that the "development" of the country required a population that could grasp the means of modern production and consumption. While some came to see Mexico's indigenous peoples as trainable workers and, to a limited extent, subjects, almost no one claimed that Indians could become full-fledged citizens of a modern state. Mestizos, however, showed some potential. Starting at the beginning of the Porfiriato, some American travelers began to write seriously about race in Mexico and what it meant to Americans as economic and political ties between the nations deepened. Out of these representations of travel to Mexico emerged several narratives of Mexican racial formation that idealized the mestizo population and the processes of *mestizaje* as the raw material for a much-needed middle class for the country. In order to paint a picture of mestizos as a population that could be assimilated into the modern state, some makers of American travel discourse began to reverse the long-standing notion that *mestizos* inherited only the worst qualities of their European and Indian progenitors. Instead, they formulated a new vision of *mestizaje*.

FIGURE 4.1. "Mestizo Types." N. H. Darton, "Mexico — The Treasure House of the World."

Frederick Ober, the author of the 1887 *Travels in Mexico*, was one of the writers who presented this new vision of *mestizaje* for a mass audience. "From a union of two races, Spanish and Indian," he wrote, "results the *mestizos,* — feminine *mestizas,* — or mixed people, and the handsomest in all Mexico. They are a gentle, docile race, loving pleasure, not always avoiding labor, cleanly in habit, and perfectly honest."[22] Ober fleshes out this vision of mestizos throughout his seven-hundred-page travelogue.[23] In his view, Indians were naïve and manageable, but mestizos more closely resembled the values of "progress" espoused throughout the late nineteenth century. Two decades after the publication of Ober's *Travels in Mexico*, N. H. Darton idealized *mestizaje* in his influential *National Geographic* article. Among stock pictures of burden bearers and other Indian *tipos*, a full page in Darton's article is dedicated to paired portraits of "Mestizo Types," photographs that speak volumes about the shift in representations of *mestizaje* that occurred during the Porfiriato (Figure 4.1). On the left, a young woman wears traditional dress, complete with a fine-looking rebozo and gold necklaces. She rests her arm on an ornate chair, a Mona Lisa smile barely discernible on her face. On the right, a man of a similar age wears a crisp white suit buttoned to his neck and holds his hat in hand. His greased hair is perfectly parted to one side. His arm rests against a pedestal table. Both man and woman pose in an elaborately furnished studio, carefully positioned among markers of middle-class *mexicanidad* (fancy furniture, oriental rugs, a fan, a floral backdrop) but still looking distinctly Indian. Darton's caption defines these two as simply "Types of Mestizos (White Father and Indian Mother), Yucatan." For the author, writing almost four hundred years after Cortés and Malintzin, the white man and the Indian woman remains the only possible parentage of the mestizo. He was not alone in this presumption. Ober claimed that "the Mestizo . . . is properly the offspring (not always properly begotten) of white father and Indian mother."[24]

While Mexican Indians appeared ubiquitously in American discourse, photographs of mestizos were another matter.[25] Despite the fact that mestizos appeared in countless images, few travelogues or articles from the Porfirian period specifically marked photographic subjects as mestizos or commodified exemplary mestizo "specimens" on picture postcards. For this reason alone, the paired images in Darton's article stand out, but they also embody a particular view of *mestizaje*, one that idealizes the mestizo subject as a reformed native. These particular examples of the mestizo body politic appear serenely civilized as they engage in the very modern practice of posing for a studio portrait. Their clothing and surroundings blend indigenous details (their clothing styles, their brown skin) with European ones (the furnishings, her fan, his hat). They are also beautiful and, to use Ober's phrase, "cleanly of habit." They appear to take proper care of their bodies, which are trim but not undernourished. The studio props include several markers of middle-class "taste," including the pedestal, heavy drape, and floral rugs. The crisp—even glowing—whiteness of their clothing lends them an air of unspoiled cleanliness. In contrast to the dominant narrative about the slatternly nature of native women, this whiteness communicates the mestizo potential for personal self-care and sexual self-control. In short, these are ideal mestizo types, evenly blending native and European elements to produce something distinctly Mexican. Descriptions and images of particularly docile and civilized-looking mestizos such as these served the idea that *mestizaje* was a solution to the supposed problem of Indian difference. This is true despite the fact that, phenotypically, these particular mestizos have an Indian appearance. Perhaps the dress and setting, when applied to native-looking bodies, should be read as an argument that *mestizaje* was as much a performance as it was a corporeal presence.

Many writers saw the whitening of the Indian population as the result of the aspirational character of the mestizo class. As Ober put it:

> Always aspiring, the Mestizo is rapidly drawing away from the Indian progenitor, and assimilates into the white race; it is said that Mestizos of the third generation cannot be fully distinguished from the Creoles themselves. . . . Not alone in point of numerical superiority, through peculiar fitness for holding political office, the Mestizos are the dominant people of Mexico to-day.[26]

Ober's sad vision of racial cleansing echoed García Cubas's claim that "not a few of the natives, . . . by their enlightenment, have joined the [mestizos], thereby founding new families with the habits and customs of the upper classes."[27] Or, as J. Hendrickson McCarty put it, "The well-to-do mestizo is inclined to disown his progenitors on the Indian side, and chooses all his associates on the white side of his family."[28] Importantly, each of these visions of Indian decline says as much about American imaginings of mestizos as it does about native people. Ober's description of the "always aspiring" mestizo is particularly illuminating here, for it captures the sense that mestizos possessed one of the most dearly held values for American Progressives around the turn of the twentieth century: the desire for self-improvement. Furthermore, these representations of mestizo upward mobility imply that marital and sexual choices were the results of rational (rather than, say, libidinal) choices. Thus, these visions of selective *mestizaje* suggest that, unlike their Indian ancestors, mestizos could function in Mexican society as *gente de razón*. Though many writers claimed to lament the extinction of the native population, they also painted it as an inevitability that would eventually benefit the nation's progress, subtly framing *mestizaje* as a panacea for Mexico's Indian dilemma.

Prominent thinkers on both sides of the border advanced the idea that Indianness was dissipating in the face of mestizos' efforts at self-improvement, including Matías Romero, the Mexican politician and diplomat who courted U.S. investment in Mexico throughout the late nineteenth century. These writers attributed the numerical rise in mestizo population to the "fact" that Indians wanted their offspring to become mestizo and had been "marrying up" in this way for centuries.

Writers referenced the positive traits of mestizos that made them healthier and lengthened their life spans. In contrast to Indians, mestizos could grasp what it meant to be a modern person and take care of their bodies accordingly. They would acquiesce to being vaccinated, for example, and could learn proper methods of cooking and housekeeping. According to many writers, mestizos also practiced self-control when it came to sex and alcohol. In other words, the mestizos were becoming the dominant race in Mexico because they deserved to be.

What did these authors hope to gain by suggesting that Indian people and some mestizos were actively choosing whiteness? Again, we must consider the politics of economic conquest. Proponents of capitalist expansionism in Mexico constantly worried about the lack of a discernible middle class in that country and what it meant for the prospects of remaking Mexico's economy in their own image. They were well aware of the economic and social divides that separated the haves from the have-nots, which posed an entirely new set of problems. American-style capitalism, though it also created huge disparities, depended in part on the presence of a middle class. Among other things, the middle class served as a market for consumer goods. Travel writers frequently complained that Indians bought very little and were too easily satisfied by just the basic necessities of life, making it difficult for them to imagine that native people could serve as a consumer market. The spread of American capitalism into Mexico required the creation of a consumer class, and it appeared to some that the mestizos were the most likely to replicate American patterns of consumption.

For this reason, the creation of a Mexican middle class can best be described as a racial project. This was certainly the case in the United States, where European ethnic groups were incorporated into whiteness in part to make them better subjects to capitalism. American travel writers frequently looked for ways to improve the Mexican Indian, an ethnoracial category incapable of constituting a middle class. Whiteness was an even more powerful way to assuage American concerns regarding Mexico's so-called race problem. In the context of economic conquest, whiteness—or what we might call "near-whiteness," which many writers claimed that light-skinned mestizos embodied—represented the capacity to function as modern capitalist subjects. Positioning Mexico as a whitening nation calmed concerns that racial difference would prevent the expansion of American capitalism beyond the southern border of the United States. Furthermore, authors' insistence that Indians and darker-skinned mestizos chose to whiten their progeny also suggested that they could make the "rational" choice of preferring whiteness over Indianness.

The predicted decline of the Mexican Indian also served the overarching goal of attracting foreigners to invest in Porfirian Mexico. García Cubas, for one, made it clear that he hoped that his description of Mexican territory and people would dispel foreigners' negative perceptions of his country and increase foreign investment. According to the author, who began the book by lamenting the misperceptions circulated by foreign travelers from Humboldt to Sartorius,

> The scarcity of the population of Mexico in comparison to its extant territory; the unrivalled geographical position of the country, between the two great oceans, the fertility and topical advantages of its lands, . . . the docile character of its inhabitants, the admirable falls of water, . . . offer the highest inducements to the establishment of manufacturing and other enterprises; the working of mines of precious metals and other useful mineral substances, . . . and in short so many and so propitious gifts as those with which nature has enriched Mexico, cause it to be one of the choicest countries in the world for colonization.[29]

Remember that this description of the country as "one of the choicest countries in the world for colonization" is followed by an ethnological overview of Mexico that concludes with the argument that the Indian population was facing a precipitous decline, even extinction. The shape of Garcia Cubas's argument encourages us to read his ideas about Indian decline as an attempt to assuage foreigners' anxieties about Mexican racial difference: investors need not worry about Indian cultural difference because Indian bodies were in the process of disappearing. García Cubas's book and similar texts created by American travelers illuminate the link between eugenic theory and economic conquest, namely, that racial improvement would open doors to economic expansion. Though it might seem counterintuitive to presume that a smaller population of workers and consumers would aid the processes that made up economic conquest, García Cubas shows that those who framed Mexico as a site for expansion did so by establishing that it was heading toward having the *right* population.

CONCLUSION

José Vasconcelos was born in 1882, around the time that Americans began to travel to Mexico in large numbers, thanks to the ever-expanding rail networks linking the two nations. As a child in the city of Oaxaca, he might have witnessed the appearance of tourist parties from time to time, groups of strangely dressed white people who would have marveled at the stout green colonial buildings, the extensive ruins at nearby Monte Albán and Mitla, or the grand old tree at Tule. Most of the Americans who wrote about race and *mestizaje* in Mexico during the Porfiriato would never hear about his vision for a final, cosmic race that would eventually populate the Americas. Nonetheless, these travelers formed and disseminated their own visions of the future of race in Mexico, visions that deserve further attention. While Vasconcelos remains required reading for anyone interested in the history of race in Mexico, travelers' accounts, some of which are nearly as provocative as Vasconcelos's, are nearly forgotten. Over the course of the Porfiriato, their views of race in Mexico underwent a radical transformation, from shock and horror at the race mixing that they saw there to a vision of mestizos as the future of the nation. However, as the next chapter argues, this latter view—and, more broadly, the politics of economic conquest—could not withstand the powerful changes Mexico would face as the Porfiriato drew to a close.

CHAPTER 5

REVERSALS OF FORTUNE: REVOLUTIONARY
VERACRUZ AND PORFIRIAN NOSTALGIA

*Mexico has been a slave-pen, a torture-chamber, a treasure-house,
and a slaughter-house.* G. L. MORRILL, *THE DEVIL IN MEXICO* (1917)

*Vera Cruz! How shall we describe it? A queer old place, strange as
any in the world, and yet on our own continent!*
HELEN J. SANBORN, *A WINTER IN CENTRAL AMERICA AND MEXICO*
(1886)

*[I]t is but a short step, when design doesn't conform to desire, from
fantasy to terror.* GREG GRANDIN, *EMPIRE'S WORKSHOP*

DURING THE PORFIRIATO, American travelers optimistically predicted that Mexico's marvelous progress and stable relationship with
the United States would continue forever. Porfirio Díaz was aging
rapidly in the final decade of his rule, however, and some timidly wondered what would happen when the man who seemed to have single-
handedly modernized Mexico could no longer rule. W. E. Carson, for
one, predicted that Mexican stability would flourish because of the
threat of American interventionism, as we saw in Chapter Two. Carson,
like countless others in the United States, saw the continuation of the
regime in Porfirio Díaz Jr. or the dictator's nephew Félix Díaz, who had
risen to the rank of general. Regardless of whom they saw as the rightful heir to the regime, American writers and other observers firmly believed that the Porfiriato would outlast its namesake. Even after John
Kenneth Turner published his famous articles exposing the dark underbelly of Porfirian law and order, making it clear that revolution was
fomenting in the north, many American writers continued to cham-

pion the elderly Díaz and to downplay any possibility of social and economic upheaval.

Well into the second decade of the 1900s, when some Americans began to question the unraveling regime, the majority of travelers painted a business-as-usual portrait of Mexico. In June of 1910, one traveler named Irvin von Keck reported in an American magazine:

> The longer we extend our stay in Mexico and the more that we travel within its romantic cities the firmer we become persuaded that Mexico is a country which has before it a future as brilliant as it is certain. Had we believed all these articles recently published by a certain class of magazines and newspapers, describing Mexico as dark as they would do Russia, we are most agreeably surprised in finding just the contrary. We find no signs of slavery or mistreatment wherever we may go for investigation. Everybody seems to live happily and contentedly.[1]

Von Keck undoubtedly turned a blind eye to the great social and economic disparities created as side effects of Porfirian "progress," but his description speaks to the fact that many Americans *wanted* to see a Mexico where everyone lived happily and contentedly despite recent reports to the contrary. The opening phrase of this excerpt—"the longer we extend our stay"—is also telling, as it applied to Americans in general. By the time his article appeared in *West Coast Magazine*, the American colonies in Mexico were larger than ever.

Despite this rosy description of Mexican stability, the Porfirian regime would finally collapse within a few months of the fabulous—and costly—national celebrations of the centennial of Mexican independence. Two American writers with dramatically opposed political views played surprisingly important roles in Díaz's undoing. John Kenneth Turner, a socialist muckraker, first traveled to Mexico in 1908 after interviewing Mexican political prisoners at the Los Angeles County Jail. His dispatches from Mexico, in which he presented a scathing view of political corruption and state violence under Díaz, appeared in American newspapers and magazines in late 1909 and 1910 and were compiled and published as *Barbarous Mexico* the following year. Turner's writings, some of which closely resemble travelogue writing, focused on what he called debt slavery in Mexico, arguing that cronyism between Díaz and American capitalists and government officials had created the conditions in which millions of Mexicans lived in bondage, tied to their debts like slaves. Turner revealed Díaz's merciless policies against the Yaqui, one particularly dramatic example of what the author called "The Diaz System" of statecraft. He did not, however, let the U.S. political and business elite off the hook, claiming that the United States had come to dominate the entire Mexican economy and political system through the complicity of Porfirio Díaz. Turner's exposé was perhaps the first criticism of the economic conquest of Mexico.

The magazine articles were widely read and hotly discussed in both the United States and Mexico. *The American Magazine* dropped the series in December of 1910, just three months into the exposé, presumably under pressure from the U.S. and Mexican governments. The publication history of Turner's book and articles is fascinating in its own right, but more pertinent to the study at hand, Turner's article helped draw attention in the United States to the brutal tactics of a dying regime. Although liberal Mexican readers probably were not shocked by Turner's accusations, many of their counterparts to the north were outraged by what they read about what was happening in Mexico. Turner provided a powerful counterpoint to the narrative that had dominated all representations of Mexico for more than three decades. While his writings met with resistance from the political and business elite in both countries, they no doubt convinced many American readers that their government should not intervene to protect the Díaz regime once the revolution came.

Although his articles and book created an international sensation and received praise in the mainstream press, Turner remained an outlier in his vociferous criticism. Few of the travelers who wrote about Mexico prior to Turner's reportage appear to have considered the dark underbelly of Porfirian modernity, as Turner himself lamented in *Barbarous Mexico*.[2] In fact, following the publication of Turner's articles, a spate of pro-Porfirian essays appeared in prominent American magazines and newspapers, including *Moody's Magazine: The Investors' Monthly*, which attempted to calm investor concerns following the publication of Turner's first articles in *The American Magazine*, *Overland Monthly*, and the *Los Angeles Times*. Above all, boosters wanted to protect U.S. investments. To do so, they criticized Turner and other detractors while reminding their readers of the economic risks of questioning the methods or endurance of the regime. In direct response to Turner's articles, Von Keck wrote:

Whatever the motives of the composer of those articles might have been, he never should have forgotten that Mexico is our next door neighbor, who without a doubt shows a great anxiety in keeping up the best relations with us. Mexico is an enormously rich country. Almost a billion dollars of American capital are most profitably invested in mines and in every kind of commercial and agricultural enterprises—and thousands of Americans have made and are still making their fortunes there. Considered only from this point of view, it certainly doesn't show a noble character to accuse and attack a country that has given us so much.[3]

Von Keck urged readers to understand that economic conquest required diplomacy. Mexico had indeed "given" Americans so much, and he, along with many others, feared that they risked losing a massive capital investment if relations between the two nations soured. His rebuttal of Turner exemplifies a spate of articles that appeared at the regime's last gasp, for the majority of pro-Díaz representations claimed that the United States was too heavily invested in Mexico to permit a revolution—and that Mexicans were too beholden to American capital to rebel. Writers like von Keck desperately tried to squelch any criticism of the regime, arguing that Turner's investigative work and the growing unrest south of the border represented only a temporary glitch in the long and lucrative dictatorship of Porfirio Díaz. Perhaps these writers and publishers did acknowledge Díaz's shortcomings in private, but they dared not criticize the regime in print.[4] Instead, they predicted that the Porfiriato would continue to the end of the president's life and even beyond.

This was, of course, a false prophecy. Neither Díaz nor *porfirismo* could surmount the forces that gathered in opposition to the regime under the banner of the antireelection movement. The movement against the reelection, led by Francisco I. Madero, gained increasing popular support through 1910 and early 1911. During that time, it became clear that Díaz, by then elderly and possibly senile, could no longer maintain the illusion of progress and stability. He officially resigned on May 25, 1911. Six days later, Díaz, along with members of his family and a small circle of friends and advisors, appeared in Veracruz to bid farewell to the nation that they had ruled for decades. He vowed to return, certain that he would be the one to restore order to the political chaos that was sure to follow his departure. The *New York Times* reported that tears rolled down the deposed dictator's face as he addressed the soldiers who guarded him at Veracruz.[5] He then boarded a private yacht owned by Weetman Pearson (later Lord Cowdray), a prominent British industrialist who was heavily invested in Mexico's oil industry.[6] While competing factions fought to control Mexico over the next decade, the exiled president and Doña Carmen lived in a comfortable Paris apartment and summer homes in the south of France. He reportedly visited on a regular basis with José Yves Limantour, his secretary of finance (and some say the political architect of the Porfiriato, though he lacked political charisma himself), who lived in exile nearby, but was plagued by grief and regret over the events that unfolded in his native land. Díaz died in Paris in 1915, long before the dust settled back in Mexico.[7]

Ideologically, James Creelman was the opposite of Turner. While Turner advocated for the full-scale social and economic transformation of Mexico, Creelman hoped that the superficial prosperity created under Díaz would continue in perpetuity. His 1908 interview with Díaz in *Pearson's*, in which the president claimed that he would not run for another term, also garnered an incredible amount of attention in both the United States and Mexico. As his rival Turner put it, the interview "was reprinted in every periodical in Mexico, and produced a profound sensation."[8] Chapter Two examined the Creelman interview as a hagiography of Díaz, but at the time of its publication the most startling thing to come out of the interview was the president's announcement that he would not run for reelection. "I welcome an opposition party in the Mexican Republic," Díaz told Creelman. "If it appears, I will regard it as a blessing, not as an evil. And if it can develop power . . . I will stand by it, support it, advise it, and forget myself in the successful inauguration of complete democratic government in the country. . . . I have no desire to continue in the Presidency. This nation is ready for her ultimate life of freedom."[9] While Díaz was known to pay lip service to his dedication to democracy, the announcement that he had no desire to continue his presidency was another thing altogether. Historians such as Díaz biographer Paul Garner have suggested that Díaz's pronouncements might have been a response to pressure from U.S. Secretary of State Elihu Root "to clarify his intentions, and even to step down in order to prepare for a peaceful transition of power."[10] Regardless of the dictator's motivations, it appeared to all (with perhaps the exception of Díaz's inner circle) that the Porfiriato was drawing to a close. Nonetheless, Creelman did not give up on his Díaz boosterism. His book *Diaz, Master of Mexico* competed with Turner's *Barbarous*

Mexico to tell the "truth" about the president, and he continued to publish pro-Díaz articles after the start of the revolution.

Soon after translations of the *Pearson's* article appeared in Mexico City newspapers, opposition groups began to look for potential candidates who could represent them in the 1910 election. Díaz, however, reneged on his claims, announcing that he would again stand for the presidency, this time against Francisco Madero, an aristocratic but left-leaning writer and politician from Coahuila. In 1909, Madero, the scion of one of the richest families in the country, had published a popular "anti-reelectionist" book titled *The Presidential Succession in 1910*. Inspired in part by the popular reception of his book, he ran for president under the slogan *sufragio efectivo, no reelección* (effective suffrage, not reelection)—strikingly similar to Díaz's own antireelectionist campaign in 1871, his first and failed attempt to win the presidency. Although Madero appealed to a wide swath of the voting public and the antireelectionist movement had gained serious momentum in 1909 and 1910, polling officials announced in September of 1910 that Mexicans had almost unanimously reelected Díaz for an eighth term. This massive electoral fraud made it clear to observers in both Mexico and the United States that Díaz's remarks to Creelman constituted nothing more than an empty political gesture. He did not, in fact, think that Mexico was ready to move away from his and his circle's "logical paternalism." Madero called for revolution and got it, dismantling a dictatorship that had ruled for almost three and a half decades. The violence and chaos that followed changed the course of Mexican history.[11]

The revolution did not, however, squelch American travel or demand in the United States for representations of Mexico. It is well known, for example, that tourists gathered near the border to watch skirmishes throughout the revolution and that they sometimes crossed into Mexican border towns to survey damages after battles and to try to catch glimpses of the insurrectionists. These modes of tourism provided only a superficial view of the troubles in Mexico, but they speak to the ongoing interest Americans displayed toward their southern neighbor. Surprisingly, travel to revolutionary Mexico did not stop at the border. Though their numbers did not match those who flocked to Mexico during the Porfiriato, Americans continued to travel into the country's interior during the revolutionary years. American popular interest in Mexico grew even stronger during this time, especially as the revolution flared and diplomatic relations between the nations deteriorated. Indeed, some claimed that it was every American's duty to immerse himself or herself in the "Mexican Question." As one magazine writer claimed in 1914, "The time has passed to regard Mexico as only strange, picturesque, and turbulent. . . . It becomes the duty of every American citizen to know Mexico, no less than the question of the tariff, the control of trusts, and the suffrage question."[12]

Indeed, more Americans did strive to know Mexico in the years following the Porfiriato, but they found an even more diverse and contradictory set of discourses regarding their southern neighbor than in previous decades. After briefly examining the ways that Mexico's image as a modernizing treasure house was supplanted by a deeply abject view of the nation, this chapter turns to the city of Veracruz to unpack the politics of what I call "Porfirian Nostalgia," a longing for the Porfiriato that dominated representations of travel to Mexico after 1911. Veracruz served as a staging ground for multiple foreign interventions, including a U.S. military occupation in 1914, making it an ideal case study for understanding how the politics of empire continued to shape how American travelers viewed Mexico in that nation's revolutionary period. Whether they called for military intervention or renewed economic dominance, travelers saw Veracruz as the embodiment of the best and worst of Mexico.

FINDING *THE DEVIL IN MEXICO*

Gulian Lansing Morrill was a flamboyant Baptist preacher from Minnesota who began to fashion himself as a globe-trotter in the late nineteenth century. As pastor of the People's Church in Minneapolis, Morrill gained notoriety for introducing theatrics to the pulpit. His sermons were known to include jokes, projected slides and moving pictures, "singers from the vaudeville houses," and even, on at least one occasion, hula dancers. One critic later noted that he was known as "the sporting people's pastor," a reference to the fact that Morrill was well known in Minnesota and beyond for incorporating popular culture and attention-grabbing stunts into his sermons and public appearances.[13] Even so, he was also something of a civic leader in the relatively new but rapidly growing city of Minneapolis. Alongside his fellow leaders of the Center Improvement Association, for example, he presented the city with its first municipal Christmas tree in 1913.[14] However, it is Morrill's large body of travel writing, rather than any testaments to his civic leadership or his preaching, that endures a century later. Using the pen name "Golightly," Morrill stood out in the crowded field of professional globetrotters by fashioning himself as a moral crusader who exposed vice wherever he traveled.[15] His travelogues take on a moralistic tone but are also wildly sensationalistic. This combination made him a popular author and speaker on the illustrated lecture circuit.[16] Morrill thus provides valuable insight into the popular view of revolutionary Mexico.

Though Morrill's early works focused on European travel and theology (he was ardently anti-Catholic), he became increasingly adventurous by the turn of the twentieth century, traveling to non-Western countries, where his thoughts on race, gender, sexuality, and empire found their ways into his writings. Travelogues based on these exploits had such telling titles as *Sea Sodoms* (1921), *Hawaiian Heathens and Others* (c. 1919), *Rotten Republics* (1916), and *Near Hell in the Far East* (c. 1923). Morrill's son Lowell illustrated most of these books with photographs that ranged from the banal to the shocking, as I will describe later in this chapter. They depict Golightly learning to throw a boomerang from an aboriginal Australian, climbing the pyramid at Cheops, dancing the hula in Hawaii, and inspecting scantily clad native women. In word and image, these works blur the line between travelogue, reportage, and manifesto, and in them Morrill appears as a startlingly contradictory character, both high-minded moralist and jingoistic voyeur.

The contradictory aspects of Golightly Morrill are most apparent in his approach to sexuality among the natives of the far-flung places that he visited. At the same time that he claimed shock and horror at what he saw in non-Western settings, he seemed to revel in seeking out "vice" in these places. Morrill's non-European travelogues featured *National Geographic*–style photographs of native women in various stages of undress to illustrate both his text and the glossy advertising sections in the backs of his books, which promoted well-known brands like Radisson hotels and Munsingwear underclothes. These images usually included sarcastic or suggestive captions that invited readers simultaneously to acknowledge and to disavow the desirability of the women featured in them. One image featuring native Hawaiian women bathing in a lake or river, for example, beckons, "Come on in, the water's fine," despite the fact that the women's expressions appear anything but inviting. Although their breasts are exposed, the women glare defiantly at the camera.[17] Morrill and his son Lowell, who took the picture, probably encountered these women while writing *Hawaiian Heathens and Others*, a typically pernicious account of his travels in the Pacific Islands. This is only one in a large body of such images that Morrill included in his books, evidence that his tongue must have been planted firmly in cheek while writing about so-called degeneracy in the non-Western world.[18] Though Morrill attempted to obscure the pleasure of looking throughout his books, his images and words make it clear that his desire for the locals, or to look at the locals, could not be contained.

Morrill published his Mexican travelogue in 1917, well into the revolution and two years after the death of Díaz in Paris. Titled *The Devil in Mexico*, it stood out as one of his most incendiary and overtly political harangues. Morrill's key theme was the need for interventionism in Mexico, rationalized through narratives of economic, sexual, and moral degeneracy. The frontispiece to the book juxtaposes a staid profile portrait of Morrill with a stark image, taken by Morrill himself, of a bandit hanging from a telegraph pole. The latter image's caption sardonically describes the scene as "a buzzard's banquet."[19] The rest of *The Devil in Mexico* follows this tone: partly pious, partly sensationalistic, and fully polemical. The travelogue also includes some strikingly comical elements (whether intentional or not), such as the author's vicious and over-the-top "Morrillisms on Mexico" and his "Mexican Alphabet," in which *M*, for example, stands for "Misrule, Mestizos, Mañana," and *T* stands for "Thieves, Treachery, Tortillas."[20] In one particularly comical scene, Morrill walks into a Presbyterian church in Veracruz and sermonizes in English, confident that the parishioners got the message even if they could not understand the words.

In another fascinating instance, the preacher's writings about Mexico inspired a humiliating public arrest that echoes C. B. Waite's brush with the law in Mexico City. On December 31, 1917, a federal marshal arrested Morrill in his home on charges that he used the United States Postal Service to distribute "obscene and improper materials through the mails."[21] He was released on $3,000 bail, but the globe-trotter's passport was confiscated a few days later in New Orleans as he was en route to Ecuador. The material in question was *The Devil in Mexico*, and it appears that the author's arrest had less to do with its naked pictures than with its political content.

Morrill challenged U.S. foreign policy throughout *The Devil in Mexico*, bitterly arguing that the government had failed to protect American citizens and their property since the start of the revolution. A particular source of ire was the evacuation of U.S. citizens from Tampico and Veracruz around the time of the Tampico Affair. Even before the events that took place in Tampico, some prominent American thinkers and businesspeople had called for intervention. In 1913,

William F. Buckley Sr., who then lived in Mexico and had just founded the new Pantepec Oil Company, demanded intervention in a letter to Colonel Edward Mandel House, the chief advisor to President Wilson.[22] Morrill, like other interventionists, believed that the government should have used military force to protect the American expatriates and their property. Unlike other interventionists, however, Morrill waged his argument in the most politically charged terms. "Mexico," he wrote,

> is the dust in our eye, the stone in our shoe, and the briar in our finger, socially, financially, and politically. U.S. treats Americans in Mexico like the Devil and the Mexicans politely tell us to go to hell. In spite of the smooth speech of Washington orators we are treated as escaped criminals and are hated and plotted against. Our trouble in Mexico is not so much from foreign enemies as it has been our home enemies at Washington who failed to protect our citizens and their interests.[23]

Morrill called for intervention in Mexico, claiming that it was the responsibility of the United States to restore the rights and property of its citizens, to establish political stability there, and to prevent Mexico from falling under German influence as the war in Europe grew ever more intense. Like many in the United States, Morrill thought that the Wilson administration should have intervened to depose the dictatorial and murderous Victoriano Huerta. Business leaders and politicians in the United States preferred Venustiano Carranza, who they believed could protect American citizens and property from insurrectionists. Morrill's indictment of the so-called failure of the U.S. government to protect its citizens abroad also speaks to his masculinist, paternalist outlook. Though Morrill openly professed that Washington was full of buffoons, he thought that the government's Mexican policy had been too soft since the end of the Porfiriato and economic conquest.

According to newspaper reports and Morrill himself in later writings, former Minnesota governor John Lind attempted to block the release of *The Devil in Mexico*, arguing to Morrill's publisher that the book "will cause great injury to the relations between our country and Mexico, and that it will materially aid German propaganda in the latter country."[24] Lind had served as a special envoy to Mexico during a diplomatic crisis in 1913, when it became clear that U.S. ambassador to Mexico Henry Lane Wilson had played a role in Victoriano Huerta's coup d'état and might have arranged the assassination of Vice President José María Pino Suárez. Morrill harshly criticized him for failing to use American influence to strong-arm Huerta out of office and dedicated a short section of *The Devil in Mexico* to describing the former governor as a "deLINDquent diplomut" and after his failed mission, one whom Mexicans saw as the "butt, the he-goat of ridicule—a common subject of censure, comment, cursing, and caricature in public and private."[25] He also called the Pershing Expedition, which mobilized almost five thousand American troops at the U.S.-Mexico border to squelch the actions of Pancho Villa and other insurrectionists in 1916 and 1917, a joke and ridiculed other American leaders for failing to exert proper authority in Mexico. Lind saw to it that Morrill was arrested and his passport confiscated. Despite these troubles, Morrill's Chicago publishers went ahead with the release of *The Devil in Mexico*. The author reported in later writings that the book was banned from many bookstores and sold only under the counter in others because the press made it known that it had been investigated by federal agents.[26]

Like C. B. Waite, who continued to photograph Indian women and children following his arrest, Morrill resumed his work following the controversy surrounding his Mexican travelogue. In 1918, he published *On the Warpath*, a travelogue about Indian country in the U.S. Southwest that began with a harangue against the "fig-leaf fanatics" who spoke out against *The Devil in Mexico* as an obscene text.[27] "My accusers," he wrote, "belong to the class . . . that mistakes prudery for piety. They would put a corset on the Venus de Milo; dress Michael Angelo's 'David' in B.V.D's; paint diapers on Raphael's cherubs; and emasculate the Bible, Shakespeare, and all literature, from Aristophanes to Zola."[28] In this typically lofty defense of himself, Morrill not only compares his own writing to great works of art but also makes it clear that he was well aware of his role as a provocateur.[29] Never one to shy from a fight and firmly entrenched in the culture of the day's yellow journalism, Morrill concluded, "I hope my book, like dynamite, will 'raise the Devil' in Mexico, where he is so firmly entrenched, and that his Satanic spirit and sway will be utterly 'razed.'"[30] From 1910 through the 1920s he continued to lecture and preach throughout the country, gaining ever more attention as an outré "morrilist." It appears that he remained an eccentric to the end: one newspaper account reported that Morrill delivered the eulogy and played the piano, both via phonograph, at his own 1928 funeral.[31]

"A WARNING TO FILTHY AND NONPROGRESSIVE COMMUNITIES"

Although Morrill's view of Mexico was anything but favorable, he, like many observers, reserved special venom for the port city of Veracruz, a locale that had long been seen as Mexico's "front door" by foreigners. Prior to Mexico's railroad era, most travelers from the United States passed through the city, which served as a major landing place for the "steamers" arriving from New Orleans, Havana, and other major ports of call. Even after the start of regular rail service, many travelers arrived at or departed from Mexico on a steamer via Veracruz. Almost every travel book written during the Porfiriato and in the following decades included a description of the rail route connecting Veracruz to Mexico City, the first and one of the most beautiful routes in the country. According to their memoirs, travelers always passed hurriedly through Veracruz, refusing to linger any longer than necessary in a city known as a breeding ground for both criminals and tropical diseases. For centuries, Veracruz had represented the best and worst about Mexico to foreign visitors. English-language descriptions of European presence in Mexico frequently begin with the founding of La Villa Rica de la Vera Cruz by Cortés on Easter Sunday, 1519. The founding of the city marked the start of Spanish colonialism. Situated on the Gulf of Mexico, the city became the ultimate contact zone, one where Mexican, Caribbean, Anglo-American, and European cultures collided and where sea passengers destined for Mexico's interior and many other parts of Latin America met one another. Veracruz also represented the staging ground for subsequent interventions by the French, Spanish, and Americans.

Foreign visitors had never been kind in their descriptions of Veracruz. They complained about its intensely tropical climate, the "northers" that stranded passengers, and what they saw as typically tropical inefficiencies in the locals' behavior. They saw the buzzards that constantly perched on rooftops all over the city as harbingers of filth and decay. As one traveler put it in the late nineteenth century, "There is little to see in Vera Cruz except the dirty streets, the turkey buzzards, which act as general garbage commissioners, and a horrible black figure of Christ, which blemishes one of the churches."[32] The people of the city fared no better, especially when writers turned their attention to the markedly mixed population of Veracruz. Above all, two tropes dominated American impressions of Veracruz during the nineteenth and early twentieth centuries: the view of *veracruzanos* as physically inferior to both

Americans and other Mexicans, and the idea that they had squandered the city's "natural advantages."

An American newspaper reporter named Thomas Rees reinforced the perception of Veracruz as a hellish place through which to pass in a travelogue titled *Spain's Lost Jewels*:

> I left after a short while, with the impression that Vera Cruz was the most dismal and melancholy place that I had ever visited. . . . It has a nice location at the foot of a long slope of hills that gradually rise to snow clad mountains. It also lies on the shore above sea level. These two advantages make it possible to have good water and good drainage, the two greatest factors in making any place beautiful and healthy, and yet for all the long years past it has been a municipal ulcer, a festering place of contagion, a hot-bed of disease, and the great breeding ground and distributing place for the fatal yellow fever to all parts of the world.[33]

In this passage, Rees, like many of his compatriots who traveled to or through the city, claims that Veracruz is naturally well positioned but has been ruined by the stewardship of the Mexicans who inhabit it, resulting in a place that is deadly to its inhabitants, its visitors, and even the world. This vision of Veracruz would have resonated with readers in 1906, considering that the United States had taken control of the construction of the Panama Canal two years earlier. This handoff occurred in large part due to the estimated 22,000 workers who succumbed to yellow fever and other tropical diseases in French attempts to build the canal. Walter Reed's research confirmed that it was mosquitoes rather than human contact or some endemic quality of the tropics that spread yellow fever. Nevertheless, Thomas Rees held fast to the notion that Veracruz, as an endemically unhealthy place, threatened the health of the traveler. In a telling rhetorical move, Rees suggests that *veracruzanos* paid a physical price for failing to profit from their "natural advantages." Many travelogue writers echoed the idea that the unhealthiness of the city—and Mexico as a whole—was connected to the character of its inhabitants, projecting their anxieties about the prospects for Mexican modernity onto the bodies and characters of the people. In the context of Veracruz, a city associated with yellow fever *and* various vices, this meant that the unhealthiness of the city reflected a deviant local population.

Progressive Era thought connected the discourse regarding filth and disease to dominant ideas about racial difference. As a former slave port and Mexico's principal Atlantic and Caribbean seaport, Veracruz had a cultural and racial makeup that had always consisted of admixture and syncretism, a fact that horrified American travelers who arrived with ideas about racial purity and segregation. Above all, travelers were surprised to find that the descendents of African slaves had mixed with the locals and influenced the culture of Veracruz. Following independence, the city became a locus for immigrants from Europe and the Caribbean as well, adding to travelers' impressions of the city as a place that blurred racial and cultural boundaries. Recall, for example, Helen Sanborn's shock when she arrived at the port in 1886 to find that, to her dismay, the people of Veracruz were "rather mixed." Others joined Sanborn in finding the mixed population of the city particularly distasteful. The difference between these representations of Veracruz and the positive views of *mestizaje* examined in Chapter Four is that, to American observers, race mixing in Veracruz looked less logical than the more purposeful and logical choices made by some Indians and mestizos to procreate with people whiter than themselves. Throughout the Porfiriato and beyond, rather than championing *mestizaje* in Veracruz, American writers treated the racial admixture observed there as another symbol of the city's degeneracy.

Beyond these narratives of health, disease, and racialized deviance, Veracruz represented Mexico's failures at modernization in a broader sense, as suggested by Rees's description above. Even at the apex of the Porfiriato, as travelers crafted a vision of Mexico as a nation at the threshold of modernity, the city stood out to some as a marker of Mexican backwardness. Rees captured this sentiment in *Spain's Lost Jewels.* "It is strange that any city should have neglected its opportunities," Rees wrote, "but here it stands, a warning to filthy and nonprogressive communities, neglected by its own people and shunned by strangers, and being left behind in the race of time."[34] Several discourses associated with Veracruz converge in this one sentence, including American perceptions that the city symbolized the worst of Mexico, that Veracruz was one of the ahistorical places in the country, and that human neglect was the source of the city's problems. Given the tendency of travelers to note the racially mixed makeup of the city, one also cannot help but wonder if a failure to properly segregate its racialized populations from one another represented one of the ways in which Veracruz had neglected its opportunities.

This hellish image of Veracruz did not, however, fit with American impulses to see Porfirian Mexico as a nation that could be incorporated into their nation's growing economic empire. A counternarrative thus appeared during the Díaz era that presented a very different view of the city and its significance to the nation. Veracruz became a different kind of staging ground, one where Mexican modernity might be established and measured. First and foremost, travelers during the Porfiriato had to contend with the long-standing view of Veracruz as an unhealthy place. Even Morrill begrudgingly admitted that Veracruz, which had been "one of the worst pest holes in the world," where it had been "not uncommon to have more than forty yellow fever deaths per day" in which "foreigners were the first to die," had cleaned up its act during the Porfiriato and become a healthier place for the traveler. In 1910, Presbyterian minister and missionary James G. Dale noted that "modern sanitation had been introduced, and now years pass without a single case of the fever."[35] Dale devoted more than a dozen pages to memorializing his fellow missionaries who had succumbed to the disease, but credited the sewers, as well as God and his own church's efforts, with creating a city that more closely resembled U.S. standards.

Throughout the Porfiriato, Americans also increasingly saw Veracruz's potential as a commercial port. In 1898, Sir Weetman Pearson, the industrialist on whose yacht Díaz would depart the nation thirteen years later, won the contract to reconstruct and refurbish the harbor. In the early twentieth century, pictures of the new and improved harbor began to appear in American writing. In direct contrast to the depiction of Veracruz as a site of contagion, these representational practices suggested that Veracruz was a testing ground for Mexico's modernization. The refurbished port represented Mexico's move toward becoming an even more accessible and profitable economic force.

These visions of a healthier, busier, and more modern Veracruz did not last long. By the second decade of the 1900s, observers from the United States reverted to the older way of seeing the city. Anxieties about health and well-being were replaced, however, by new fears about the revolution's effects on Mexicans' capacities to adhere to modern subjecthood. In the aftermath of economic conquest, images and narratives emerged that painted post-Porfirian Mexican subjects as innately resistant to American industrial modernity.

"THE HOT CARESSES OF A TROPICAL ATMOSPHERE": GOLIGHTLY IN THE VENEREAL CITY

A few years into the Mexican Revolution, Morrill depicted Veracruz as a place that looked nothing like a laboratory for Mexican modernity. Adapting Rees's view of the city as a "warning to filthy and non-progressive communities," he saw the city as the embodiment of Mexico's revolutionary chaos and a perfect rationale for U.S. interventionism. At the core of this criticism was the long-standing view of Veracruz as a place in which modernity could never take hold, whether due to climate, history, or the racial makeup of the population. Morrill attributed the city's failure to modernize to all three. Although there had been a glimmer of hope that Veracruz could modernize under Díaz, the city and its port stood as testaments to Mexico's and Mexicans' failures to fully benefit from the decades of economic conquest that preceded the revolution. Moreover, American observers wrote their anxieties about Mexican modernity onto the bodies of the city's inhabitants.

For Morrill, Veracruz's dysfunction as a modern space was linked to his sexualized vision of its inhabitants. The following appears in *The Devil in Mexico* under the title "Disease and Depravity":

> V C in Vera Cruz stands for Venereal City. "El Dictamen" is the leading newspaper. It only has four pages, yet whole columns are filled with advertised cures for syphilis, locomotor ataxia, and all the ills that licentious Latin America is heir to. The space we give to weather reports on the front page, or to special news with extra headlines, is given here to the nauseating ads. . . . On the main street I saw merry, curious groups of men, women, and children earnestly gazing in shop windows at photographs of patients cured of filthy diseases. Under each photograph was a name and address which the crowd was making a mental note of for future reference. . . . L A in Latin America stands for licentious animals.[36]

In this passage and elsewhere, Morrill lays bare his brutal vision of Veracruz as a space of sexual degeneracy, one that would shock the more prudent visitors from the north. He ends the description of sexual depravity with a rather telling pronouncement. "If Vera Cruz had a 'safety first' eugenic bureau similar to the one in Wisconsin," he wrote, "there would be few legal weddings." Elsewhere in the book he estimated and lamented that 75 percent of Mexican children were born out of wedlock.

Throughout nineteenth- and twentieth-century American history, but especially in the Progressive Era, marriage, family planning, and sexual healthiness served as markers of one's potential to be modern. Indeed, the "eugenics bureau" Morrill mentions looked to some in 1917 like the height of American modernity, as government-run eugenics programs attempted to apply scientific methods to the otherwise messy—and less than modern—process of human procreation. So Morrill's description here marked the residents of Veracruz as less than modern, a representational move that would have also served as a subtle argument for intervention. Whereas the dominant interventionist argument rallied around the American capital investment in Mexico and the U.S. citizens still resident there, a line of reasoning Morrill employed at length in *The Devil in Mexico*, he also bases his argument for intervention partly on the sexual degeneracy of the Mexicans.

Morrill's description of the sexual dangers found in Veracruz extended beyond the *veracruzanos*. In his view, the sexual appetites of the locals posed a threat even to subjects with better self-control. In other words, the Venereal City was contagious. "In Vera Cruz," Morrill claimed, "the principal male pastime is talk of girls and not of God. . . . Even Americans who stay here very long fall into the same habit."[37] This twists the classic colonial fear that white women needed protection from sexually aggressive natives by suggesting that white male sexuality was susceptible to contamination. Influenced by the local culture and the steamy climate, they might transgress the self-control that was the cornerstone of middle-class white U.S. values. This is reminiscent of Tweedie's claim, at the turn of the twentieth century, that "Mexico is not the place for a weak boy inclined to drink or play cards. The country and the climate would simply spell damnation for him."[38] It is interesting that Morrill and Tweedie, both of whom saw the presence of white men as a civilizing force for Mexican life, would present the sexual propriety of Americans as something fragile here. By suggesting that American men could be corrupted by the locals when visiting Veracruz, Tweedie and Morrill disrupt the supposedly unshakable vision of American manhood espoused by Theodore Roosevelt and other political and cultural workers of the day, the proponents of the "strenuous life" mentioned in Chapter Two. But perhaps this representational move has less to do with perceptions of American manhood than with ideas about Mexican degeneracy. Both authors, along with many others from the period, construct Mexican masculine perversions—those of the sexual variety as well as perversions of personality such as gambling and alcoholism—as a natural product of the sultry climate, making perversion seem like an endemic, intractable element of Mexican culture. The idea that even American men could fall prey to tropical temptations would have underscored the view of Veracruz as the Venereal City.

Such a view of Veracruz in particular and Mexico in general was intimately connected to ideas about gender and sexuality that appeared in American popular culture during the Progressive Era, especially those that imagined white femininity and sexual purity to be under constant threat. The cultural figure of the New Woman explored in previous chapters was always in danger of becoming a "fallen woman," especially in cities, where reformers increasingly attempted to manage feminine propriety through legislation and philanthropy. Muckraking journalists like Stephen Crane, whose *Maggie: A Girl of the Streets* would help to usher in the Progressive Era, constructed the fallen woman as a rallying point for urban reform. For these and other influential reformists, including photographer Jacob Riis and Jane Addams, the downside to modernity was that it created the urban conditions that took women out of the domestic sphere and into the city streets. Because the fallen woman was such a popular trope in the United States, representations of women in revolutionary Mexico would have resonated with American readers.

In *The Devil in Mexico*, Morrill forcefully transferred the fallen-woman trope to Mexico and another type of urban space, the harbor. One remarkable scene depicted the desperation and humiliation of fallen *veracruzanas* at the docks:

WHARF RATS

The arrival of a Ward Liner at Vera Cruz draws beggars as molasses does flies. The old and young, from baby to grandma, dirty, half-dressed, horrible hags and pretty girls. . . . They beg for bread, clothes, money, or anything that the sailors or passengers may give them. Begging and thieving is their profession. . . . The girls greedily grabbed cigarets [*sic*] and smoked them. Sailors at the port holes looked on, laughed, leered, and threw buns, bones, fruit, and garbage at them, making it seem like a country fair pastime where visitors throw eggs at the coon's head target in the sheet. . . . Wharf rats rolled over and over and fought for the filthy food flung them, attempting to hide it in their rags, or steal it from each other. This is the submerged tenth; the scum that flows down from the city to the sea; the human dirt waiting to be swept off by disease into the dust-bins of the grave.[39]

This bleak scene exemplified the views of travelers who interpreted the social chaos of the revolution in gendered and sexualized terms. Here and throughout Morrill's Mexican travelogue, women represent the worst in Mexican society. They are prostitutes, thieves, and beggars and, as they are here, compared to animals condemned to extinction. This section of *The Devil in Mexico* exemplifies abject femininity's place in colonial discourse. As a generation of works in postcolonial studies has shown and other chapters of this book have addressed, proponents of the imperial project frequently articulated their ideas about colonized groups and their relationship to power through representations of women and their sexuality. For Morrill, the failure of the *veracruzanas* at the wharf to adhere to U.S. forms of capitalism, gender, and good behavior rationalized U.S. interventionism. The scene is an extension of the earlier scene depicting Morrill's entrance to Veracruz and his supposed horror at seeing the advertisements for cures for venereal diseases. The women that he saw at the harbor reflect Morrill's beliefs about Mexican female degeneracy under revolutionary conditions, namely that women's fallen conditions reflected, more broadly, the national condition. The racial dimensions of this encounter are clear in the author's comparison of the women to the "coon's head target," a humiliating and racist game in which white fairgoers aimed at black caricatures to win prizes at country fairs in the United States.

But what about desire in a scene like this one? In order to unpack how desire works in this scene and throughout *The Devil in Mexico*, it is important to return to the pleasures found in the act of looking. At the same time that Morrill denounced sexual degeneracy, he clearly relished the view of those whom he saw as fallen women. In the back pages of *The Devil in Mexico*, where the narrative falls away and a gallery of Morrill's globe-trotter images appear among advertisements, there are two images of topless women within a few pages of one another. In the first, two seated women identified as "Siva Siva Dancers—Samoa" stoically return the camera's gaze, not unlike the women bathing topless in the photograph mentioned earlier. The second image, appearing opposite an ad for Royal Lemon Compound, a laundry soap, features a Salvadoran washerwoman and Morrill himself. The dark-skinned woman stands at the edge of a river, with clothes strewn about on boulders that line the water's edge. Morrill appears from out of the left of the frame, looking jaunty in a jacket, cap, and long white tie. He hands the woman something, perhaps payment for a washing or a tip for allowing his son Lowell to take her picture. The image is captioned "'Clothes' Quarters," a play on the woman's profession and the fact that this is a rare glimpse of contact between a white man and a seminaked native woman. The viewer sees Morrill look at the woman and is invited to take in the spectacle of her bare breasts. Although Morrill seems to enjoy this view, his description of the women at the Veracruz harbor is an example of the contradictory nature of his views of sexuality. The abjectification of the women reflects the fine line between desirability and danger that has haunted American representations of Mexican women since the nineteenth century. His description constructed Mexican women—especially poor and Indian women—as spectacles for the presumably white and male American gaze. Morrill was, in fact, quite adept at this mode of representation, considering his fondness for holding up women of color as the objects of desire and ridicule. He made a career as a writer by holding up women in this way. In this sense, he reminds one of C. B. Waite, whose work operated at a similar nexus of desire and derision. Though Waite held a very different view of Mexico—one no doubt influenced by the fact that he lived and thrived in Porfirian Mexico—his photographic oeuvre nonetheless communicates similar things about the desire to look at native women and, as we have seen, the potentially violent aspects of looking.

Unlike Waite, who fled Mexico just a few years prior to Morrill's visit, the latter's "wharf rats" reiterated American anxieties about revolutionary Mexico's relationship to the United States.[40] Morrill despised the fact that the Porfiriato had come to an end and advocated throughout this book for U.S. interventionism. In this sense, Morrill's highly sexualized view of Veracruz is not about sexuality at all, but about the unruliness of the Mexicans and American anxieties regarding the future of economic conquest. In the passage immediately following the "wharf rats" scene, Morrill scans farther down the harbor to reveal the connections between industrial decay and the "ruined" women:

> Turning our eyes from these human remains, we glanced at the mechanical ones at the dock. Hoisting cranes that might have lasted fifteen years with care were rusting away in five. Only a few were in use. Once all were busy day and night, now during the war there were just a few and only when the boat arrives. Other ruins we saw were those of ship-skeletons on the shore when we entered the harbor.[41]

Once again, as we saw in Chapter One, an American traveler explicitly compared Mexican women to ruins. But unlike Americans during the Porfiriato, who used the trope of ruins to heighten Mexican women's desirability, Morrill conflated female degeneracy with industrial decay. The ruins of Mexico's shipping industry, which thrived under Díaz, and the "human ruins" stood for the same thing: the excesses wrought by the revolution.

PORFIRIAN NOSTALGIA

These scenes from *The Devil in Mexico* reflect a desire on the part of many American observers to return to the order, progress, and opportunities for capitalist development that the Porfiriato had come to represent in the United States over several decades, a desire that many authors and photographers mapped onto the bodies of Indian women. A desire to return to the Porfiriato seems, in fact, to be the raison d'être for much of the travel discourse that appeared in American popular culture following Díaz's departure. Morrill set the tone for his travelogue in its preface:

> God has blessed Mexico as one of the wealthiest and most beautiful countries in the world and man has cursed it. The country has gone back to the days before Porfirio Diaz. Mexico is the white man's burden—a burden of famine, fever, poverty, ignorance, war, and superstition. . . . We were our brother's keeper in the Philippines and Cuba, and our responsibility includes intervention in Mexico whenever it may be necessary. This Tropic of Cancer country is a tropical cancer, and it may be that the only cure is Uncle Sam's sword.[42]

In just a few sentences, the author sets the stage for his strident claims that the United States must intervene in Mexican affairs, making it clear that such an action would be a natural extension of expansionism in Cuba and the Philippines and that military interventionism was the proper protocol for unruly wards of America's growing empire. Although this preface is rich for a number of reasons, I am most interested in his claim that Mexico had "gone back to the days before Porfirio Diaz." This is a manifestation of what I call "Porfirian Nostalgia": the public desire on the part of some Americans to return to the economic, political, and cultural relations created by the long rule of Díaz. The previous chapters have established that Americans developed an elaborate and contradictory vision of Mexico during the Porfiriato, one that played up the regime's self-fashioned national fantasy but revised it to fit with the politics of economic conquest. Those who espoused Porfirian Nostalgia constructed the revolution as the violent antithesis to the "New Mexico" predicted by those who called for U.S. expansion and intervention south of the border. Morrill was one of the more outspoken adherents of this representational practice. Many others joined him, including some unlikely allies.

James Creelman published an early iteration of Porfirian Nostalgia in the April 1911 edition of the *North American Review*, a brief article published a month before the ex-president fled to France that looked back on Mexican history to explain the coup against Díaz. Creelman advanced a race-based argument that Mexico had never been ready for democracy. In his view, Mexico needed Díaz because its native and mixed native population had neither the interest in nor the capacity for self-government. One strategy for reminding American readers of this supposed fact was to aggrandize the man who had just yielded power to his foreign secretary, Francisco León de la Barra.[43] "The bitterest foe of the Mexican Government," Creelman wrote in 1911, "must confess that Porfirio Diaz has led his people out of confusion, almost uninterrupted strife, poverty, brigandage and misery; that he has made one nation of the Mexicans . . . enriching the country greatly through swiftly increasing industry and commerce."[44] Despite the fact that many Americans had come to see the regime as corrupt and oppressive, Creelman wanted his readers to see that the Porfiriato had transformed a dangerous backwater into a thriving economy with a cohesive national identity. He continued to endorse the regime even as it entered its final throes. Creelman reminded readers that Díaz never denied his undemocratic practices but reiterated that these were means to a more prosperous end for the nation. Three years following his interview with the president, the author continued to champion the man whom he had called the "the master and hero of modern Mexico" in his *Pearson's* article, which, ironically, had played a significant role in Díaz's undoing. That earlier article had helped politicize the same proletariat that Creelman now claimed was uninterested in the democratic process. In other words, Creelman held on to the Porfirian dream for years into the revolution.

The most famous proponent of Porfirian Nostalgia was, surprisingly, Jack London. One of the most popular and prolific American writers of the early twentieth century, London had been a socialist agitator since

1896 and wrote about class struggle throughout his career. Like every active socialist in the United States, he watched the events unfolding in Mexico after 1910 very closely. He also drew literary inspiration from the revolution. His short story "The Mexican" (1911) took a sympathetic view of Mexicans and their revolution by telling the story of a scrappy boxer who wins a large sum of prize money to support the activities of the Junta Revolucionaria Mexicana.[45] A few years later, however, he published a series of articles in *Collier's* that still inspire controversy among London scholars because of their baldly interventionist and racist account of the occupation of Veracruz. Though these articles superficially championed Indian peons as political underdogs and lamented their oppression over the previous four hundred years, they also espoused the racist rhetoric of the day. For example, in his second dispatch for *Collier's*, titled "With Funston's Men," London referred to native people as "short, squat, patient-eyed, long-enduring," as "lowly, oxlike creatures," and as "descendants of the millions of stupid ones who could not withstand the several hundred ragamuffins of Cortez."[46] Over the course of his articles, London concludes, like so many of his contemporaries who preceded him to Mexico, that Mexicans were unfit to rule themselves. This unfitness led to the argument that U.S. occupation could only improve Veracruz and Mexico.[47] He claimed, for instance, that Veracruz "was cleaned and disinfected as it had never been in all its history." Some of London's contemporaries, and later his daughter Joan, expressed shock and horror that the otherwise firmly socialist London would produce articles that promoted the interests of American businesses and the politics of U.S. imperialism through such racist rhetoric.

One of London's *Collier's* articles stands out as particularly mired in the author's conflicted views on race and *mestizaje*.[48] Titled "The Trouble Makers in Mexico," it claimed that "the educated Mexicans, the wealthy Mexicans, the business and shopkeeping Mexicans, hail American intervention with delight" and passionately villainized the nation's mestizos as the fomenters of a false revolution. Mestizos were, in fact, the titular "trouble makers," referred to by London as "half-breeds" and "half-casts" in his article. (Creelman had similarly called them "part Indians" and "hybrids.") "Like the Eurasian," London wrote, the mestizo "possess all the vices of their various commingled bloods and none of the virtues."[49] At its core, London's *Collier's* article presents the revolution as a racial problem, one in which a degenerate racial minority (the mestizos) incites the nation's racial majority (Indians are presented in the article, not surprisingly, as a fallen race) to undo the progress created under what the author calls a "capitalist dictatorship." In other words, London's racism ultimately prevented him from championing the world's first socialist revolution.

In "The Trouble Makers in Mexico," London fashioned himself as an interventionist who regretted the end of the Porfiriato, a move that riled the political left in the United States. "There is no other Porfirio Diaz in sight," he wrote, unwittingly answering authors from the previous decades who wondered what would happen after the dictator died or was forced from office. London's impulse to look for another Díaz ignored the fact that Díaz was a mestizo, a member of the very group that London blamed for the social and political upheaval in Mexico. The famous author claimed, in fact, that mestizos were ill equipped to practice self-government, but he seems to have excluded Díaz from his formulation. As if in direct conversation with the boosters who claimed that Díaz could practice political manhood, London claimed that "they are not in a world of men, these half-breed trouble makers. They are child-minded and ignoble-purposed. The stern stuff of manhood, as we understand manhood, is not in them."[50] This masculinist view of citizenship and subjectivity served as an argument against the revolution but also illustrates the gendered dimensions of Porfirian Nostalgia. London repeated a representational pattern that scholars have long traced in colonial literary and cultural production, namely, the effeminization of native men to justify intervention. This logic relies, of course, on the misogynistic and homophobic notion that the "unmanly" are unfit for self-government and require intervention from more masculine outsiders.

All iterations of Porfirian Nostalgia hinged on the idea that the United States had "lost" Mexico in one way or another. Morrill, for one, framed the Porfiriato as an era in which generous U.S. citizens (and *not* their government) had heeded Díaz's invitation to come to Mexico, develop the country, and make their personal fortunes. This is another example of economic conquest painted as a humanitarian effort. According to Morrill,

> Mexico gave us the Macedonian cry, through the lips of Porfirio Diaz, "Come over and help us." It was heard and we hustled. . . . Americans who went were honorable. Of course they were able to make money — they went for that very purpose — but at the same time they enabled the Mexicans to help themselves, for their wages were increased and

matters of education, sanitation and care of the sick were improved. Heretofore, there had been but two classes and our men made possible a "third estate," or middle-class between the master and the slave.[51]

In Morrill's view, Americans had gone to Mexico with the best of intentions but were rejected by Mexicans who were not ready for social transformation. "As usual," Morrill concluded, "jealous and ungrateful Mexico hated any one who made her industrious or better."[52] From the vantage point of 1917, Morrill could look back and claim that Americans had done their best to improve Mexico—and make themselves rich at the same time—but that Mexico had been too ungrateful to appreciate these efforts. Doing so enhanced his call for the U.S. to intervene and restore Porfirian order south of the border.

Porfirian Nostalgia instantiates historian Louis A. Pérez's claim that an expectation for gratitude shaped U.S. policy in Latin America following the events of 1898. According to Pérez, some Americans felt that Cubans should have been grateful for, among other things, the new modern infrastructure installed by American occupying forces. Pérez claims that colonizers "historically have sought validation in the self-proclaimed role as transmitters of progress and civilization, to which 'natives' were proclaimed beneficiary and for which they were expected to display proper appreciation, most appropriately through submission to the colonial benefactors."[53] Although travelers and other observers could not claim to have liberated the Mexicans, as the subjects of Pérez's essay did in the Cuban context, they did see themselves as the creators—or at least the financiers—of Mexican modernity. Writers repeatedly credited their compatriots and their capital as the progenitors of Mexican modernity and joined Morrill in claiming that Mexico had been too "jealous and ungrateful" to maintain its ties as a sister republic to the United States and its economy. Thus, during the Porfiriato, many Americans felt that Mexicans should be grateful for their economic and cultural interventions. For Americans who felt this way, or the ones who traveled in their footsteps, the Mexican Revolution was a betrayal of all of the "good" that economic conquest had done. Only ungrateful people could let their cranes rust and their women degenerate into "the submerged tenth; the scum that flows down from the city to the sea; the human dirt waiting to be swept off by disease into the dust-bins of the grave."

SAILORS AS TOURISTS: U.S. OCCUPATION AND PLEASURE

I have argued throughout *Americans in the Treasure House* that capitalist development was a form of interventionism, but the Mexican Revolution opened the door to other forms of intervening in Mexican affairs. It is well documented, for example, that U.S. ambassador to Mexico Henry Lane Wilson helped orchestrate Huerta's coup d'état (actions that led to his dismissal from the post, leading Woodrow Wilson to send John Lind to Mexico as his personal envoy). Military action would also come into play during this time. In 1914, John J. Pershing assumed command of the Army Eighth Brigade at Fort Bliss to secure the U.S.-Mexico border, a move that reflected deepening American anxieties about Mexico and an increasingly militaristic approach to the "Mexican Problem."[54] Relations between the countries reached a new low in April of that year. Once again, as it had during the Mexican-American War, Veracruz served as the staging ground for a U.S. military occupation in Mexico.

The occupation of Veracruz was the result of a tragicomedy of errors involving American sailors, a miscommunication with Mexican officials, and wounded national pride. It started in Tampico, an industrial city on the Gulf of Mexico north of Veracruz. Tampico and its environs were home to a considerable concentration of U.S. citizens due to the immense investment of American firms in the local oil industry. As Morrill put it, "Until oil was discovered in the vicinity, Tampico was an unimportant port. Now oil tanks with their industry and wealth seem to have grown up like mushrooms in a night."[55] By 1914, Tampico had already boomed, making the city a strategic location for American investment and settlement, and many foreigners working the oil industry remained in residence there during the revolution. The state of Tamaulipas, of which Tampico is the principal seaport, had the largest population of resident American citizens in all of Mexico. The Taft and Wilson administrations had watched the area closely, worried that American lives and property were at risk as the political situation worsened in Mexico. Wilson resisted intervening into these affairs for the first year of his presidency, despite the fact that several members of his cabinet hailing from Texas had been urging the president to take action. Eventually, an opportunity to intervene—but only a highly dubious one—presented itself.

On April 9, 1914, nine American sailors were taken into custody by federalist troops as they attempted to retrieve fuel from a Tampico warehouse. It seems that Mexican soldiers misunderstood their intentions and were unable to communicate across the language barrier. Although the commander at Tampico quickly released the sailors and issued a formal apology, he refused to comply with U.S. demands for the raising of the American flag on Mexican soil and a twenty-one-gun salute. Soon thereafter President Woodrow Wilson asked Congress for permission to stage an armed invasion of the area, but by the time Congress authorized Wilson's request, U.S. warships had landed in Veracruz. In an initial battle, 22 Americans and more than 150 Mexicans were killed, many of whom were civilians who bravely took up arms to fight off invading forces from a powerful nation. Afterward, U.S. forces remained in Veracruz for seven months. The image of the American flag hoisted over the city on April 27 became a popular postcard and an icon of U.S. imperialism in Mexico (Figure 5.1).

The visual culture of Veracruz's occupation consisted mostly of jingoistic postcards like this one but also included postcards that captured encounters between American military personnel and Mexican people. These souvenir cards were not mass-produced but printed in small numbers by Mexican and American entrepreneurs who saw a market among the homesick military personnel. The sailors themselves could also make postcards, as the Kodak 3A had been introduced in 1903 just for this purpose. The most compelling among the countless images made by and for American sailors in Veracruz centered on two main themes: the violent aftermath of the U.S. military occupation, including countless images of sailors posing with dead bodies, and the activities of sailors looking for a good time.[56]

The latter category of images produced some surprising results. Some postcards quite explicitly exploited the stereotypes associated with both sailors and *mexicanas*, especially those that focused on lonely sailors and their encounters with local women and girls. Encounters between American men and Mexican women were highly mediated in representations of travel to Porfirian Mexico, as previous chapters have shown, but the sense of distance between travelers and locals no longer dominated under the conditions of revolution and occupation. Now white American men were free to admire (or, as we have seen and will see below, to abjectify) Mexican women from a closer proximity, as they did in a number of photographs of sailors taken in Veracruz in 1914. One such image, which appears in Paul J. Vanderwood and Frank N. Samponaro's study of American picture postcards documenting the Mexican Revolution, shows a group of young sailors "at home"

FIGURE 5.1. American forces raising flag in Veracruz, 1914. DeGolyer Library, Southern Methodist University, Dallas, Texas.

FIGURE 5.2. Postcard of sailors with local women, Veracruz. Paul J. Vanderwood and Frank N. Samponaro, *Border Fury.*

with two well-dressed Mexican women in what appears to be a military camp (Figure 5.2). The women look uncomfortable, but the men seem to be having a grand time, their arms draped around each other and the women. One of the women diverts her gaze away from the camera and holds her arms stiffly at her side. The other woman looks directly into the camera but places one hand on the top of her head and the other behind the small of her back in a strange and enigmatic display. In the background, other men carry on with business as usual, suggesting that this was not a rare scene at camp.

This postcard does not explicitly depict the chaos or violence of military intervention but is nonetheless a record of the cultural politics of intervention. It captures the fact that some sailors saw local women as a diversion from the work of occupying the city or lack of work, since the visual record of the occupation abounds with images of sailors at leisure. Vanderwood and Samponaro claim that "Mexican young ladies seemed to interest some military personnel mainly as cultural artifacts" in a very brief description of this image.[57] This seems to me to ignore the politics of desire at play when occupying forces place local women in front of a camera for display—in an image intended to be sent back home to the occupying nation, no less. As Edward W. Said, Malek Alloula, and many contributors to postcolonial feminist studies have shown, actions like these were a cornerstone of imperialist and neoimperialist discourses following the discovery of photography. To suggest that the sailors saw the women as cultural artifacts elides the fact that sexual domination has long been an integral part of imperialist relations.[58]

Other images from 1914 made it even clearer that occupied Veracruz became a playground for the American sailors who remained following the seizure of the city. One postcard, for example, featured a cartoon drawing of a white sailor lounging on a plank that is wedged between two palm trees and dreaming of a beautiful fair-skinned woman with bare shoulders. At the other end of the bench sits a squat woman with a rebozo and dark skin. She is clearly not the sailor's dream girl, but she eyes him longingly—a finger raised to her mouth, as if she can taste him—and says "amo."[59] The caption reads, "Senoritas in Vera Cruz are different from what we thought."[60] This card echoes the trope of Indian ugliness explored in Chapter Three and makes explicit that some sailors arrived in Veracruz with something other than anthropological interest in the local women. In other words, the view of Mexican women—and, in particular, Indian women—as both desirable and abject that predominated during the Porfiriato extended into the revolutionary period.

Magazine coverage of the occupation underscored the image of Veracruz as a playground for American sailors. Writing in *Everybody's Magazine*, war reporter Frederick Palmer described soldiers at leisure as a pleasure-seeking fraternity. "Every afternoon the sailors come ashore in liberty parties to enjoy the freedom of the streets through which they swept in the extinction of snipers," Palmer wrote. "The broad esplanade of the Sanidad pier is a medley of boat-calls and sailor joshing and laughter," he continued, as if Veracruz were a resort town rather than the site of a hostile foreign intervention. This depoliticizing description makes the occupation seem like something social and fun rather than an iteration of American empire. Like all on-the-ground correspondents, Palmer was charged with drawing a story out of Veracruz despite the fact that very little happened in day-to-day operations. At one point, Palmer explicitly compares the sailors to tourists:

> Having taken the city by force of arms, he proceeds to take it again with his money and good-nature. . . . Nimble and young and boyish,

with his easy gait and his hail-fellow-well-met comradeship, heat can not stale his wit and humor. It is difficult when you see him ashore to think of him as a fighting man at all. He is a tourist; an American, whether from the Maine or the Mississippi coast, who has become the playboy of the world.[61]

In this telling description, Palmer lays bare the link between military operations and pleasure. Harking back to the period just before the war, when economic conquest was in full swing, he also acknowledges that spending money was one way to take the city. Although the author does not explicitly include local women as one of the pleasures pursued by sailors, focusing instead on souvenir shopping and other innocent pastimes, it is not difficult to imagine that he saw the *veracruzanas* as another resource for the enjoyment of the bored troops. The presence of local women would have underscored the sailor's new status as a "playboy of the world." Such a notion is apparent in the picture post-card culture that flourished among the sailors themselves. This should not, however, suggest that the locals appreciated either the American occupation, the so-called improvements made to their city, or the exploits of American sailors.

Another remarkable image dating from the U.S. occupation offers what might be read as a visual allusion to Morrill's "wharf rats" scene. It depicts more than a dozen sailors, guarded by another sailor, casually eating from their mess kits on a street in Veracruz (Figure 5.3). Several of the sailors pause from their meal to smile at the photographer. Just beyond the sailor standing guard, more than two dozen local women and children look on with hungry expressions and empty baskets. They are begging for scraps of food. Behind them, yet another sailor also stands guard, his rifle slung casually at his hip. A handwritten caption reads "Mexican Women and Children Begging Food from U.S. Sailors—Vera Cruz, Apr. '14." The postcard memorializes the uneven and uneasy relations between invading American troops and *veracruzanos*. The women in this image function more like Morrill's "wharf rats" than the beautiful women depicted in other images from the occupation of Veracruz. Rather than playfully posing with them, the sailors keep their distance—so much so that a sailor with a rifle guards them from the women and children. Being destitute, desperate, and dark-skinned, the begging women depicted in the picture might be seen as fulfilling American visions of the fallen Mexican woman. This is a photographic glimpse of the women described so grimly in *The Devil in Mexico* and

FIGURE 5.3. Women begging for food in occupied Veracruz. Andreas Brown, American Photographic Collection, The Getty Research Institute, Los Angeles.

elsewhere throughout the second decade of the 1900s. The sailors certainly do not seem to be taking them or their plight very seriously.

However, perhaps there is another way to read this photograph, one that resists the abjectification of *veracruzanas*. Do these women and children merely line up to beg for food? Or can their behavior be read as a performance of resistance? It is well known that women in Veracruz took up arms against the invading forces from the north, just as women in other parts of Mexico took active roles in fighting against federal troops and *yanqui* invaders. Although I am reluctant to read this image as an unequivocal sign of revolutionary womanpower (the glaringly uneven power relations apparent in the photograph will not allow me to do so), there are subtle cues that the women in the postcard are not merely passive victims of the occupation or of exploitation. These women are not only objects for the gazes of sailors or the viewer. In the face of occupying forces, they appear to refuse the passivity associated with Mexican women. One woman near the left edge of the picture, her face covered by a rebozo, raises her hand in a gesture that might be read as pleading, exasperated, or incensed. It is clear that she refuses to take no for an answer. Likewise, another young woman, also in the front line of begging, stands with a hand planted squarely on her hip. Several of the children stare intently at the sailors, suggesting that they are unintimidated by the white men in their midst. These signs might suggest that begging—an act presumed to represent the most abject subject position, especially considering Morrill's description of the women at the harbor—can also be read as an act of resistance against the presence of these foreign men and the broader politics of empire that they represent. Although it is doubtful that the creators, senders, and recipients of the postcard might have seen it this way, it is possible that this postcard shows that the women of Veracruz were neither pretty props nor fallen women but active resisters to U.S. military occupation.

Not surprisingly, the appearance of picture postcards like the ones described here coincided with a spate of jingoistic magazine articles that took a racialized view of the occupation. Popular magazines like *The Nation* and *Collier's* provided forums for writers to think out loud about the meanings of the intervention. Many of these writers were travelers, too, since they went to Veracruz personally to inspect the actions of military personnel there. London's article appeared in *Collier's* just two months into the occupation but did not explicitly deal with the events in Tampico or Veracruz. Even so, his racist view of Indians and "half-breeds" would have interested American audiences seeking to make sense of the situation in Mexico—and the role that racial difference would play in military endeavors south of the border. Race-baiting in these articles, which reached much wider audiences than picture postcards, was particularly potent because many presumed the racial superiority of occupying forces.

The writings of Frederick Palmer, the war correspondent who equated occupying sailors with tourists, are again illustrative here. Palmer had covered the Greco-Turkish War, the Philippine-American War, the Boxer Rebellion, and the Boer War before he landed in Veracruz in 1914.[62] The editors of *Everybody's Magazine* claimed that these experiences had given him "an understanding of alien peoples, a realization of the futility of war, a point of view."[63] In a series of articles published in the magazine, Palmer's point of view was fixed not on alien peoples or the futility of war but on the experiences of the more than six thousand military personnel stationed in Veracruz—soldiers, sailors, and marines awaiting a declaration of war from Woodrow Wilson. Palmer took a keen interest in the everyday activities of these men and argued throughout his reportage that war would stimulate a higher form of manhood in the fighters.

Among other themes, Palmer emphasized modernization efforts in Veracruz, another theme that helped rationalize U.S. intervention. Throughout the Porfiriato, as we have seen, American magazine writers championed Díaz's modernization projects as a civilizing agent for Veracruz. "He caught the spirit of the expanding industrial age," Palmer wrote of Díaz. "Foreign capital came with its offers and he accepted them. . . . The land was webbed with railways and telegraph wires manned by foreigners, and foreigners opened up the wealth of the mines. Mexico prospered."[64] In the absence of Díaz, the *científicos*, and other agents of rational development, however, Palmer and his peers saw an opening for the United States to resume its role in shaping Mexican modernity. Instead of conquest through capitalist investment and development, these writers suggested that U.S. military intervention could continue the modern development of Mexico. Palmer, for his part, blended Porfirian Nostalgia with the notion that the United States would pick up where Díaz left off. "Vera Cruz is an example of [Díaz's] policy of exotic improvements," he wrote in one article, "which expressed his desire to keep Mexico apace with the forms of civilization; more, it is proof of our moral influence on this hemisphere."[65] Another article claimed that "for three years Mexico has seemed bent on destroying all that she had built under Diaz."[66] These various reflections on Veracruz and American influence suggest yet again that Mexicans had "moral influence" and capital investment from the United States to thank for the glimpse of modernity that the nation enjoyed under Díaz. However, Mexicans' inclination to destroy what had been built under Díaz implied that they possessed an unruly nature and that American military intervention served a higher purpose.

Palmer's view of the occupation was, at its core, one that championed benevolent imperialism. He suggested that the occupation reflected the ascendancy of the United States as a global power, one that could use military prowess to instill "the American spirit," as he called it, in disparate parts of the world. Above all, he saw the occupation of Veracruz as a way to test the politics and practices of administering U.S. imperialism. He claimed, for example, that once the initial battle had ended, the American sailors "became gentle, considerate masters," a theme that he employed throughout his coverage in *Everybody's Magazine* and was loaded with racist and imperialist connotations.[67] This meant that the occupying forces had learned, through other imperial adventures, how to behave like proper colonial administrators. In none of Palmer's reportage does he describe the conditions depicted by G. L. Morrill or in the picture postcard of women and children begging for scraps of food in Veracruz. Instead, he suggests that the people of Veracruz were better off because of their gentle, considerate masters. "Our single-minded policy [to peacefully take control of Veracruz], aiming only to help him cure his own ills, he takes as weakness. . . . He will not let us help him until we give him first the proof of our strength, as we had to give the Filipinos." Apparently the troops stationed at Vera-cruz agreed with this imperialist sentiment. "We must teach them how to respect us," one marine officer told Palmer, "and then we must teach them how to behave."[68] This last turn of phrase, that Americans would teach the residents of Veracruz (and, presumably, Mexico) how to behave, is particularly telling in relation to the politics of Porfirian Nostalgia. It seemed to many that Mexicans had learned proper behavior under the conditions of economic conquest but had forgotten how to behave since the fall of Díaz. In the eyes of observers like Palmer and his interviewee, military occupation would restart the educational process.

One should remember that Palmer already had firsthand experience observing the imperialistic practices of the U.S. government and military, as he had covered the American war with the Philippines. In addition to the reference above, Palmer compared the occupation to U.S. military operations in the Philippines at several points in his series of articles for *Everybody's Magazine*. Overall, Palmer painted a picture of a military with a pedagogical need of its own, namely, that it needed to learn how to behave like a legitimate imperial presence. He noted, for example, that American sailors in Veracruz were less prone to drunkenness than they had been in the Philippines, where they failed to display high levels of self-control. "Vera Cruz," Palmer wrote, "is the mirror to American qualities and ethics. One comes to Vera Cruz to get acquainted with the United States."[69] In other words, to Palmer, the occupation of Veracruz represented the best of American intentions, especially the impulse to civilize less developed corners of the world.

Still, despite these allegedly lofty intentions and the imperialist lessons learned by the U.S. military and its personnel, the occupation was over in just seven months. While American forces occupied Veracruz, Huerta fell and Carranza, whom some Americans saw as more palatable, assumed the presidency. John Lind (Morrill's "DeLINDquent Diplomut") helped to broker a peace deal that resulted in American forces leaving Veracruz in November. At that time, American ships and the servicemen they carried quietly left Veracruz. The occupation of that city lasted only seven months, but if press coverage from the time is to be believed, it represented a turning point in the history of U.S.

imperial power. Although the event is little remembered in the United States, it seemed to some at the time that Americans should take solace in the fact that the mere presence of U.S. armed service members could force revolutionary Mexico to behave itself. The exhibits at the Museo Nacional de las Intervenciones in Mexico that commemorate this strange but memorable event in the history of relations between the United States and Mexico stand as a reminder that this American intervention lives on in Mexican historical memory.

CONCLUSION

In one of the epigraphs that introduce this chapter, Greg Grandin reminds us that it is "but a short step, when design does not conform to desire, from fantasy to terror." This is an apt description of what happened in American representations of Mexico when the triumphs of economic conquest melted away and the oppressive underpinnings of Porfirian modernity were finally exposed to the American public. As we have seen in previous chapters, Americans constructed an elaborate fantasy about how American capitalist expansion would transform both Mexico and the United States during the Porfiriato. But the beginning of the Mexican Revolution marked an intense shift, one in which the fantasies about the future of American progress turned to disgust. In this chapter I have argued that, as a result of this shift, subsequent representations of Mexico were tinged with nostalgia for the Porfiriato and all that it represented to the proponents of economic conquest.

The chapter focused on Veracruz as the key example of a place that inspired both intense horror and a longing for a return to the Porfirian order. Whereas Americans had come to see the city as a healthier and modernizing space during the Porfiriato, writers like Gulian Lansing Morrill transformed it into a savage "venereal city" in the years that followed. Perceptions of Veracruz as a degenerate city also helped pave the way to a short-lived but deeply symbolic U.S. military occupation in those years. However, Veracruz is just one of the places in Mexico that fascinated travelers, photographers, and writers from 1910 to the 1930s and inspired American desires for a return to the old Porfirian order. Others could have easily served as my case study here. Mexico City, for example, was the location of the much-photographed *decena trágica* in February of 1913, ten days of some of the most brutal fighting of the revolution. Hundreds of photographs from the *decena trágica* appeared in American magazines and newspapers or circulated as picture postcards, including those that featured the mutilated and charred remains of combatants. These images certainly helped advance the idea that revolutionary Mexico looked like hell on earth. Conversely, the U.S.-Mexico border served as a site of revolutionary tourism, with spectators lining the Rio Grande or descending upon Tijuana to view skirmishes and their aftermaths. In contrast to images from the *decena trágica*, visual and literary representations of this mode of border tourism made the revolution appear like yet another tourist attraction. Despite the fact that other cities could have served as the focus of this chapter, Veracruz has been useful because it represents one of the most dramatic places to observe the mixture of desire and derision that tinged American views of revolutionary and postrevolutionary Mexico, views that were closely tied to the promises and failures of economic conquest. Indeed, the so-called Venereal City served as a powerful locus of Porfirian Nostalgia in the second decade of the 1900s and beyond, one of the places where Americans looked for and found the devil in Mexico.

Americans in the Treasure House has shown that travelers played a powerful role in shaping American ideas about Mexico during the Porfiriato and in its aftermath. Travel discourse that circulated in the United States imagined many Mexicos, ranging from a dangerous backwater to a rapidly modernizing "sister republic." Above all, travel discourse subtly but firmly placed Mexican subjects—from lowly peons to Porfirio Díaz himself—within the orbit of American imperialism. Representational practices like those examined throughout this book also bled into the new medium of motion pictures soon after the end of the Porfiriato, when villains labeled as "greasers" populated early westerns. Silent films like *Broncho Billy and the Greaser* (1914), in which perennial cowboy hero Broncho Billy Anderson soundly defeated a greaser with intentions to rob him and rape his blond paramour, proposed that Mexican character was a problem not only for Mexico's development but also within the borders of the United States. The more than one million Mexicans who migrated to the United States to escape the violence and chaos of the Mexican Revolution from 1910 to the 1920s were forced to contend not only with the modes of representation examined throughout this book but with a new spate of cultural forms that imagined Mexican people as primitive villains who could not adapt to the law and order that supposedly characterized American life.

This does not mean, however, that U.S. investors and politicians lost sight of Mexico as a field for capitalist expansion. Contrary to what one might suspect, U.S. economic domination continued throughout the revolution and into the 1920s. As Gilbert G. González and Raul A. Fernandez have put it, "The 1910 civil war . . . neither derailed nor significantly threatened the strategic position held by the United States; on the contrary, the [economic interests of] the latter emerged from the war not only unscathed but also even stronger."[1] Other scholars have shown that foreign firms such as Weetman Pearson's Aguila oil company became much more profitable in the aftermath of the war. By the time the civil unrest in Mexico began to wind down around 1920, American proponents of economic conquest reintroduced the idea that Mexico was a treasure house waiting to be tapped by a more enterprising and ingenious nation.

Travel discourse again supported this project, for travelers returned to the idea that Mexico was a treasure house waiting to be exploited for pleasure and profit. Frank G. Carpenter's travelogue, *Mexico* (1924), painted a strikingly different portrait of Veracruz than did either Morrill or the sailors stationed there in 1914, one that is more paradisiacal than infernal. "Although it has borne the brunt of repeated attacks from the sea, and submitted to a series of occupations by foreign invaders," he writes,

> Vera Cruz remains to this day one of the most typically Spanish cities of Mexico. Seen from the harbour, its low buildings seem hardly to rise above ocean level, while behind it and around it are vast stretches of green plains. Its waterfront has docks wonderfully constructed of great blocks of stone, and so long, that a walk to the end of them is tiring in the blazing sun.
>
> Their equipment includes giant cranes, railroad tracks, and every modern device for loading and unloading cargoes moving by ship or train. The port works, as well as the asphalt-paved streets, water supply, and sewers were put in by an English firm, and it must be conceded that they did a good job. Many a larger town in the States has fewer modern port facilities and an uglier waterfront than this entrance to present-day Mexico.[2]

In this view of Veracruz, written just seven years after Morrill's, foreign developers again take the credit for the development of Veracruz. The markers of Porfirian modernity—including cranes, railroad tracks, asphalt-paved streets, and sewers—make an encore appearance, perhaps to urge the reader in the 1920s that Mexico was again open for business (for that, after all, was the theme of so many travelogues from the 1870s to 1911). In stark contrast to the "wharf rats" discussed in the previous chapter, Carpenter claimed, "The only scavengers that we saw were the buzzards which flocked here in such numbers that they darkened the sky."[3]

Paired photographs, one placed right above the other, illustrate Carpenter's vision of Veracruz as a sort of industrial paradise (Figure C.1). The top picture offers an aerial view of the harbor, busy with boat traffic but orderly. A huge ship sits at its modern dock, while, in the background, large cranes looming on the horizon suggest prosperity. Below this photograph, a second image depicts the palm-lined front drive of a large hacienda in the state of Veracruz. "The *hacendado* of the rich hot lands of Vera Cruz," reads the caption, "lives in one of the garden

Once the starting point of Spanish galleons laden with silver wrested from the conquered Aztecs, Vera Cruz is to-day the chief port of a free people through which they exchange goods with the rest of the world.

The *bacendado* of the rich hot lands of Vera Cruz lives in one of the garden spots of the earth. Large scale operations and much capital are required for profitable cultivation of coffee, sugar, and rubber.

FIGURE C.1. The port of Veracruz juxtaposed with an hacienda. Frank G. Carpenter, *Mexico*.

spots of the earth. Large scale operations and much capital are required for profitable cultivation of coffee, sugar, and rubber." Although this photograph represents a very different built environment than the one directly above it, it suggests that the paradisiacal garden (an old trope common to colonial travel writing) is readily compatible with industry and commerce. It reminds readers that the hacienda is not merely a garden but an enduring economic system. By emphasizing that tropical goods required large-scale investment, the caption seems to both discourage casual speculation in Mexico and reassert the view of Mexico as a place ripe for economic exploitation.

These two images, along with their captions and Carpenter's other descriptions of Veracruz, suggest a remarkable reversal of Morrill's "Venereal City" and countless other representations of Veracruz that appeared through the decades. It is especially telling that Carpenter would pair an image of the industrial port with an image of an hacienda. Once again, agriculture and industry became the main tropes associated with the opportunities for Americans south of the border. Once the chaos of the revolution began to wind down, American observers returned to the idea that Mexico could be a profitable "garden spot" for Americans.

They also returned to the idea that Mexico could be a place for fun in addition to profit. In the 1930s, an American woman named Lillian Beebe compiled a photographic album documenting the previous decade of the life that she shared with her husband, Orion. The Beebes lived in Minatitlán, a small industrial city southeast of Veracruz, for most of this time. Orion was plant manager for more than twenty years at the Royal Dutch Shell compound there. The album, which consists of more than eleven hundred photographs, tells the story of their life in Minatitlán and their many travels throughout Mexico and the United States. From the more than 1,100 pictures that Lillian carefully selected and pasted into the album's pages, it appears that the Beebes enjoyed a life of swimming pools, golf outings, and day trips. Several pages of the album, focusing on a trip taken in 1930, find the Beebes behaving like giddy tourists and taking part in the sporting life that made this part of the country famous among foreigners living in Mexico. They clown around as they boat and picnic with another American couple, pose triumphantly with giant tarpon catches, and ride horses through the countryside. Most fascinatingly, the Beebes also engage in ethnoracial playacting by dressing up and posing as Mexican Indians. Seven such images appear on one page of the album. Lillian Beebe wears the *blusa*

FIGURE C.2. The Beebes playing Indian. Orion and Lillian G. Beebe Photograph Album, c. 1925–1930. Nettie Lee Benson Latin American Collection, University of Texas Libraries, University of Texas at Austin.

and sarong skirt of a campesina, her hair tucked under a long black plaited wig. He wears the stark white pajamas of an Indian peasant, a poncho, and a straw sombrero. A smudgy black beard is painted on his face. They both wear the *huaraches* ubiquitous in Indian Mexico. The most surprising aspect of these costumes is how detailed and elaborate they are. Great care seems to have been taken in making them look as authentic as possible.

The couple simply stand and pose in their native garb in the majority of these pictures, but three of the photographs reproduce the *tipos* images popular throughout the Porfiriato and in its aftermath (Figure C.2). In one of the photographs, Mrs. Beebe holds a basket to her head. In another, she kneels and pretends to work a metate, re-creating the image of native womanhood that had long circulated in American representations of Mexico. In a third image, Mr. Beebe jokingly chugs from a bottle, acting like the stereotypically drunken native. Both Orion and Lillian Beebe seem to enjoy playing Indian, as did other expatriates and tourists who posed in similar fashion.[4] My purpose in highlighting these images and Carpenter's descriptions is to show that, at least in the eyes of some Americans, postrevolutionary Mexico again resembled the treasure house that Americans created for themselves during the Porfiriato. The 1930s saw a loosening of social restrictions, and the Beebes appear to be having fun (which, sadly, cannot be said for the Americans who appear in the previous decades of travel discourse, though my idea of "fun" might be limited by my twenty-first-century perspective). More importantly, the decade saw a return to popular visions of Mexico as a destination for both pleasure and capitalist development. Travel promoters seeking to profit from the Egyptological craze that followed the discovery of King Tutankhamun's tomb in 1922 again began to market Mexico as the "Egypt of the New World."

Foreign investment picked up again, too, until President Lázaro Cárdenas declared in 1938 that, in accordance with Article Twenty-Seven of the Constitution of 1917, all mineral and oil reserves found within the country belonged to the Mexican people. This expropriation inspired a surge in Mexican nationalism—as well as renewed tensions between the nations. Still, the perceived pattern of Mexico moving closer to and further from the United States had been firmly established and would remain as such for the remainder of the century and into the next.

Even Americans who have never traveled south or browsed a *Lonely Planet* or *Fodor's* guide to Mexico tend to recognize Mexican travel discourse from the middle decades of the twentieth century. Starting in the 1930s, the Mexican government produced a slew of materials encouraging American consumers to visit their southern neighbors. Midcentury posters, the likes of which now adorn the walls of a certain type of Mexican restaurant in the United States, featured, among other themes, light-skinned señoritas and impossibly fecund gardens, both of which marketed Mexico as a trip to paradise. While I cannot deny the kitsch appeal of these materials (and the fact that they are often downright beautiful examples of graphic design), I have found that older representations of travel to Mexico are even richer reflections of Mexico's complex place in the American imagination. These materials include everything from a spate of elaborate travelogues lovingly dedicated to Porfirio Díaz to a provocative set of photographs depicting Indian women and girls that landed a well-known American photographer in a Mexico City jail. Porfirian travel discourse might have lacked the buxom models and the visual pop that have allowed later tourism materials to endure as part of how we see Mexico, but their power to shape our collective imagination endures in subtler ways.

In recent years, however, Mexico seems to have moved increasingly far from America's comfort zone. Spectacularly brutal drug violence, to cite the most glaring contributing factor, has shifted perceptions of the Mexican beach vacation and seriously affected the nation's tourism industry, especially after seventeen people were killed in a single day in Acapulco in the spring of 2010.[5] Early in the following year the U.S. State Department broadened its Mexican travel advisory, advising Americans to avoid Tamaulipas, Michoacán, and parts of nine other states. The effects of this warning and the broader sense that Mexico is now a danger zone have been far reaching, affecting, among other things, the nation's all-important tourism economy. Though it shares the world's most frequently crossed border with the United States, Mexico again seems very far away to many Americans.

FINALLY, A PERSONAL REFLECTION. I, too, am a traveler. I have been a tourist in Mexico many times. Unlike a lot of the children who grew up near me in a Midwestern Chicano enclave, who packed into family cars headed south each summer from a very early age to visit grandparents and other relatives, I first went to Mexico as a tourist when I was a teenager and somehow talked my parents into letting me spend a week in Cancún with my brother and some friends. Years later, when we were in graduate school, my then-boyfriend Aaron and I were always on the lookout for inexpensive ways to escape the frigid Minnesota winter. Often, the cheapest way to get out of town was to follow the paths of the "snowbirds" (Minnesotans who live mostly in the north but take long vacations during the colder months or spend their winters in a second home) by flying to Mexico. Despite the fact that I was working on a dissertation about American travelers south of the border, I demonstrated an uncanny knack for silencing the researcher within and simply seeking out the best stretches of beach on the strip of sand and resorts that the guidebooks now call the "Riviera Maya." On one of these trips, however, as we lay on rented chairs soaking up Playa del Carmen's amazing light, my scholarly interests came face-to-face with my vacation.

After a cruise ship docked at the posh but sterile new development near the beach, several of its college-age passengers swarmed the part of the beach that we had claimed several hours earlier. These were typical American college kids, who annoyed us in the usual ways: blaring music, drunken shouting, barking orders at the *meseros* who constantly refreshed their drinks. Aaron and I were nearing the limits of our patience when a Mexican girl in a bathing suit walked past our strip of sand. She looked to be about fourteen years old. One of our rowdy neighbors made a cartoonishly lurid display of lust in her direction, screaming in English to his friends that the girl might be young but possessed everything he needed to suit his needs. The women in his party groaned and rolled their eyes, but his male companions saw the comments and gestures as an occasion to raise their Coronas for a toast. They had apparently found the Mexico that they were looking for.

As I recount this more than five years later, my blood still boils when I think about that young man's behavior on the beach that day. But I also realize his behavior does reflect a certain logic, given the ways of seeing Mexico developed by travelers that I have delineated in this book. In *Americans in the Treasure House*, I have assumed that travelers' visions of Mexico have long depended on the paradox of Mexico as a simultaneously desirable and dangerous place to visit, an infernal paradise next door. These paradoxes sometimes incorporated sex and sexuality. We have seen, for example, that one American man claimed to have fallen in love with a poor Indian girl featured in a photograph from the ruins at Mitla, while some writers claimed that native Mexican women were so abject that they were worthy not even of black men. While I have only scratched the surface of the sexual dimensions of the touristic encounter, the behavior of the man on the beach at Playa del Carmen is a minor (though irritating) iteration of what some tourists have come to expect in Mexico, namely, that Mexican bodies will serve as a source of pleasure for tourists and, ultimately, will represent an important part of the nation's resources. If the history of travel discourse tells us anything, it is that complex forms of pleasure, desire, and fear shape cultural relations between the United States and Mexico. One hundred years after the Porfiriato, those of us on the U.S. side of the border are still trying to answer the question "What is Mexico?"

INTRODUCTION

1. Turner, "The Slaves of Yucatan," 525. These articles were eventually published in book form as *Barbarous Mexico*. The first installment was published in *The American Magazine*, but that publication dumped the series due to furor created by Turner's incendiary (and now classic) indictment of Díaz.

2. Tweedie, *Mexico as I Saw It*, 1.

3. Díaz was influential enough to be the namesake of both a period in Mexican history (the Porfiriato) and the adjective describing that period ("Porfirian").

4. See *Strange Lands Near Home* (Boston, 1902).

5. The Mexican tourism industry is well aware of the connection between travel and knowledge production. Recent official mottoes promoted by FONATUR, the tourism arm of the federal government, include "México: Closer Than Ever" and "México: The Place You Thought You Knew." The latter motto is especially pertinent to my discussion of travelers as cultural workers. I am indebted to the small but growing body of critical scholarship on the politics of travel that has followed the publication of Mary Louise Pratt's *Imperial Eyes* in 1992.

6. Pratt, *Imperial Eyes*, 4. Pratt's emphasis on the mid-eighteenth to mid-nineteenth centuries (with a brief foray into the 1980s) shows that travel writing provided crucial frameworks through which people in Europe came to see places and people in the United States as objects of imperialism. I am indebted to Pratt's groundbreaking study in countless ways.

7. Recent scholarship on travel to Mexico, such as Dina Berger's, has focused more intensely on the cultural politics of travel following the advent of a large-scale tourism industry in Mexico in the 1920s and after than it has on the Porfiriato. While this is important work, the Porfiriato deserves more attention as a key moment in the history of tourism, an industry that today accounts for the fourth-largest source of foreign exchange for the country (according to the World Bank). Twenty million foreigners visit Mexico each year, a mass movement of people with its roots in the Porfiriato.

8. Turner, *Barbarous Mexico* (1911 edition), 252; emphasis in the original.

9. Pletcher, *Rails, Mines, and Progress*, 3.

10. González, *Culture of Empire*, 6. My debt to González's work here and in other writings will be clear in the pages that follow.

11. Ibid., 3.

12. I refer here to the increased emphasis in American studies, ethnic studies, Latin American studies, and other disciplines on research that exceeds and crosses national boundaries. While any intellectual buzzword runs the risk of having only a short shelf life, the transnational turn seems to represent a paradigm shift for many of these fields. For a precise and influential description of the "transnational turn," see Shelly Fishkin's 2004 American Studies Association Presidential Address.

13. The opening of rail lines was marked by a lavish ceremony presided over by

President Manuel González, the military general and Díaz protégé who served as president from 1880 to 1884. Though this event is arguably as momentous as the laying of the golden spike at Promontory Point, Utah, in May of 1869, it does not remain a part of the popular memory in the United States or Mexico. Nor was the joining of U.S. and Mexican rail lines commemorated in art or on postage stamps and the like by either government.

14. Even as late as 1909, *Terry's Guide to Mexico*, the first and most influential Mexican guidebook, stated in its foreword that "although Mexico lies contiguous to the United States, it is much less accurately known to Americans than its importance warrants" (iii). One might argue that this still rings true today.

15. I borrow the concept that Mexico was both very close and quite alien to the United States from Streeby's 2000 essay on representations of the bandit Joaquín Murrieta in *Post-Nationalist American Studies*. Streeby argues in that piece that American studies has emphasized "the American 1898" as a flashpoint in the history of U.S. imperialism but must also more fully consider what she calls "the American 1848." This point is well taken, but this book demonstrates that Mexico helps to connect 1848 and 1898 as key moments in the history of American empire.

16. On Mexico's place in the pre-Porfirian American imagination, see Streeby's *American Sensations*.

17. Hart, *Empire and Revolution*, 122. This fact is a reflection on what Daniel Lewis calls "iron horse imperialism."

18. Steele, *To Mexico by Palace Car*, 7.

19. Ibid., 7–8.

20. Comparisons between Mexico and Egypt were rampant during the latter part of the Porfiriato. This mode of Orientalism would be revisited in the 1930s, as evidenced by a new spate of pamphlets and brochures that used Egyptian motifs to promote Mexico as a travel destination. The Warshaw Collection in Business Americana at the National Museum of American History holds several interesting examples.

21. Carson, *Mexico: Wonderland of the South*, 171. Carson's description implies distinct class differences between the worldly travelers who had been to Europe and the Americans who marveled at churches and other sites on their first trips abroad. The travelogues analyzed in this book similarly construct their readers as everyday Americans who might never have been abroad. In this sense, Mexico appears to have been a middle-class destination.

22. As is well documented elsewhere and therefore won't be discussed at length here, the Díaz regime relentlessly granted land concessions and mineral rights to foreign firms. Díaz's plan to modernize the nation depended in large part on his willingness to acquiesce to the demands of foreign capital.

23. See Pletcher, *Rails, Mines, and Progress*. Pletcher provides a fascinating account of the cultural work performed by seven of the highest-profile promoters of capitalist investment in Porfirian Mexico. I am more interested in travel discourse as a more subtle method of boosterism for American capitalist development in Mexico.

24. Pletcher counted diplomats, tycoons, and utopian reformers among these promoters, all of them prominent men who saw Mexico as an ideal place for U.S. capitalist investment. Not all of these men were invested in railroads, but the rail industry was by far the biggest object of U.S. capitalist investment. By 1911, railroads

accounted for more than 61 percent of all American investments in Mexico (roughly $644 million; see Pletcher, 313).

25. Epes Randolph, "A New Western Empire," *Los Angeles Times*, November 28, 1909.

26. Bishop, *Old Mexico and Her Lost Provinces*, quoted in Pletcher, *Rails, Mines, and Progress*, 28.

27. A good example can be found in Harriott Wight Sherratt's description of her ride to the falls of San Juanacatlán, which was then the second-largest waterfall in Mexico but is now virtually extinct due to environmental degradation. "Our traveling companions on the trip were an interesting company," wrote Sherratt. "There was a bright-faced young Frenchman, a low-browed, unprepossessing Spaniard, a German commercial traveler, two courtly and affable Mexicans, a coffee planter from the Isthmus of Tehuantepec who claimed citizenship in Kansas, and ourselves. There were all the materials for a successful composite photograph" (Sherratt, *Mexican Vistas*, 264). The same could be said for many of the other encounters like this one that appeared in travelogues written by Americans.

28. Darton, "Mexico—the Treasure House of the World," 492.

29. Hart, *Empire and Revolution*, 236.

30. Olivier Debroise mentions Spaulding in *Mexican Suite*, 81. Francisco Montellano describes Terry in *C.B. Waite, fotógrafo*, 26. *Terry's Guide to Mexico* would survive many editions and was published until the middle of the twentieth century.

31. Wright, *Picturesque Mexico*, 445. Wright, the daughter of slave owners, became somewhat famous in the United States for traveling thousands of miles across Mexico and South America, including across the Andes, on mule back. She was the widow of Hinton P. Wright, a Chief Justice of the Georgia Supreme Court who died in 1886.

32. Ibid.

33. *Los Angeles Times*, July 27, 1902, 16. Interestingly, this is the first mention in the article that Sinaloa had any population at all. Like the producers of a significant portion of promotional discourse, the article's author, Clinton Johnson, focuses on climate, flora, fauna, and mineral deposits, neglecting to mention anything about the Sinaloans except for their friendliness to foreign investors. The politics of representational practices like these is discussed below.

34. Rice, *Mexico: Our Neighbor*, 76.

35. Ibid., 75.

36. Ibid., 76.

37. Ibid., 108–109.

38. Ibid.

39. Dale, *Mexico and Our Mission*, 195.

40. Ibid., 196.

41. It should be noted that elite Mexicans published a few books in this genre. Chief among them was Matías Romero, a Mexican diplomat who worked closely with American business concerns to promote capitalist development throughout the late nineteenth century. Romero published articles in magazines like *National Geographic*, as well as a number of books, demonstrating that he was a cultural worker as well as a politician and businessman. Romero's *Geographical and Statis-*

tical Notes on Mexico (1898) touted the fortunes that could be made by developing his nation's resources but adopted a skeptical tone regarding American emigration to Mexico.

42. Hamilton, *Hamilton's Mexican Handbook*, 2.

43. Ober, *Travels in Mexico and Life among the Mexicans*, vii.

44. Wright, *Mexico: A History of Its Progress and Development*, 444.

45. *Los Angeles Times*, June 7, 1883, 2.

46. Hundreds of snapshots that I surveyed in researching this book depict American "colonists" climbing mountains, hunting and fishing, touring, and relaxing in one another's sumptuous homes. These images suggest that the good life was one of the many perks of the economic conquest.

47. Art historians and literary analysts have plumbed the topic of fruit as a metaphor for human fertility as well as imperialism for some time (pun intended). Psalm 127:3 describes children as the "fruit of the womb."

48. Indeed, the mechanics and meanings of rail travel to Mexico have inspired several scholarly works, including Daniel Lewis's *Iron Horse Imperialism* and, most recently, a fascinating dissertation by Michael Matthews exploring the "civilizing mission" facilitated by the trains.

CHAPTER ONE

1. The letter, dated January 4, 1911, can be found in the Archivo Histórico de la Universidad Iberoamericana, and the photograph is archived at the Centro de Estudios de Historia de México.

2. Quoted in Montellano, *C. B. Waite, fotógrafo*, 123.

3. Ibid., 25. Montellano laments the fact that no known image of Waite survives in U.S. or Mexican archives and that the details of Waite's life are so sketchy.

4. Ibid., 25; translation mine.

5. Ibid., 28.

6. See Terry, *Terry's Guide to Mexico*, xxx.

7. Montellano, *C. B. Waite, fotógrafo*, 29–30; translation mine.

8. As Montellano notes, Waite's life following his departure is unclear. It seems that he returned to Los Angeles with his wife and daughters, but he does not appear to have continued his photographic work in the United States. See Montellano, *C. B. Waite, fotógrafo*, 71.

9. These ten days, the most brutal in the history of the Mexican Revolution, are referred to as the *decena trágica*. The visual documentation of this brief but bloody period will be addressed again in Chapter Five.

10. The Mexican Revolution represents a pivotal moment in the history of photojournalism, as documented by the broad and varied body of Mexican scholarship on the visual cultures prompted by the war. It is ironic that Waite would contribute to Mexican photojournalism of the Revolution, since for decades he had carefully constructed a static and pro-Díaz view of Mexico.

11. Their status as foreigners might also have sometimes helped these men secure commissions from the Porfirian establishment. It is well documented that the Mexican elite emulated Europe throughout the Porfiriato and oftentimes considered anything foreign to be superior.

12. Debroise, *Mexican Suite*, 79.

13. Ibid., 4. This is not to say that Debroise does not take Waite et al. seriously as social actors, just that he does not see them as artists.

14. On the significance of ruins to early tourism in Mexico, see Dina Berger's *The Development of Mexico's Tourism Industry* and Christina Bueno's chapter in *Holiday in Mexico* (Dina Berger and Andrew Grant Wood, eds.).

15. Montellano, *C. B. Waite, fotógrafo*, 19.

16. Without further commentary, Montellano describes this man's gaze as "enamored" (*C. B. Waite, fotógrafo*, 18).

17. hooks, *Black Looks*, 23.

18. Our conceptualization of womanhood in the contemporary United States is, of course, different from that of Zapotec women in the early twentieth century. While we would call some of these women "girls," since they appear to be in their teens, they would have been considered fully grown in their own culture. As such, I consider them as women in this analysis.

19. I am reminded here of the photo that serves as the cover of Robert J. C. Young's *Colonial Desire*, an 1897 photograph of white men in Africa draping their arms around the shoulders and waists of some African women and children, and am compelled to point out that this image was, within a broader colonial context, hardly exceptional. It seems that men posed like this in a variety of colonial settings. Still, the image from Mitla is exceptional within the Mexican context, where visiting white men rarely posed with native people in this way.

20. See Mraz, *Looking for Mexico*, Chapter One.

21. *Terry's Guide to Mexico*, for example, devoted special sections to beggars and thieves in its 1909 guidebook and subsequent editions.

22. Montellano, *C. B. Waite, fotógrafo*, 81. Also cited in Mraz, *Looking for Mexico*, 34. Waite wrote this as the caption of a photograph of a very old man carrying a large bundle of sticks.

23. See Mraz, *Looking for Mexico*, 35.

24. Quoted in Hernández, *Postnationalism in Chicana/o Literature and Culture*, 48, and Montellano, *C. B. Waite, fotógrafo*, 38.

25. Rodríguez Hernández, "Niños desnudos en el porfiriato," 46–48.

26. Ibid., 48.

27. Rodríguez Hernández claims that the paper's description of the images does not match the smiling children that we encounter in Waite's nudes, implying that nudity—and not poverty—was the problem with the pictures. I believe that both themes would have been dangerous to the Porfirian agenda.

28. This article is reproduced in full in Montellano, *C. B. Waite, fotógrafo*, 38; translation mine.

29. While the historical record is vague about the destination, one suspects that Waite tried to send his packet to the United States, since Americans were by far the most avid consumers of his work.

30. Hernández and Montellano each reproduce a number of these images culled from Mexican archives. Other photographers like Winfield Scott produced similar images, but Waite was far and away the master of the form.

31. Goldman, "'Golden Age of Gay Porn,'" 242.

32. For an important feminist critique of Alloula's *Colonial Harem*, see Rey

Chow's essay "Where Have All the Natives Gone." Chow reminds us that we must be careful not to assert that men of color should reinforce patriarchal relations through protecting women of color from the colonial gaze.

33. Spivak, "Can the Subaltern Speak?," 296–297.

34. A. Smith, *Conquest*, 10.

35. Brown, *Tour of the 400*, 145–146.

36. Sontag, *On Photography*, 14.

37. The only description of this group is found on page 22 of *Indians of Southern Mexico*, where Starr details the women's clothing.

38. John Mraz has argued this point in his analysis of the nation's tremendously popular illustrated press. The exceptions were found in the *notas rojas* (red notes), which consisted of sensationalized police news. Mraz, *Looking for Mexico*, 44–47 and 51–53.

39. Maximilian, the Austrian archduke backed by Napoleon III and doomed from the start, was named Emperor of Mexico in 1864. His rule lasted just three years, but in that time the common people of Mexico became a source of fascination among French and other European consumers of *cartes de visite* and travel albums.

40. It is important to note here that typological photographs were only one means by which to measure corporeal difference. Anthropometry, including craniometry, served as an early tool of physical anthropology. The photograph was an important tool for these endeavors, including Starr's. Stephen Jay Gould's *Mismeasure of Man* is the classic text debunking the scientific racism of anthropometry.

41. Debroise, *Mexican Suite*, 120.

42. This is true from the *casta* paintings of the eighteenth century to the present. Debroise compares Mexicans' interest in *tipos* in the middle to late nineteenth century to the popularity of wax dolls and figurines that depicted Indians and working people (see *Mexican Suite*, 116–120). In both cases, representing the bottom of the social hierarchy seems to have offered middle-class and elite Mexicans a way to see and make sense of their society.

43. I would argue, based on the presence of Aubert images in archives in the United States, that Aubert's *tipos* also found their way into North American popular culture.

44. *Los Angeles Times*, April 13, 1902. From a clipping archived at the Braun Research Library.

45. Ober, *Travels in Mexico*, 275. The politics of representing the Mexican Indian as an animal-like worker ("dog-trots" and unbelievably large loads in this example) are explored later in this book.

46. *New York Times*, May 30, 1897.

47. *Los Angeles Times*, April 13, 1902.

48. Benham, "They Carry Loads," *Los Angeles Times*, September 24, 1899.

49. Carson, *Mexico: Wonderland of the South*, 189.

50. Sherratt, *Mexican Vistas*, 223–224.

51. González, *Culture of Empire*, 56.

52. William Beebe, quoted in González, *Culture of Empire*, 57.

53. Ober, *Travels in Mexico*, 464.

54. The tropes associated with ruins have remained consistently dominant throughout the history of travel to Mexico up to the present day. At the time of this

writing, the global portal page of visitmexico.com (the official site of the Consejo de Promoción Turística) featured a dramatic and beautiful photograph of El Castillo at Chichén Itzá.

55. *The Land of the Montezumas* was the title of a travelogue by Cora Hayward Crawford. Other writers referred to Mexico with names like *Aztec Land* (Ballou) and similarly Aztec-themed monikers.

56. "A New Western Empire," *Los Angeles Times*, November 28, 1909.

57. Morris, *A Tour in Mexico*, 40.

58. Sherratt, *Mexican Vistas*, 44.

59. McCarty, *Two Thousand Miles*, 98.

60. Ibid., 5.

61. Carson, *Mexico: Wonderland of the South*, v.

62. Blake and Sullivan, *Mexico: Picturesque, Political, Progressive*, 80.

63. Creelman, "President Diaz"; also, Lyle, "Mexico at High Tide," *The World's Work*, 9183.

64. McCarty, *Two Thousand Miles*, 98.

65. Anzaldúa, *Borderlands/La Frontera*, 25.

66. Brady, "The Fungibility of Borders," 177.

67. Russell, *Red Tiger*, 336.

68. Morrill, *The Devil in Mexico*, 346.

69. Creelman, "President Diaz," 237.

70. Several scholars have noted the irony that Wheatley, a slave, would create such an enduring emblem of Americanness.

71. Wexler, *Tender Violence*, 60.

72. Wexler is most interested in white women photographers of the late nineteenth and early twentieth centuries. It is important to note that few, if any, white women published photographs of Mexico during the nineteenth century.

73. The same can of course be said for women in other parts of what some now call the Third World, especially in parts of Africa and Oceania. Women in those settings served as easy subject matter for topless photos like those that would come to fill the pages of *National Geographic* and similar ethnological and pseudo-ethnological magazines.

74. See Rogin, "The Sword Became a Flashing Vision," 158.

75. Tweedie, *Mexico as I Saw It*, 275. This image looks strangely artificial, and it's quite possible that someone cut and pasted Tweedie's image onto the locomotive. Whether or not this is the case, the image retains its representational power.

76. *El Universal*, May 20, 1925. Quoted in Montellano, *C. B. Waite, fotógrafo*, 216.

CHAPTER TWO

1. Creelman, "President Diaz," 253.

2. Frank McLynn, quoted in Fox and Allyn, *Revolution of Hope*, 7.

3. Lummis, *Awakening of a Nation*, 103–104.

4. Turner, *Barbarous Mexico*, 205.

5. Wright, *Picturesque Mexico*, 101.

6. Wright, *Mexico*, 144.

7. For more on Lummis's biography and his status as "foremost writer on the

Southwest," see Chapter Four of Padget's *Indian Country*. Curiously, Padget makes no mention of Lummis's writings on Mexico despite the fact that *The Awakening of a Nation* might be his most enduring work.

8. Lummis, "The Mexican Wizard," 309.

9. Rice, *Mexico: Our Neighbor*, 92.

10. Tweedie, *Mexico as I Saw It*, 76.

11. Wright, *Picturesque Mexico*, 103.

12. *Los Angeles Times*, October 6, 1907.

13. "Gray Eagle of Mexico Sails to Make New Home in Spain," *Los Angeles Times*, June 1, 1911.

14. "Porfirio Diaz," *Los Angeles Times*, June 3, 1915.

15. Creelman was a major contributor to the American edition of the magazine. The article did not appear in the original London edition of *Pearson's Magazine*.

16. See Lomnitz, "Chronotypes," 220.

17. Cited in Mraz, *Looking for Mexico*, 72.

18. Creelman, "President Diaz," 232.

19. A copy held by the library of the University of California Santa Barbara, distributed by the Mexican National Packing Company, circulated under the title "Porfirio Diaz, Regenerator of Mexico."

20. Creelman, "President Diaz," 274.

21. Ibid., 277.

22. González, *Culture of Empire*, 7.

23. Carson, *Mexico: Wonderland of the South*, 206.

24. Ibid., 207.

25. Turner, *Barbarous Mexico*, 259–261.

26. Gillpatrick, *The Man Who Likes Mexico*, 117.

27. Hugo G. Nutini provides a fascinating account of the Mexican aristocracy from the colonial period to the 1990s in *The Wages of Conquest*. Although much more could be written in this chapter about the broader social world of the upper classes in Porfirian Mexico, I focus here on only the two most recognizable of its members.

28. Gillpatrick, *The Man Who Likes Mexico*, 118.

29. Garner, *Porfirio Díaz*, 127.

30. See Mraz, *Looking for Mexico*, Chapter One.

31. Rice, *Mexico: Our Neighbor*, 24.

32. Gillpatrick, *The Man Who Likes Mexico*, 111.

33. Creelman, "President Diaz," 232.

34. Tweedie, *Mexico as I Saw It*, 129.

35. Godoy, *Porfirio Diaz*, 98.

36. Wright, *Picturesque Mexico*, 102–103.

37. These three markers of proper subjecthood are not the only ones that would have helped travelers categorize people as "proper subjects" or "improper subjects." They are simply three of the key aspects of character that travelers during the late nineteenth and early twentieth centuries wrote about when grappling with the question of whether Mexicans could become modern subjects. Subsequent chapters will explore the role that race plays in this question. Incidentally, today's travelers might replace the term "progress," as I have used it here, with "development." Travelers still

look for signs of modernity and progress when they visit the so-called developing world. As anyone who has read English-language accounts of Mexico knows, countless contemporary travel memoirs and guidebooks continue to rehash the idea that Mexicans stand at the cusp of modernity, with one foot in the modern day and one in a mythical, mystic past.

38. Gillpatrick, *The Man Who Likes Mexico*, 125.

39. See Roosevelt, *The Rough Riders*, 22.

40. Roosevelt, *Winning of the West*, 3:45–46; quoted in Bederman, *Manliness and Civilization*, 182–183.

41. Lummis, *Awakening of a Nation*, 104–105.

42. Tweedie, *Mexico as I Saw It*, 5.

43. Benjamin and Ocasio-Meléndez, "Organizing the Memory," 329.

44. Howell, "Mexico, Past and Present," 183. Howell went on to say that the "qualities inherited from both parents are indicated by the remarkable character he developed in the many vicissitudes of his eventful life" (183–184). The politics of framing *mestizaje* as the result of a white father and Indian mother will be more fully examined in Chapter Four.

45. Wright, *Picturesque Mexico*, 92.

46. Tweedie, *Maker of Modern Mexico*, 354–355.

47. Creelman, "President Diaz," 241.

48. Hoganson, *Fighting for American Manhood*, Chapter Six.

49. Lummis, *Awakening of a Nation*, 114.

50. Creelman, "President Diaz," 242.

51. Although Americans were, by and large, still unaware of the fact, Díaz also maintained a status as an Indian killer. His oppression of the Yaqui and other indigenous people represents one more thing that he and Roosevelt had in common. Both presidents superficially celebrated native people at the same time that they acted aggressively toward them.

52. Lummis, "The Mexican Wizard," 310.

53. Creelman, "President Diaz," 235–236.

54. Creelman, *Diaz, Master of Mexico*, 6.

55. I refer to her as "Carmelita" throughout this section to distinguish her from her husband and because it is in keeping with how travelers described her during this period.

56. Wright, *Picturesque Mexico*, 118.

57. Lummis, *Awakening of a Nation*, 114.

58. Ibid., 116.

59. Sherratt, *Mexican Vistas*, 114. This metaphor of sisterly relations echoes Sherratt's call, in the book's introduction, for greater American interest in Mexico. "I have in these pages . . . endeavored to bring our neighbor over the way a little nearer to us, hoping that we might someday know her better and learn to feel for her the interest of a sympathizing elder sister" (19).

60. Tweedie, *Maker of Modern Mexico*, 349.

61. Lummis, *Awakening of a Nation*, 5.

62. They also made little note of Delfina Ortega, Díaz's niece and first wife, who died following complications from giving birth to her seventh child with Díaz in 1880. Only two of the seven children survived infancy. Garner notes that there "can

be little doubt that this tragic family history derived from consanguinity" (*Porfirio Díaz*, 49).

63. Foster wrote newspaper and magazine articles promoting American business interests and the Porfirian regime. See, for example, "The New Mexico," an article that he wrote for *National Geographic* in 1902.

64. Howell, "Mexico, Past and Present," 185.

65. Ibid.

66. Tweedie, *Mexico as I Saw It*, 147. Queen Alexandra had been born a Danish princess and married the Prince of Wales in 1868. She became Edward VII's queen consort of the United Kingdom upon Queen Victoria's death in 1901. State portraits of Carmelita and Queen Alexandra from around the turn of the twentieth century do bear a striking resemblance to one another.

67. Martin, *Mexico of the Twentieth Century*, 64. Book review from January 26, 1907.

68. Tweedie, *Maker of Modern Mexico*, 289.

69. Creelman, "President Diaz," 275.

70. Carson, *Mexico: Wonderland of the South*, 207.

71. Martin, *Mexico of the Twentieth Century*, 1:vii; emphasis mine.

72. Creelman, "President Diaz," 237.

73. Ibid.

74. Ibid., 258.

75. Ibid., 259.

76. Marie Robinson Wright published a photograph of the same smiling boy in a sailor suit in 1911. See *Mexico*, 143.

77. Fornaro, *Diaz, Czar of Mexico*.

78. Niederkorn, "Mother Jones Speaks Out for Convicted Caricaturist," *New York Times*, November 29, 1909.

CHAPTER THREE

1. See Allan Punzalan Isaac's *American Tropics* for a fascinating analysis that connects Boy Scout novels to media representations of Andrew Cunanan. On imperialism in the late-nineteenth and early-twentieth-century literary imagination, see especially Amy Kaplan and Donald E. Pease's *Cultures of United States Imperialism*.

2. Kipling, *The Complete Verse*, 261.

3. Prendergast, "Railroads in Mexico," 276.

4. On Bourke, see José David Saldívar in *American Studies: An Anthology*, 27–28.

5. Leopold's misadventures in the Congo inspired outrage from many prominent Americans, including Mark Twain and Booker T. Washington, and, most famously, inspired Joseph Conrad's *Heart of Darkness*.

6. Bourke, "The American Congo," 594.

7. Howland, "A Mexican City," 26.

8. McCarty, *Two Thousand Miles*, 47.

9. I will drop the quotation marks around the word *race* in the interest of clarity, but in doing so I do not mean to reify race as a biological fact or Indian racial difference as real in any biological sense.

10. On tolerance regarding interracial sex, see, for example, Phillip D. Morgan's essay "Interracial Sex in the Chesapeake and the British Atlantic World, c. 1700–1820." Morgan suggests that interracial sex was tolerated, even "fashionable," in Jamaica but was held in contempt in the colonial United States.

11. White, *Our New Possessions*, 265.

12. Ibid., 371.

13. Debroise, *Mexican Suite*, 45.

14. Wright, *Picturesque Mexico*, 380.

15. These works, titled *Picturesque Mexico* and simply *Mexico*, are so bald in their effusive praise of Mexico, Díaz, his advisors, and the women of *la clase alta* and so lavishly produced that one wonders whether Wright was working for the Mexican government.

16. Travelers from the U.S. Southwest would have had some firsthand experience with Mexican racial difference, but the vast majority of travel writers examined here came from the Midwest or the Eastern Seaboard. This is probably because the uniting of rail lines in the 1880s inspired a number of travelers from the U.S. interior to make the trek south of the border.

17. Omi and Winant, *Racial Formation*, 56.

18. For a more extensive discussion of "pure" versus "political" knowledge, see Said, *Orientalism*, 9–15.

19. Omi and Winant, *Racial Formation*, 71; emphasis in original.

20. It has always been difficult to count the number of indigenous Mexicans, as writers acknowledged even during the Porfiriato. "These figures are only approximately accurate," wrote James Dale in 1910 regarding his estimate of the Indian population, "for the Indians of the remote mountain districts shun the census gatherer, suspecting that the government is seeking to impose an extra tax." Dale, *Mexico and Our Mission*, 19.

21. Said, *Orientalism*, 206.

22. Turner, *Barbarous Mexico*, 289.

23. For a fascinating interpretation of *The North American Indian*, see Gidley, in *Edward S. Curtis and the North American Indian, Incorporated*, who calls the project "the largest anthropological enterprise ever undertaken" (3). Gidley also points out that Curtis was part of a bigger—though often uncredited—team of ethnologists, Native American informants, and technicians. Thus, when I write of Edward S. Curtis, I really refer to the team of people that Gidley calls "The North American Indian, Incorporated."

24. Harris, *Travel-Talks*, 1–2.

25. McCaa, "The Peopling of Mexico," 277.

26. Dozens of such postcards are reproduced in Montellano's *C. B. Waite: La época de oro de las postales en México*, which, unlike the Montellano volume mentioned above, focuses specifically on Waite's picture postcards.

27. Terry, *Terry's Guide to Mexico*, 1909 edition, lxxx. This sentiment persisted until at least the 1938 edition (the most recent that I have consulted), as the same text appeared through many subsequent editions of Terry's famous guide.

28. G. Brown, *Tour of the 400*, 37.

29. Morris, *A Tour in Mexico*, 310.

30. Garland-Thomson, *Staring: How We Look*, 6.

31. Tweedie, *Mexico as I Saw It*, 230.

32. Ibid., 278.

33. Ibid.

34. Ibid., 156.

35. Ibid., 158.

36. Ibid., 73. Tweedie goes on to say in this passage that if "mere animal existence [is] a joy, the native Mexican has surely reached Elysium."

37. Jenks, "Centrality of the Eye," 1.

38. Starr, preface (no page number) to *In Indian Mexico*. Another Starr book, *The Physical Characters of the Indians of Southern Mexico* (1902), exhaustively details the anthropologist's 1890s fieldwork by illustrating his methods and findings through prose, photographs, and scientific-looking charts. In this book, which opens with a color skin chart drawn from Franz Boas, Indian physical difference becomes the object of intense clinical scrutiny. I am particularly struck by the fact that the camera explicitly served as an anthropometric tool throughout Starr's work.

39. See Foucault's *Birth of the Clinic*.

40. See correspondence between Lummis and Starr archived at the Braun Research Library, part of the Autry National Center for the Study of the American West.

41. Starr, *In Indian Mexico*, 396.

42. Ibid., 398.

43. This should not suggest, however, that the boundaries of whiteness were ever fully enforced in the legal or popular arenas. Mixed-race people, for example, have challenged the supposedly clear distinctions between the white and the non-white throughout U.S. history, as have entire national and ethnic groups (such as Japanese-, Arab-, Jewish-, and Mexican-Americans) whose relationship to whiteness is ambiguous.

44. The idea that Indians were a fallen race because of Spanish colonialism demands scholarly attention beyond what I can devote here. Many travelers who went to Mexico around 1898 used the "fallen" status of Indian people to decry Spanish colonialism as a particularly brutal mode of domination—and as an argument for war against Spain to "liberate" its colonial possessions in the Caribbean and the Pacific.

45. Or, "God wants it." Bourke, "The American Congo," 607.

46. Shah, *Contagious Divides*, 10.

47. For a particularly insightful interpretation of the Pears' ads, see McClintock, *Imperial Leather*.

48. Carson, *Mexico: Wonderland of the South*, 195.

49. See Montellano, *C. B. Waite, fotógrafo*, 41.

50. Tweedie, *Mexico as I Saw It*, 73.

51. Conkling, *Mexico and the Mexicans*, 121.

52. Ibid., 163.

53. Bederman, *Manliness and Civilization*, 25.

54. *Los Angeles Times*, April 18, 1909. Clipping archived at the Braun Research Library.

55. Starr, "Physical Characters," 82.

56. Tweedie, *Mexico as I Saw It*, 451. Not surprisingly, Tweedie focuses more on business opportunities than on beauty in this section of the book. The isthmus, only

125 miles at its narrowest point, was then the best route for transporting goods between the Atlantic and the Pacific Oceans.

57. Campbell, *Mexico: Tours through the Egypt of the New World*, 77–78.

58. Said, *Orientalism*, 207. This is a useful framework for understanding the politics of representing Indian women in Porfirian Mexico, but my research departs from Said's view of Orientalism as "an exclusively male domain." As addressed throughout this book, American women contributed greatly to travel discourse and the view that Mexico was a conquerable (in both economic and sexual senses) domain.

59. "The Poor in Mexico," *Los Angeles Times*, September 22, 1901, 4R.

60. Carson, *Mexico: Wonderland of the South*, 192–193.

61. *Los Angeles Times*, November 12, 1905. Clipping archived at the Braun Research Library.

62. "Playing the bear" refers to the custom of a young man's persistent public courtship of a young woman in Mexico, which included romantic gestures such as serenades and visits to the woman's balcony. The intended end of this protracted set of actions was marriage. Illustrations and descriptions of Mexicans playing the bear appear in a wide variety of travel discourse. Almost every travelogue devotes at least a few lines (or pictures) to the custom, and images of young men playing the bear illustrate countless postcards dating from the first decade of the twentieth century. Typically, the young woman is protected by a barred window but gamely encourages a man who strums a guitar or offers tokens of his affections.

63. Ober, *Travels in Mexico*, 279. As we will see later, Ober counted lighter-skinned mestizos among the "better classes" and predicted that Indian difference would disappear altogether through a form of racial Darwinism.

64. Dale, *Mexico and Our Mission*, 31.

65. When this image was published as a hand-colored picture postcard, Waite's identifying information was cropped out of the frame. A print archived at the De-Golyer Library at Southern Methodist University affirms this photograph as one of Waite's.

66. Terry, *Terry's Guide to Mexico*, lx.

67. Sherratt, *Mexican Vistas*, 85.

68. Morrill, *The Devil in Mexico*, 119.

69. The author, journalist David Goodman Croly, claimed to be an abolitionist promoting marriage across black-white racial lines. He published the pamphlet anonymously.

70. Scholars of African American studies have, of course, long traced desire in representations of black subjects, but I am interested here in overt, public declarations of the Indian body as desirable for the white gaze. In particular, I am interested in whether travel writers could overtly construct the Indian as desirable for white readers.

71. Flippin, *Sketches*, 39; emphasis in original.

72. Sherratt, *Mexican Vistas*, 106.

73. Flippin, *Sketches*, 40.

74. Ibid.

75. Creelman, "President Diaz," 240.

76. Ibid., 241.

77. Mayer, *Mexico as It Was*, 170–171; emphasis in original.

78. Lummis, *Awakening of a Nation*, 5.

79. Creelman, "Underlying Causes," 601–602.

80. Ibid., 603.

81. Ibid., 607. Curiously, Creelman more explicitly addressed black suffrage at the beginning of the article. "The American people look on complacently," he wrote, "while their negro fellow citizens are deprived of their constitutional right to vote in order that the supremacy of the white race may be insured in Southern states. Even the descendents of the New England abolitionists have come virtually to acquiesce in the situation, recognizing the fact that white men will not consent to live under a negro government. Toleration of this practice has become in this sense a national policy" (ibid., 597). This might appear to be an antiracist harangue on Creelman's part, but it soon becomes clear that the writer is making an argument that suspending the rights of nonwhite people is politically expedient and ultimately benefits the nation. He also seems to want to point out the hypocrisy of Americans who supported the democracy movement in Mexico.

82. This is true despite the fact that, as Nicole M. Guidotti-Hernández has shown, Mexico explicitly followed U.S. Indian policy as a model, with its policies against the Yaqui the potent symbol of its oppression of native people. While the topic of Mexican governmental suppression and aggression against native people is beyond the scope of this book, it must be noted that the Porfirian regime did mimic U.S. strategies to contain native peoples as well as North American ideas about eugenics and white supremacy, which guided Díaz's many ill-fated attempts to attract permanent white colonies in Mexico.

83. Bourke, "The American Congo," 592.

84. Carson, *Mexico: Wonderland of the South*, 187.

85. Ober, *Travels in Mexico*, 275.

86. Rice, *Mexico: Our Neighbor*, 24.

87. Carson, *Mexico: Wonderland of the South*, 193.

88. I cannot help but note here a parallel between this view of Mexican Indianness and constructions of white womanhood in the United States. In the north, many men (and, to be fair, many women as well) posited that white women possessed positive qualities but were not "ready" for full citizenship. Still, despite this parallel, this book has shown that white women travelers from the United States, such as Susan Hale, routinely engaged in this infantilizing mode of representation.

89. S. Hale, *Mexico*, 412.

90. Prendergast, "Railroads in Mexico," 276.

91. Enock, *Mexico*, 257.

92. Porfirian treatment of the Yaqui was the subject of much of Turner's exposé, *Barbarous Mexico*. On Mexican and U.S. violence against the Yaqui, see Guidotti-Hernández.

93. Blake, *Mexico: Picturesque, Political, Progressive*, 80.

94. Morris, *A Tour in Mexico*, 80.

95. Carson, *Mexico: Wonderland of the South*, 187–188.

96. Ibid., 187.

97. See Briquet Album, Image No. 30, Benson Latin American Collection.

98. Darton, "Mexico—The Treasure House," 495.

99. Here I use the term "rationalization" in the Weberian sense, to refer to the push to make the work performed by native people more specialized and efficient. Weber and many who followed him noted that rationalization of labor led to a re-organization of work and life, helping to make the rationalized worker a more modern person.

100. Foster, "The New Mexico," 24.

101. Foucault, *Discipline and Punish*, 136.

102. White, *Our New Possessions*, 371; emphasis mine.

103. "A New Western Empire," *Los Angeles Times*, November 28, 1909.

104. Anti-Catholicism reached its peak in the United States as immigration from Europe increased in the mid- to late nineteenth century. While this is beyond the scope of the study at hand, it is clear that anti-Catholic sentiments were already in place in the hearts and minds of American observers of Catholic Mexico.

105. Durham, "Characteristic," 502.

106. Wells, "A Bit of Mexico," 14.

107. Pascoe, quoted in Haven, *Our Next-Door Neighbor*, 464.

108. Haven, *Our Next-Door Neighbor*, 105.

109. Turner, *Barbarous Mexico*, 283. Turner claims, "If the rulers of the land had been enlightened and had given the Mexican the barest glimpse of brightness outside the church the sway of the priest might have been less pronounced than it is today" (283).

110. McLynn, *Villa and Zapata*, 11.

111. Garner, *Porfirio Díaz*, 121.

112. Ibid., 122. As Garner notes, this strategy would eventually backfire, as Protestant pastors, critical of the dictator's various conciliations to the Catholic Church (as well as other inhumane and antidemocratic policies), played a prominent role in the Mexican Revolution.

113. Durham, "Characteristic," 503.

114. Hale, *Mexico*, 414.

115. Dale, *Mexico and Our Mission*, 90.

116. See Debroise, *Mexican Suite*, for further analysis of the uses of the studio portrait in Mexican self-fashioning.

117. Dale, *Mexico and Our Mission*, 133.

118. Strong, *Our Country*, 28. Wendy J. Deichmann Edwards notes that *Our Country* sold 175,000 copies in the 1880s, attesting to Strong's popularity as an authority on the civilizing power of mission work (Edwards, "Forging an Ideology for American Missions," 191).

119. M. Romero, *Geographical and Statistical Notes*, 76.

CHAPTER FOUR

1. Sanborn, *A Winter in Central America*, 228.

2. It is perhaps more accurate to say that the tragic mulatto's popularity book-ended the Porfiriato, since a number of books and plays appeared from the 1840s to the 1860s (e.g., Lydia Marie Child's "The Quadroons" [1842] and "Slavery's Pleasant Homes" [1843], short stories credited with establishing the genre; William Wells Brown's *Clotel, or The President's Daughter* [1853]) and again in the 1910s and 1920s

(e.g., the infamous portrayal of racial mixing in the film *The Birth of a Nation* [1915]; the musical *Showboat*, which premiered in New York in 1927; Nella Larsen's *Quicksand* and *Passing*, also in the late 1920s). *Iola Leroy*, one of the first novels written by an African American woman, appeared in 1892 and closely followed the tragic mulatto genre, as did other popular texts from around this time. The trope of the tragic mulatta was already firmly established and would have tremendous staying power in American popular culture, lingering until at least the late 1950s, when Douglas Sirk made the second film adaptation of Fanny Hurst's *Imitation of Life*.

3. Along with other scholars, Annette Gordon-Reed's work on the Hemings family and its relationship to Thomas Jefferson illuminates the mixed-race origins of the United States. The fact that the Hemings-Jefferson case still incites debate and controversy speaks to the long endurance of denials of race mixing in American history.

4. Historians of race are careful to remind us that Mexican racism against people of mixed African origin has been long-standing, powerful, and pervasive. Baltasar Fra Molinero has argued that in "the racially mixed Mexican society of the first part of the 18th century Mulattoes and Blacks stood out as the object of most acts of repression on the part of the civil and ecclesiastical authorities." See http://abacus.bates.edu/~bframoli/pagina/alegria.html.

5. McCarty, *Two Thousand Miles*, 215.

6. Roediger, *How Race Survived*, 151.

7. Darwin, cited in Said, *Orientalism*, 201.

8. See Galton, *Inquiries into Human Faculty and Its Development*.

9. As Shawn Michelle Smith shows in *American Archives*, Galton made use of photographs to mark and catalogue human difference. In this way, the visual artifacts created by travelers to Porfirian Mexico resemble those produced by Galton and his field workers.

10. García Cubas, *Republic of Mexico*, 61. García Cubas goes on to give several examples of tribes that have rapidly decreased in population and then to detail causes of this decline, including bad child-bearing and -rearing practices, their resistance to vaccination, and premature marriage. Not surprisingly, each of these factors was closely related to modern subjecthood. Overall, García Cubas seems to claim that Indian people were facing extinction because they could not adapt to modernity. As he put it, "If we consider the Indian from the time he is born or even before his birth, we shall only find a series of lamentable wretchedness" (ibid., 62).

11. Ibid., 128; emphasis in original.

12. Terry, *Terry's Guide to Mexico*, lx.

13. García Cubas, *Republic of Mexico*, 129.

14. Ober, *Travels in Mexico*, 272.

15. Chicana scholarship on Malinche is too extensive to recount here, so it must suffice to point out that Chicana feminist scholarship (and, significantly, Chicana feminist art) has attempted to recast the story with Malintzin as, in Candelaria's terms, a "feminist prototype." Likewise, queer scholars have challenged Paz's subtle homophobia in the assertion that to be fucked inherently means to be dominated, humiliated, and defeated. Fine examples of revisionist interpretations of the Malinche story appear in Rolando Romero and Amanda Nolacea Harris's edited volume *Feminism, Nation and Myth: La Malinche*.

16. Ober, *Travels in Mexico*, 280.

17. The woman known as Pocahontas did, of course, bear a mixed-race child with her English husband, John Rolfe. Thomas Rolfe was born in 1615. Despite the fact that an extraordinary number of people in the United States claim descent from Thomas Rolfe and millions claim some trace of Indian ancestry, mixed-race Native American heritage does not have the same political meaning as it does in Mexico, where mestizos belong to the dominant racial group both in terms of size and political/social power.

18. Creelman, "President Diaz," 251.

19. One surprising exception to the oversimplification of *mestizaje* is found in the guidebook *Terry's Guide to Mexico*, which quotes a pamphlet from the International Bureau of American Republics, stating, "The Mexican of to-day has the blood of more races in his veins than any other American. Iberian, Semite, Hamite, Goth and Vandal, Roman and Celt, mingled their blood in that stream of brave and adventurous men who first set eyes on Yucatan in 1517, and who conquered Mexico in 1522. Like Spain from the remotest time, Mexico soon became the meeting-ground of races, of peoples, of languages, and of religion" (1911 edition, lxi).

20. See David Eng's *Racial Castration* for an in-depth study of racialized masculinity.

21. Caballeros, *charros*, and similar cultural figures were closer to middle-class travelers' own social standings, values, and norms than were peons. Still, with very few exceptions, mestizo men seem to have been off-limits as objects of desire for traveling men and women. Of course, I can only account for travelers' narratives and not their actual sexual practices.

22. Ober, *Travels in Mexico*, 43. Several editions of this book, which Ober copyrighted in 1883, circulated throughout the 1880s. I refer here to the 1887 edition published by Estes and Lauriat of Boston.

23. It is pertinent to point out that dozens of line drawings illustrate Ober's book, many of them depicting Mexican women. There seems to be, however, a sharp divide between women marked as Indian and women from *la clase alta* in these images. The women described as "beautiful" are distinctly light-skinned and European in appearance. One such drawing, apparently adapted from a photograph, depicts what Ober calls "the beautiful creole" standing in what looks like a window, wearing jewels and a tightly corseted Victorian dress (277). Similarly pink-cheeked and well-dressed women adorn the cover of *Travels in Mexico*. So while Ober championed *mestizaje*, and mestizas in particular, the illustrations seem to omit the physical presence of mestizas by focusing on the opposite ends of the hierarchy of race and class that defined Mexican society.

24. Ober, *Travels in Mexico*, 280.

25. M. Bianet Castellanos has pointed out to me that, in the context of the Yucatán, the term *mestizo* does not always refer to people of mixed ancestry but might refer to a native person who wears certain folk costumes. While this is true, my emphasis in this chapter is on *American* representations of mestizos and *mestizaje*. Since Darton referred explicitly to racial admixture in his description of these photographs, it is fair to assume that he meant "mestizo" in the sense that I use it throughout this book. See also Gabbert's *Becoming Maya*.

26. Ober, *Travels in Mexico*, 281.

27. García Cubas, *Republic of Mexico*, 16.

28. McCarty, *Two Thousand Miles*, 215.

29. García Cubas, *Republic of Mexico*, 5-6.

CHAPTER FIVE

1. Von Keck, "Mexico of To-day," 245.

2. One might presume that the obsessive focus on impoverished Mexicans could be read as a critique of the regime, but almost every writer examined here saw Díaz's policies as the way to lift the majority of Mexicans out of poverty. In other words, they saw Díaz as the solution to a problem that predated his rule, ignoring the fact that the gulf between rich and poor Mexicans actually widened during the Porfiriato.

3. Von Keck, "Mexico of To-day," 245.

4. This is true even of Díaz supporters who otherwise spoke out against oppression of native people in the United States. The tireless booster Charles F. Lummis is a good example of this. In the first few years of the twentieth century, Lummis published a series of articles sharply criticizing U.S. policy toward the Hopi and other tribes of the Southwest, especially in the wake of a 1901 Supreme Court decision allowing the removal of three hundred native people from the area around Warner's Ranch, California (published in his *Out West* magazine and compiled in 1968 as *Bullying the Moqui*). Despite Lummis's deeply felt commitment to defend native people from ongoing U.S. aggression and colonialism, he, like many other writers of the time, chose to ignore Díaz's oppression of the Yaqui and other indigenous groups in Mexico. In Creelman's famous article, Díaz identified the Yaqui and the Maya as the two tribes that remained hostile to his nation-building efforts.

5. "Gen. Diaz Departs and Warns Mexico," *New York Times*, June 1, 1911.

6. Pearson was the owner of Pearson Conglomerate, a leading construction firm in the United Kingdom that eventually came to control several important companies and large swaths of land in Mexico. In 1889, Díaz invited him to Mexico to build a transoceanic rail line. While laying track, his crew discovered one of the world's largest oil fields, the Potrero del Llano. He created the Mexican Eagle Petroleum company, which became one of Mexico's largest firms. Amazingly, the Aguila Company, as it was known, survived the ouster of Díaz and actually became more profitable after 1910, as its heavy investments in the petroleum infrastructure began to pay off.

7. Though Porfirio Díaz never fulfilled his vow to return to his native land, his wife Carmen did return to Mexico City in 1934. She remained there until her death ten years later.

8. Turner, *Barbarous Mexico*, 149.

9. Creelman, "President Diaz," 242.

10. Garner, *Porfirio Díaz*, 213.

11. It would be difficult to overestimate the significance of the revolution, a social, political, and cultural reformation that reverberated far beyond Mexico itself. Mexican migration to the United States—a massive movement of people that I will address in this book's conclusion—is just one of the many ways that the revolution's effects were felt beyond Mexico's borders.

12. Palmer, "What It All Means in Mexico," 815.

13. See Rone, *A History*, 339–341. Rone, a devout Baptist, lamented Morrill's "misused brilliant intellect" and claimed that Morrill would resort to "anything that could be done to secure a crowd" in his "church theater." He also noted, "Because of such pretentious displays [as speaking on the lecture circuit, officiating at stunt weddings, etc.] he was denied admittance into the self-respecting churches."

14. As documented in a photograph held by the Minnesota Historical Association (GT4.81 p80).

15. I, for one, was not convinced that, with a name like Golightly Morrill (and a son named Lowell Morrill), Morrill was a real person until I came across evidence documenting his life at the Minnesota Historical Society. All doubts were dispelled when, well into my dissertation research, one of Morrill's descendents contacted me. He had found online the details of a talk that I gave on Morrill's work in 2005. I subsequently interviewed the wife of Morrill's deceased grandson and other descendents in Minneapolis.

16. Morrill's popularity is difficult to quantify, but several pieces of evidence suggest that he was a somewhat well-known figure in the United States. These include the wide-scale dissemination of his travelogues (they are still held in the general collections of libraries across the United States), the fact that popular presses published them and mainstream companies advertised in them, the suspicions that he aroused in prominent government officials such as John Lind (as we will see), and the fact that national newspapers reported on Morrill's exploits and his death in 1928.

17. I do not want to overstate the agency of the women featured in this image, but it is possible that their expressions reflect a subtle mode of resistance to the white men with the camera. They appear neither delighted to see the camera nor amused by the interruption.

18. Notably, the images that appear in the back pages of Morrill's later travelogues do not correspond with the theme of the books. This suggests that the author or his publishers saw the advertising section as a sort of free-for-all in which the most provocative images from all of Morrill's travels might appear.

19. This image appears later in the book with the caption "A Mexican Landscape," identified as Charcas in the state of San Luis Potosí. Morrill wrote that "I shot him with the Kodak though he was already dead" (*The Devil in Mexico*, 159).

20. These "Morrillisms" are perhaps only comical in intent (or in retrospect), but funny or not, they are undeniably over-the-top. Some typically juicy examples include: "Intervention eventually, why not now?"; "The Mexican face is an open book where low appetite is written in big, bold letters"; "Mexican people and insects are noxious and obnoxious"; and, to summarize, "What's the matter with Mexico? Everything!" Some are downright threatening, such as, "Make the Mexican who insults the Stars and Stripes wear stripes and 'see stars.'" The book goes on like this for thirty-six pages. Certainly, Morrill's thoughts might be dismissed as the work of one eccentric provocateur, but his popularity as a speaker and writer suggests that he was not too far from mainstream perceptions of Mexico.

21. *Minneapolis Journal*, January 1, 1918.

22. Buckley would go on to live and work in Mexico until 1921, when he was expelled by the Obregón government. In the meantime, he rose to prominence as an expert on Mexico, testifying before the U.S. Senate Subcommittee on Foreign Rela-

tions as an expert on that country in 1919. Five years earlier, Victoriano Huerta had appointed Buckley as a Mexican delegate to the Niagara Falls Peace Conference, in which Argentina, Brazil, and Colombia mediated peace between the United States and Mexico.

23. Morrill, *The Devil in Mexico*, 133. Here "U.S." refers to "Uncle Sam."

24. John Lind, quoted in Morrill, *On the Warpath*, 18. The possibility that Mexico could partner with Germany was a matter of great concern to the U.S. government and body politic in 1917. In January of that year, the United States intercepted the infamous Zimmerman Telegram, which proposed an alliance between Germany and Mexico should the United States enter World War I.

25. Morrill, *The Devil in Mexico*, 134.

26. Morrill, *On the Warpath*, 28.

27. The title *On the Warpath* cleverly refers to both a stereotypical view of Indian country and Morrill's own battles with censorship.

28. Morrill, *On the Warpath*, 7.

29. It also begs the question of whether Morrill thought that his book had been suppressed because of its sexual or its political content. Although Morrill professed throughout the book that he had been singled out because he dared to criticize the government, this passage uses the sexual skittishness of the "fig-leaf fanatics" to underscore his point. Perhaps this represents a subtle admission on Morrill's part that his depictions of native women inspired a sexual gaze rather than a morally outraged one. Either way, this short passage does illustrate that, despite his outrageous prose and subject matter, Morrill was nonetheless an erudite writer.

30. Morrill, *On the Warpath*, 24.

31. *Los Angeles Times*, December 13, 1928.

32. Sherratt, *Mexican Vistas*, 166.

33. Rees, *Spain's Lost Jewels*, 106–107.

34. Ibid., 108.

35. Dale, *Mexico and Our Mission*, 12.

36. Morrill, *The Devil in Mexico*, 117.

37. Ibid., 117.

38. Tweedie, *Mexico as I Saw It* (1911 edition), 245. Importantly, Tweedie couched her warning in boosterism that was typical during the Porfiriato. "But for any lad with a good business head and some training," she continued, "there are many openings."

39. Morrill, *The Devil in Mexico*, 104–105.

40. Granted, one might read Waite's images from the *decena trágica* as a critique of the revolution, but Waite never explicitly criticized Mexico, even after the Porfiriato came to a close.

41. Morrill, *The Devil in Mexico*, 105.

42. Morrill, preface to *The Devil in Mexico*, no page number.

43. Díaz and León de la Barra were not political adversaries, but the Treaty of Ciudad Juárez, which ended the first stage of the Mexican Revolution, called for León de la Barra to assume the presidency until elections could be held later in 1911.

44. Creelman, "Underlying Causes," 596–597.

45. "The Mexican" first appeared in the *Saturday Evening Post* on August 19, 1911, but has been reprinted in dozens of anthologies and collections since its initial publication. It was filmed in 1952 as *The Fighter* (Herbert Kline, dir.).

46. London, "With Funston's Men," 145.

47. Jack London, quoted in Reesman, *Jack London's Racial Lives*, 280.

48. Jeanne Campbell Reesman provides a fascinating account of the author's constantly shifting and contradictory views on race in *Jack London's Racial Lives*. As Reesman's biography shows, London held deeply conflicted views on race. Though the author was raised in part by an African-American neighbor and former slave, a woman to whom he dedicated several books, he also boasted again and again about his Anglo-Saxon pedigree.

49. Reprinted at http://carl-bell-2.baylor.edu/~bellc/JL/TheTroubleMakersOf Mexico.html. London writes of mestizos that "they are what the mixed breed always is—neither fish, flesh, nor fowl. They are neither the white men nor Indians."

50. "The stern stuff is in the pure-blooded Indians," London conceded, "but it manifests itself all too rarely, else it would be impossible for the many millions of Indians to have endured slavery for four hundred years at the hands of their tiny groups of masters" (http://carl-bell-2.baylor.edu/~bellc/JL/TheTroubleMakersOf Mexico.html).

51. More than that, the reference to the "Macedonian cry," which, in turn, is a reference to Acts 16:6–10, figures economic conquest as a religious mission that resonates with Morrill's evangelicalism.

52. Morrill, *The Devil in Mexico*, 132.

53. Pérez, "Incurring a Debt of Gratitude," 362.

54. This is more than two years before the famous "Punitive Expedition," in which Pershing and his troops sought to punish Pancho Villa and his men for raids on Columbus, New Mexico.

55. Morrill, *The Devil in Mexico*, 125.

56. Soldiers stationed along the U.S.-Mexico border also made a habit of posing with hanged insurrectionists and other dead Mexicans. As Vanderwood and Samponaro's *Border Fury* shows, soldiers sent these postcards home in large numbers. Vanderwood has argued in *The Americas* that picture postcards serve as important historical evidence of the actions of U.S. militarymen in Veracruz and, more broadly, of the occupation itself.

57. Vanderwood and Samponaro, *Border Fury*, 154.

58. The connections between sexual domination and military occupation were again made clear ninety years later, in the 2004 scandal surrounding prisoner abuse at Abu Ghraib prison in Iraq. In this more recent case, U.S. troops stationed at Abu Ghraib were accused of raping, torturing, and killing Iraqi prisoners. Once again, visual culture played an important role in the affair, for photographs of sexualized prisoner abuse (especially those of Army reservist Lynndie England posing in front of shackled, hooded, and naked prisoners who were forced to masturbate and engage in other sexual humiliations) inspired public outcry regarding Iraq and the politics of occupation. The U.S. occupation of Veracruz produced no explicit photographs or sexual scandals, but we might nonetheless acknowledge that in both instances sexualized visions of the natives helped affirm American power.

59. As Vanderwood and Samponaro point out, "'amo' . . . might be shorthand for 'te amo'—'I love you,' or 'amo' could also mean 'master'" (*Border Fury*, 155).

60. This postcard is mentioned by Vanderwood in *Border Fury* and in his article in *The Americas*. Needless to say, the Americans still living in the Veracruz area were

not so amused by the events of 1914. Thousands were forced to flee as anti-American sentiment made their presence there untenable. Overall, more than 60,000 Americans evacuated Mexico as a result of the occupation and its aftermath (*Border Fury*, 150). According to historian John Eisenhower, prior to the Tampico incident, "American lives and American commercial interests did not seem threatened by any of the factions fighting in Mexico" (*Intervention!* 79). The Tampico incident and subsequent occupation of Veracruz represent a shift in U.S.-Mexico relations and the end of any hope of continuing the economic conquest. In just a matter of months, the processes that I have described in previous chapters of this book were undone.

61. Palmer, "Watchful Perspiring at Vera Cruz," 66.

62. Palmer worked as a war correspondent over an astonishingly long fifty-year career, spanning from the Greco-Turkish War to the atomic bomb tests off the Bikini atoll in 1946 (see Haverstock, *Fifty Years at the Front*). He also published several novels and an autobiography.

63. Palmer, "The American Spirit in Veracruz," 806.

64. Palmer, "What It All Means in Mexico," 816.

65. Palmer, "Watchful Perspiring at Vera Cruz," 68.

66. Palmer, "What It All Means in Mexico," 814.

67. Palmer, "The American Spirit in Vera Cruz," 807.

68. Palmer, "What It All Means in Mexico," 820.

69. Palmer, "Watchful Perspiring at Vera Cruz," 66.

CONCLUSION

1. González and Fernandez, *A Century of Chicano History*, 68.

2. Carpenter, *Mexico*, 212.

3. Ibid.

4. The Benson Latin American Collection at the University of Texas holds several personal scrapbooks from the 1920s and 1930s in which Americans appear dressed as Mexicans. The Stumpf album, described in Chapter Two, is one of them.

5. See http://www.timesonline.co.uk/tol/news/world/us_and_americas/article 7061705.ece.

BIBLIOGRAPHY

ARCHIVES AND LIBRARIES

Braun Research Library, Autry National Center, Los Angeles
Center for Southwest Research Pictorial Collections, University of New Mexico
Centro de Estudios de Historia de México, Mexico City
DeGolyer Library, Southern Methodist University, Dallas
    Lawrence T. Jones III Texas Photographs Collection
Getty Research Institute, Los Angeles
    Special Collections
Harry Ransom Humanities Research Center, University of Texas at Austin
    Jimmy Hare Lantern Slide Collection
Library of Congress, Washington, D.C.
Library Special Collections, Texas State University at San Marcos
    Southwestern and Mexican Photography Collection
Minnesota Historical Society, St. Paul
Mudd Library, Yale University, New Haven
National Museum of American History, Smithsonian Institution, Washington, D.C.
    Warshaw Collection of Business Americana
Nettie Lee Benson Latin American Collection, University of Texas at Austin
    Abel Briquet Photographs (Brisbin Photo Album), c. 1887
    Albert J. Schmidt Collection of Lantern Slides, c. 1904–1921
    Black Photograph Collection No. 1363B
    Chase Littlejohn Photograph Album, c. 1900–1925
    Ella K. Daggett Stumpf Photograph Album, 1902
    James E. Long Photograph Collection, c. 1907–1919
    Mexican Views, 1885
    Miscellaneous Photographs
    Orion and Lillian G. Beebe Album, c. 1925–1930
    P. S. Glenn Photograph Album, 1913
    Rene D'Harnoncourt Photograph Collection, 1900–1925
    Tabasco Rubber Plantation Photograph Collection, c. 1904

PUBLISHED MATERIALS

Acuña, Rodolfo. *Occupied America: A History of Chicanos.* 5th ed. New York: Longman Publishing, 2003.
Aguirre, Robert D. *Informal Empire: Mexico and Central America in Victorian Culture.* Minneapolis: University of Minnesota Press, 2005.
Alarcón, Daniel Cooper. *The Aztec Palimpsest: Mexico in the Modern Imagination.* Tucson: University of Arizona Press, 1997.

Albers, Patricia, and William James. "Travel Photography: A Methodological Approach." *Annals of Tourism Research* 15, no. 1 (1988): 134–158.

Alloula, Malek. *The Colonial Harem.* Translated by Myrna Godzich and Wlad Godzich. Minneapolis: University of Minnesota Press, 1986.

American Studies: An Anthology. Edited by Janice A. Radway, Kevin K. Gaines, Barry Shank, and Penny von Eschen. Hoboken, NJ: Wiley Blackwell, 2009.

Anderson, Benedict. *Imagined Communities: Reflections on the Origin and Spread of Nationalism.* London: Verso, 1983.

Anderson, Mark C. "'What's to Be Done with 'Em?' Images of Mexican Cultural Backwardness, Racial Limitations, and Moral Decrepitude in the United States Press, 1913–1915." *Mexican Studies/Estudios Mexicanos* 14, no. 1 (Winter 1998): 23–70.

Anzaldúa, Gloria. *Borderlands/La Frontera: The New Mestiza.* 2nd ed. San Francisco: Aunt Lute Books, 1999.

Aubertin, J. J. *A Flight to Mexico.* London: Kegan Paul, Trench, Trubner, 1882.

Ballou, Maturin M. *Aztec Land.* Boston and New York: Houghton Mifflin, 1890.

Barron, Clarence W. *The Mexican Problem.* Boston and New York: Houghton Mifflin, 1917.

Barthes, Roland. *Camera Lucida.* Translated by Richard Howard. New York: Hill and Wang, 1981.

———. *Image, Music, Text.* Translated by Stephen Heath. New York: Hill and Wang, 1977.

Bederman, Gail. *Manliness and Civilization: A Cultural History of Gender and Race in the United States, 1880–1917.* Chicago: University of Chicago Press, 1995.

Beecroft, John. *Kipling: A Selection of His Stories and Poems.* New York: Doubleday, 1956.

Beezley, William. *Judas at the Jockey Club and Other Episodes of Porfirian Mexico.* 2nd ed. Lincoln: University of Nebraska Press, 2004 (1987).

Bender, Steven W. *Greasers and Gringos: Latinos, Law, and the American Imagination.* New York: NYU Press, 2003.

Benham, George A. "They Carry Loads." *Los Angeles Times,* September 24, 1899.

Benjamin, Thomas, and Marcial Ocasio-Meléndez. "Organizing the Memory of Modern Mexico: Porfirian Historiography in Perspective, 1880s–1980s." *Hispanic American Historical Review* 64, no. 2 (1984): 323–364.

Berger, Dina. *The Development of Mexico's Tourism Industry: Pyramids by Day, Martinis by Night.* New York: Palgrave Macmillan Press, 2006.

Berger, Dina, and Andrew Grant Wood, eds. *Holiday in Mexico: Critical Reflections on Tourism and the Tourist Encounters.* Durham: Duke University Press, 2010.

Berkhofer, Robert F., Jr. *The White Man's Indian: Images of the American Indian from Columbus to the Present.* New York: Alfred A. Knopf, 1978.

Birkinbine, John. "Our Neighbor, Mexico." *National Geographic* 22, May 1911, 475–508.

Bishop, William Henry. *Old Mexico and Her Lost Provinces.* New York: Harper and Brothers, 1883.

Blake, Mary Elizabeth, and Margaret F. Sullivan. *Mexico: Picturesque, Political, Progressive.* Boston: Lee and Shepard, 1888.

Bourdieu, Pierre. *Practical Reason.* Stanford: Stanford University Press, 1998.

Bourke, John G. "The American Congo." *Scribner's Magazine* 15, no. 5, May 1894, 591–610.

Brady, Mary Pat. "The Fungibility of Borders." *Nepantla: Views from the South* 1, no. 1 (2000): 171–190.

Brennan, Mary Caroline Estes. "American and British Travelers in Mexico, 1822–1846." Ph.D. diss., University of Texas, 1973.

Briggs, Laura. *Reproducing Empire: Race, Sex, Science, and U.S. Imperialism in Puerto Rico.* Berkeley: University of California Press, 2002.

Britton, John A. *Revolution and Ideology: Images of the Mexican Revolution in the United States.* Lexington: University Press of Kentucky, 1995.

Brown, Grace Owen. *The Tour of the 400 to Mexico.* Chicago: Hartzell, Lord, 1907.

Brown, Jonathan C. "Foreign and Native-Born Workers in Porfirian Mexico." *American Historical Review* 98, no. 3 (June 1993): 786–818.

Caballero, Manuel. *México en Chicago.* Chicago: Knight, Leonard, 1893.

Calderón de la Barca, Frances. *Life in Mexico during a Residence of Two Years in That Country.* New York: E. P. Dutton, 1941 (first published in Boston and London, 1843).

Campbell, Reau. *Campbell's New Revised Complete Guide and Descriptive Book of Mexico.* Chicago: Rogers and Smith, 1909.

———. *Mexico: Tours through the Egypt of the New World.* New York: C. G. Crawford, 1890.

Candelaria, Cordelia. "La Malinche, Feminist Prototype." *Frontiers: A Journal of Women's Studies* 5, no. 2 (Summer 1980): 1–6.

Cantú, Lionel. "Border Crossings: Mexican Men and the Sexuality of Migration." Ph.D. diss., University of California-Irvine, 1999.

———. "De Ambiente: Queer Tourism and the Shifting Boundaries of Mexican Male Sexualities." *GLQ: A Journal of Lesbian and Gay Studies* 8, no. 1–2 (2002): 139–166.

Cardoso, Lawrence A. *Mexican Migration to the United States, 1897-1910.* Tucson: University of Arizona Press, 1980.

Carnes, Cecil, and Fred Carnes. *You Must Go to Mexico: Down the Pan American Highway with Cecil and Fred Carnes.* Chicago: Ziff Davis, 1947.

Carpenter, Frank G. "Buried Treasures." *Los Angeles Times,* June 21, 1913.

———. *Mexico.* Garden City: Doubleday, 1924.

Carson, W. E. *Mexico: Wonderland of the South.* New York: Macmillan, 1909.

Case, Alden Buell. *Thirty Years with the Mexicans: In Peace and Revolution.* New York: Fleming H. Revell, 1917.

Chamberlain, George Agnew. *Is Mexico Worth Saving?* Indianapolis: Bobbs-Merrill, 1920.

Chesnutt, Charles W. "The Future American." *Boston Evening Transcript,* August 18, 1900. Reprinted in *Theories of Ethnicity,* edited by Werner Sollors, 17–33. New York: New York University Press, 1996.

Chow, Rey. "Where Have All the Natives Gone?" In *Feminist Postcolonial Theory: A Reader,"* edited by Reina Lewis and Sara Mills, 324–349. New York: Routledge, 2003.

Coatsworth, John H. *Growth Against Development: The Economic Impact of Railroads in Porfirian Mexico.* Dekalb: Northern Illinois University Press, 1981.

Conkling, Howard. *Mexico and the Mexicans.* New York: Taintor Brothers, Merrill, 1883.

Crane, Stephen. *Maggie, a Girl of the Street.* New York: D. Appleton, 1896.

Crawford, Cora Hayward. *The Land of the Montezumas.* 2nd ed. New York: John B. Alden, 1889.

Creelman, James. *Diaz, Master of Mexico.* New York: D. Appleton, 1911.

———. "President Diaz: Hero of the Americas." *Pearson's Magazine* 19, no. 3 (March 1908): 231–277.

———. "Underlying Causes of the Mexican Insurrection." *North American Review*, April 1911, 596–608.

Dale, James G. *Mexico and Our Mission.* Lebanon: Sowers Printing, 1910.

Darton, N. H. "Mexico—the Treasure House of the World." *National Geographic* 18, August 1907, 493–519.

Dawson, Alexander S. "Mexico, the Treasure House of the World: Perceptions of Economic Development in Porfirian Mexico, 1876–1910." Master's Thesis, University of Calgary, 1991.

Debroise, Olivier. *Mexican Suite: A History of Photography in Mexico.* Translated by Stella de Sá Rego. Austin: University of Texas Press, 2001.

De León, Arnoldo. *They Called Them Greasers: Anglo Attitudes Toward Mexicans in Texas, 1821–1900.* Austin: University of Texas Press, 1983.

Deloria, Vine, Jr. *Custer Died for Your Sins: An Indian Manifesto.* Reprint. Norman: University of Oklahoma Press, 1988 (1969).

D'Harnoncourt, René. *Mexicana: A Book of Pictures.* New York: Alfred A. Knopf, 1931.

De Kal, Courtenay. "The Commercial Conquest of Sinaloa." *The Nation*, May 24, 1906.

Duclós Salinas, Adolfo. *The Riches of Mexico and Its Institutions.* St. Louis: Nixon-Jones Printing, 1893.

Durham, Kate H. "The Characteristic of the Mexican People." *The Home Missionary* 62, no. 11, March 1890, 502–503.

Dyer, Richard. *White.* New York: Routledge, 1997.

Edwards, Wendy J. Deichmann. "Forging an Ideology for American Missions: Josiah Strong and Manifest Destiny." In *North American Foreign Missions, 1810–1914: Theology, Theory, and Policy*, edited by Wilbert R. Shenk, 163–191. Grand Rapids, MI: William B. Eerdmans Publishing, 2004.

Edwards, William Seymour. *On the Mexican Highlands.* Cincinnati: Jennings and Graham, 1906.

Eisenhower, John S. D. *Intervention! The United States and the Mexican Revolution, 1913–1917.* New York: Norton, 1993.

Eng, David L. *Racial Castration: Managing Masculinity in Asian America.* Durham: Duke University Press, 2001.

Enloe, Cynthia. *Bananas, Beaches, and Bases: Making Feminist Sense of International Politics.* Berkeley: University of California Press, 1990.

Enock, C. Reginald. *Mexico: Its Ancient and Modern Civilization, History and Political Conditions, Topography and Natural Resources, Industries and General Development.* London: T. Fisher Unwin, 1909.

Eperjesi, John R. *The Imperialist Imaginary: Visions of Asia and the Pacific in American Culture.* Hanover, NH: Dartmouth College Press, 2005.

Espiritu, Yen Le. *Asian American Panethnicity: Bridging Institutions and Identities.* Philadelphia: Temple University Press, 1992.

Fann, K. T., and Donald C. Hodges. *Readings in U.S. Imperialism.* Boston: Porter Sargent Publisher, 1971.

Fassett, O. F. *Diary of a Journey to Mexico and California.* St. Alban's: Wallace Printing, 1888.

Ferguson, Roderick A. *Aberrations in Black: Toward a Queer of Color Critique.* Minneapolis: University of Minnesota Press, 2003.

Fiol-Matta, Licia. *A Queer Mother for the Nation: The State and Gabriela Mistral.* Minneapolis: University of Minnesota Press, 2002.

Fishkin, Shelly Fisher. "Crossroads of Culture: The Transnational Turn in American Studies—Presidential Address to the American Studies Association, November 12, 2004." *American Quarterly* 57, no. 1 (March 2005): 17–57.

Flandreau, Charles Malcomb. *Viva Mexico!* New York: D. Appleton, 1908.

Flippin, J. R. *Sketches from the Mountains of Mexico.* Cincinnati: Standard Publishing, 1889.

Fornaro, Carlo de. *Diaz, Czar of Mexico; an Arraignment.* Philadelphia: International Publishers, 1909.

Foster, John W. "The New Mexico." *National Geographic* 13, January 1902, 1–24.

Foucault, Michel. *The Birth of the Clinic: An Archaeology of Medical Perception.* Translated by A. M. Sheridan Smith. New York: Vintage Books, 1975.

———. *Discipline and Punish: The Birth of the Prison.* New York: Vintage Books, 1979.

———. *The History of Sexuality: An Introduction.* New York: Vintage Books, 1990.

Fox, Vicente, with Rob Allyn. *Revolution of Hope: The Life, Faith, and Dreams of a Mexican President.* New York: Viking, 2007.

Franck, Harry A. *Tramping through Mexico, Guatemala, and Honduras.* New York: Century, 1916.

Franck, Harry A., and Herbert C. Lanks. *The Pan American Highway from the Rio Grande to the Canal Zone.* New York: D. Appleton-Century, 1940.

Fregoso, Rosa Linda. *Bronze Screen: Chicana and Chicano Film Culture.* Minneapolis: University of Minnesota Press, 1993.

Frost, Susan Toomey. *Timeless Mexico: The Photographs of Hugo Brehme.* Austin: University of Texas Press, 2011.

Gabbert, Wolfgang. *Becoming Maya: Ethnicity and Social Inequality in Yucatán since 1500.* Tucson: University of Arizona Press, 2004.

Galton, Francis. *Inquiries into Human Faculty and Its Development.* New York: E. P. Dutton, 1907.

García Cubas, Antonio. *The Republic of Mexico in 1876.* Translated by George F. Henderson. Mexico: "La Enseñanza" Printing Office, 1876.

Gardiner, Clinton Harvey. "Foreign Travelers' Accounts of Mexico, 1810–1910." *The Americas* 8 (January 1952): 321–351.

Garland-Thomson, Rosemarie. *Staring: How We Look.* New York: Oxford University Press, 2009.

Garner, Paul. *Porfirio Díaz.* Profile in Power Series. London: Pearson, 2001.

Gates, Charles H. *A Private Train through Old Mexico by Daylight.* Toledo: Gates Tour Company, 1912.

———. *A Tour through Mexico with a Camera*. Toledo: Gates Tour Company, 1904.

Gidley, Mick. *Edward S. Curtis and the North American Indian, Incorporated*. Cambridge: Cambridge University Press, 1998.

Gillpatrick, Wallace. *The Man Who Likes Mexico*. New York: Century, 1911.

Gobineau, Arthur. *Essay on the Inequality of the Human Races*. Edited by Adrian Collins. New York: H. Fertig, 1967.

Godoy, José F. *Porfirio Diaz, President of Mexico: The Master Builder of a Great Commonwealth*. New York: Knickerbocker Press, 1910.

Goldman, Jason. "'The Golden Age of Gay Porn': Nostalgia and the Photography of Wilhelm von Gloeden." *GLQ: A Journal of Lesbian and Gay Studies* 12, no. 2 (2006): 237–258.

González, Gilbert G. *Culture of Empire: American Writers, Mexico, and Mexican Immigrants, 1880–1930*. Austin: University of Texas Press, 2004.

———. "The Ideology and Practice of Empire: The U.S., Mexico, and the Education of Mexican Immigrants." *Cultural Logic* 4, no. 1 (2000). http://clogic.eserver.org/.

González, Gilbert G., and Raul A. Fernandez. *A Century of Chicano History: Empire, Nations, and Migration*. New York: Routledge, 2003.

Gonzalez, Juan. *Harvest of Empire: A History of Latinos in America*. New York: Penguin Books, 2000.

Goolsby, William Berlin. *Guide to Mexico for the Motorist*. Dallas: Pan-American Press, 1936.

Gordon-Reed, Annette. *The Hemingses of Monticello: An American Family*. New York: W. W. Norton, 2009.

Gould, Stephen Jay. *The Mismeasure of Man*. New York: W. W. Norton, 1981.

Grandin, Greg. *Empire's Workshop: Latin America, the United States, and the Rise of the New Imperialism*. New York: Metropolitan Books, Harry Holt, 2006.

Guide and Handbook for Travelers to Mexico City and Vicinity. Mexico City: American Book and Printing, 1924.

Guidotti-Hernández, Nicole. *Unspeakable Violence: Remapping U.S. and Mexican National Imaginaries*. Durham: Duke University Press, 2011.

Gunn, Drewey Wayne. *Mexico in American and British Letters: A Bibliography of Fiction and Travel Books, Citing Original Editions*. Metuchen, NJ: Scarecrow Press, 1974.

Gupta, Akhil, and James Ferguson. "Beyond 'Culture': Space, Identity, and the Politics of Difference." In *Culture, Power, Place: Explorations in Critical Anthropology*, edited by Akhil Gupta and James Ferguson, 33–51. Durham: Duke University Press, 1997.

Haines, Michael R., and Richard H. Steckel, eds. *A Population History of North America*. Cambridge, UK: Cambridge University Press, 2000.

Hale, Edward Everett, and Miss Susan Hale. *A Family Flight through Mexico*. Boston: D. Lothrop, 1886.

Hale, Susan. *Mexico*. New York: G. P. Putnam's Sons, 1901.

Hall, Byron. "Baja California." *Los Angeles Times*, December 8, 1907.

Hamilton, Leonidas Le Cenci. *Hamilton's Mexican Handbook*. Boston: D. Lothrop, 1883.

Hannavy, John. *Encyclopedia of Nineteenth-Century Photography*. New York: Taylor and Francis Group, 2008.

Hardy, Osgood. "Ulysses S. Grant, President of the Mexican Southern Railroad." *Pacific Historical Review* 24, no. 2 (May 1955): 111–120.

Harris, Dean. *Here and There in Mexico.* Chatham, Ontario: Con. E. Shea, n.d.

———. *Travel-Talks.* Chatham, Ontario: Con. E. Shea, n.d.

Hart, John Mason. *Empire and Revolution: The Americans in Mexico since the Civil War.* Berkeley: University of California Press, 2002.

Haskin, Frederic J. "Americans in Mexico." *Los Angeles Times*, December 7, 1902.

Haven, Gilbert. *Our Next-Door Neighbor: A Winter in Mexico.* New York: Harper and Brothers, 1875.

Haverstock, Nathan A. *Fifty Years at the Front: The Life of War Correspondent Frederick Palmer.* Washington, D.C.: Brassey's, 1996.

Hendler, Glenn. *Public Sentiments: Structures of Feeling in Nineteenth-Century American Literature.* Chapel Hill: University of North Carolina Press, 2001.

Hernández, Ellie D. *Postnationalism in Chicana/o Literature and Culture.* Austin: University of Texas Press, 2009.

Hoganson, Kristin L. *Fighting for American Manhood: How Gender Politics Provoked the Spanish-American and Philippine-American Wars.* Yale Historical Publications Series. New Haven: Yale University Press, 1998.

hooks, bell. *Black Looks: Race and Representation.* Boston: South End Press, 1992.

Howell, Edward J. *Mexico: Its Progress and Commercial Possibilities.* London: W. B. Whittingham, 1892.

———. "Mexico, Past and Present." *Journal of the Society of Arts* 41, no. 2 (January 27, 1893): 181–195.

Howland, Marie. "A Mexican City." In *Strange Lands Near Home*, edited by M. A. L. Lane, 26–35. Boston: Ginn and Company, 1902.

Hutchinson, Elizabeth. *The Indian Craze: Primitivism, Modernism, and Transculturation in American Art, 1890–1915.* Durham: Duke University Press, 2009.

Ingersoll, Ralph A. *In and Under Mexico.* New York: Century, 1924.

Isaac, Allan Punzalan. *American Tropics: Articulating Filipino America.* Minneapolis: University of Minnesota Press, 2006.

Jacobson, Matthew Frye. *Barbarian Virtues: The United States Encounters Foreign Peoples at Home and Abroad, 1876–1917.* New York: Hill and Wang, 2000.

Jayes, Janice Lee. *The Illusion of Ignorance: Constructing the American Encounter with Mexico, 1877–1920.* Lanham, MD: University Press of America, 2011.

Jenks, Chris. "The Centrality of the Eye in Western Culture: An Introduction." In *Visual Culture*, edited by Chris Jenks, 1–25. New York: Routledge, 1995.

Johns, Michael. *The City of Mexico in the Age of Díaz.* Austin: University of Texas Press, 1997.

Johnson, Clinton. "Wealthful Sinaloa." *Los Angeles Times*, July 27, 1902.

Joseph, Gilbert M., and Timothy J. Henderson, eds. *The Mexico Reader: History, Culture, Politics.* Durham: Duke University Press, 2002.

Kaplan, Amy. *The Anarchy of Empire in the Making of U.S. Culture.* Cambridge: Harvard University Press, 2005.

———. "Violent Belonging and the Question of Empire Today." *American Quarterly* 56, no. 1 (March 2004): 1–18.

Kaplan, Amy, and Donald E. Pease, eds. *Cultures of United States Imperialism.* Durham: Duke University Press, 1994.

Kaplan, Caren. *Questions of Travel: Postmodern Discourses of Displacement.* Durham: Duke University Press, 2000.

Kipling, Rudyard. *The Complete Verse.* London: Kyle Cathie, 1990.

Kramer, Paul A. *The Blood of Government: Race, Empire, the United States, and the Philippines.* Chapel Hill: University of North Carolina Press, 2006.

Lawrence, D. H. *Mornings in Mexico.* London: Martin Secker, 1930.

Lewis, Daniel. *Iron Horse Imperialism: The Southern Pacific of Mexico, 1880-1951.* Tucson: University of Arizona Press, 2007.

Limón, José E. *American Encounters: Greater Mexico, the United States, and the Erotics of Culture.* Boston: Beacon Press, 1998.

―――. *Dancing with the Devil: Society and Cultural Poetics in Mexican American South Texas.* Madison: University of Wisconsin Press, 1994.

Lomnitz, Claudio. "Chronotypes of a Dystopic Nation: Cultures of Dependency and Border Crossings in Late Porfirian Mexico." In *Globalizing American Studies,* edited by Brian T. Edwards and Dilip Parameshwar Gaonkar, 209–239. Chicago: University of Chicago Press, 2010.

London, Jack. "The Trouble Makers in Mexico." *Collier's* 53 (June 13, 1914): 13–14, 25.

―――. "With Funston's Men." *Collier's* 52 (May 23, 1914): 9–13.

Love, Eric. "White Is the Color of Empire: The Annexation of Hawaii in 1898." In *Race, Nation, and Empire in American History,* edited by James T. Campbell, Matthew Pratt Guterl, and Robert G. Lee, 75–102. Chapel Hill: University of North Carolina Press, 2007.

Lummis, Charles F. *The Awakening of a Nation: Mexico of To-day.* New York: Harper and Brothers, 1904.

―――. *Bullying the Moqui.* Edited with an introduction by Robert Easton and Mackenzie Brown. Prescott, AZ: Prescott College Press, 1968.

―――. "The Mexican Wizard." *Land of Sunshine* 11, no. 6, November 1899, 309–316.

Lutz, Catherine A., and Jane L. Collins. *Reading National Geographic.* Chicago: University of Chicago Press, 1993.

Lyle, Eugene P., Jr. "Mexico at High Tide." *The World's Work* 14, no. 4, August 1907, 9179–9196.

MacHugh, Robert Joseph. *Modern Mexico.* New York: Dodd, Mead, 1914.

Manasalan, Martin F., IV. *Global Divas: Filipino Gay Men in the Diaspora.* Durham: Duke University Press, 2003.

Martin, Percy F. *Mexico of the Twentieth Century.* New York: Dodd, Mead, 1907.

Marx, Leo. *The Machine in the Garden: Technology and the Pastoral Ideal in America.* New York: Oxford University Press, 2000 (1964).

The Massey-Gilbert Blue Book of Mexico. Mexico City and St. Louis: Massey-Gilbert, 1901.

Matthews, Michael. "Railway Culture and the Civilizing Mission in Mexico, 1876–1910." Ph.D. diss., University of Arizona, 2008.

Mayer, Brantz. *Mexico as It Was and as It Is.* New York: New World Press, 1844.

McCaa, Robert. "The Peopling of Mexico from Origins to Revolution." In *A Population History of North America,* ed. Michael R. Haines and Richard H. Steckel, 241–304. Cambridge, UK: Cambridge University Press, 2000.

McCarty, J. Hendrickson. *Two Thousand Miles through the Heart of Mexico.* New York: Phillips and Hunt, 1888.

McClintock, Anne. *Imperial Leather: Race, Gender, and Sexuality in the Colonial Contest.* New York: Routledge, 1995.

McCollester, Sullivan Holman. *Mexico Old and New: A Wonderland.* 2nd ed. Boston: Universalist Publishing House, 1897. Reprinted 1899; pages cited refer to the 1899 edition.

McLynn, Frank. *Villa and Zapata: A History of the Mexican Revolution.* New York: Carroll and Graff, 2000.

Memmi, Albert. *The Colonizer and the Colonized.* Boston: Beacon Press, 1967.

Merrill, Dennis. *Negotiating Paradise: U.S. Tourism and Empire in Twentieth-Century Latin America.* Chapel Hill: University of North Carolina Press, 2009.

Mexican Central Railroad. *Facts and Figures about Mexico and Her Great Railway System.* 5th ed. Mexico City: Mexican Central Railway Company, 1906.

"Mexican Curiosities and Types." *Los Angeles Times*, October 2, 1938, G2.

Mexico Otherwise: Modern Mexico in the Eyes of Foreign Observers. Edited by Jürgen Buchenau. Albuquerque: University of New Mexico Press, 2005.

Middleton, P. Harvey. *Industrial Mexico: 1919 Facts and Figures.* New York: Dodd, Mead, 1919.

Mitchell, Pablo. *Coyote Nation: Sexuality, Race, and Conquest in Modernizing New Mexico.* Chicago: University of Chicago Press, 2000.

Molina-Guzmán, Isabel. *Dangerous Curves: Latina Bodies in the Media.* New York: NYU Press, 2010.

Montellano, Francisco D. *C. B. Waite, fotógrafo: Una mirada diversa sobre el México de principios del siglo XX.* Mexico City: Editorial Grijalbo, 1994.

———. *C. B. Waite: La época de oro de las postales en México.* Mexico City: Círculo de Arte, 1998.

———. "C. B. Waite, profesión fotógrafo." Master's Thesis, Universidad Nacional Autónoma de México, 1989.

Mora-Torres, Juan. *The Making of the Mexican Border: The State, Capitalism, and Society in Nuevo León, 1848–1910.* Austin: University of Texas Press, 2001.

Morgan, Phillip D. "Interracial Sex in the Chesapeake and the British Atlantic World, c. 1700–1820." In *Sally Hemings and Thomas Jefferson: History, Memory, and Civic Culture*, edited by Jan Ellen Lewis and Peter S. Onuf, 52–84. Charlottesville: University of Virginia Press, 1999.

Morrill, Gulian Lansing (G. L.). *The Devil in Mexico.* Chicago: M. A. Donohue, 1917.

———. *Hawaiian Heathens and Others.* Chicago: M. A. Donohue, c. 1919.

———. *On the Warpath.* No identifiable publisher, 1918.

———. *Rotten Republics; A Tropical Tramp in Central America.* Chicago: M. A. Donohue, 1916.

———. *Sea Sodoms: A Sinical [sic] Survey of Haiti, Santo Domingo, Porto Rico, Curaçao, Venezuela, Guadeloupe, Martinique, Cuba.* Minneapolis: Pioneer Printers, 1921.

———. *Tracks of a Tenderfoot: In Africa, Asia, and Europe.* Minneapolis: Minnesota Blank Book, 1902.

Morris, Mrs. James Edwin. *A Tour in Mexico.* New York: Abbey Press, 1902.

Mraz, John. *Looking for Mexico: Modern Visual Culture and National Identity.* Durham, NC: Duke University Press, 2009.

Murphy, Kevin P. *Political Manhood: Red Bloods, Mollycoddles, and the Politics of Progressive Era Reform*. New York: Columbia University Press, 2008.

The National Commission from the United States of Mexico to the Pan-American Exposition, Buffalo. *A Few Facts About Mexico*. Buffalo: White-Evans-Penfold, 1901.

Navarro, Juan N. "Mexico of Today." *National Geographic* 12, April–May 1901, 152–157 and 176–179.

Niederkorn, William S. "Mother Jones Speaks Out for Convicted Caricaturist." *New York Times*, November 29, 1909.

Nkrumah, Kwame. *Neo-Colonialism: The Last Stage of Imperialism*. New York: International Publishers, 1965.

Noriega, Chon A. *Shot in America: Television, the State, and the Rise of Chicano Cinema*. Minneapolis: University of Minnesota Press, 2000.

Nutini, Hugo G. *The Mexican Aristocracy: An Expressive Ethnography*. Austin: University of Texas Press, 2004.

———. *The Wages of Conquest: The Mexican Aristocracy in the Context of Western Aristocracies*. Ann Arbor: University of Michigan Press, 1995.

Ober, Frederick A. *Travels in Mexico and Life among the Mexicans*. Boston: Estes and Lauriat, 1887.

Olsson-Seffer, Pehr. "Agricultural Possibilities in Tropical Mexico." *National Geographic* 21, December 1910, 1021–1040.

Omi, Michael, and Howard Winant. *Racial Formation in the United States: From the 1960s to the 1990s*. New York: Routledge, 1994.

Overmyer-Velázquez, Mark. *Visions of the Emerald City: Modernity, Tradition, and the Formation of Porfirian Oaxaca, Mexico*. Durham: Duke University Press, 2006.

Padget, Martin. *Indian Country: Travels in the American Southwest, 1840–1935*. Albuquerque: University of New Mexico Press, 2004.

Palmer, Frederick. "The American Spirit in Veracruz." *Everybody's Magazine* 30 (June 1914): 814–820.

———. "Watchful Perspiring at Vera Cruz." *Everybody's Magazine* 31 (July 1914): 65–197.

———. "What It All Means in Mexico." *Everybody's Magazine* 30, no. 6 (June 1914): 814–820.

Pan American Petroleum and Transport Company. *Mexican Petroleum*. New York, 1922.

Parlee, Lorena M. "Porfirio Díaz, Railroads, and Development in Northern Mexico: A Study of Government Policy toward the Central and National Railroads, 1876–1910." Ph.D. diss., University of California—San Diego, 1981.

Pearce, Roy Harvey. *Savagism and Civilization: A Study of the Indian in the American Mind*. Rev. ed., second printing. Baltimore: The Johns Hopkins University Press, 1967.

Pérez, Louis A., Jr. "Incurring a Debt of Gratitude: 1898 and the Moral Sources of United States Hegemony in Cuba." *American Historical Review* 104, no. 2 (April 1999): 356–398.

Pletcher, David M. *Rails, Mines, and Progress: Seven American Promoters in Mexico, 1867–1911*. Ithaca: Cornell University Press, 1958.

Poole, Deborah. "An Image of 'Our Indian': Type Photographs and Racial Sentiments in Oaxaca, 1920–1940." *Hispanic American Historical Review* 84, no. 1 (2004): 37–82.

Potter, Russell A. *Arctic Spectacles: The Frozen North in Visual Culture, 1818–1875*. Seattle: University of Washington Press, 2007.

Pratt, Mary Louise. *Imperial Eyes: Travel Writing and Transculturation*. New York: Routledge Press, 1992.

Probert, Frank H. "The Treasure Chest of Mercurial Mexico." *National Geographic* 30, July 1916, 33–68.

Prendergast, Francis E. "Railroads in Mexico." *Harper's*, July 1888, 276–281.

Quiroga, José. *Tropics of Desire: Interventions from Queer Latino America*. New York: New York University Press, 2000.

Rafael, Vicente L. *White Love and Other Events in Filipino History*. Durham: Duke University Press, 2000.

Reed, John. *Insurgent Mexico*. New York: D. Appleton, 1914.

Rees, Thomas. *Spain's Lost Jewels: Cuba and Mexico*. Springfield: Illinois State Register, 1906.

Reesman, Jeanne Campbell. *Jack London's Racial Lives: A Critical Biography*. Athens: University of Georgia Press, 2009.

Reinsch, Paul S. "A New Era in Mexico." *The Forum* 32, no. 5 (January 1902): 528–538.

Renda, Mary A. *Taking Haiti: Military Occupation and the Culture of U.S. Imperialism, 1915–1940*. Chapel Hill: University of North Carolina Press, 2000.

Rice, John H. *Mexico: Our Neighbor*. New York: John W. Lovell, 1888.

Riis, Jacob. *How the Other Half Lives: Studies among the Tenements of New York*. New York: C. Scribner's Sons, 1890.

Rodríguez Hernández, Georgina. "Niños desnudos en el porfiriato." *Luna Córnea* 9 (1996): 44–49.

Roediger, David R. *How Race Survived U.S. History: From Settlement and Slavery to the Obama Phenomenon*. London: Verso, 2008.

Rogers, Thomas L. *Mexico?: Sí, Señor*. Boston: Mexican Central Railway Co. and Collins Press, 1894.

Rogin, Michael. "The Sword Became a Flashing Vision": D. W. Griffith's *The Birth of a Nation*." *Representations* 9 (Winter 1985): 150–195.

Romero, Matías. *Geographical and Statistical Notes on Mexico*. New York: G. P. Putnam, 1898.

———. *Mexico and the United States*. New York: G. P. Putnam, 1898.

Romero, Rolando, and Amanda Nolacea Harris, eds. *Feminism, Nation and Myth: La Malinche*. Houston: Arte Público Press, 2005.

Rone, Wendell H. *A History of the Daviess-McLean Baptist Association in Kentucky, 1844–1943*. Owensboro, KY: Messenger Job Printing, 1944.

Roosevelt, Theodore. *The Rough Riders*. New York: Scribner's, 1899.

———. *The Winning of the West*. 4 vols. New York: G. P. Putnam's Sons, 1889–1896.

Rose, Gillian. *Visual Methodologies*. London: Sage Publications, 2001.

Rowe, John Carlos. "Post-Nationalism, Globalism, and the New American Studies." In *Post-Nationalist American Studies*, edited by John Carlos Rowe, 23–37. Berkeley: University of California Press, 2000.

Russell, Phillips. *Red Tiger: Adventures in Yucatan and Mexico*. Norwood: Plimpton Press, 1929.

Russell, Thomas H. *Mexico, In Peace and War*. Chicago: Reilly and Britton, 1914.

Rydell, Robert W. *All the World's a Fair: Visions of Empire at American International Expositions, 1876–1916*. Chicago: University of Chicago Press, 1984.

Said, Edward W. *Orientalism*. New York: Vintage Books, 1979.

Sanborn, Helen J. *A Winter in Central America and Mexico*. Boston: Lee and Shepard Publishers, 1886.

Sánchez, George J. *Becoming Mexican American: Ethnicity, Culture, and Identity in Chicano Los Angeles, 1900–1945*. New York: Oxford Press, 1993.

Schaeffer-Grabiel, Felicity. "Flexible Technologies of Subjectivity and Mobility across the Americas." *American Quarterly* 58, no. 3 (September 2006): 891–914.

Schell, William, Jr. *Integral Outsiders: The American Colony in Mexico City, 1876–1911*. Wilmington, DE: SR Books, 2001.

Schmitt, Karl M. "American Protestant Missionaries and the Díaz Regime in Mexico, 1876–1911." *Journal of Church and State* 25, no. 2 (1983): 253–277.

Schoonover, Thomas D. *Mexican Lobby: Matías Romero in Washington, 1861–1867*. Lexington: University of Kentucky Press, 1986.

Scully, Michael, and Virginia Scully. *Motorists' Guide to Mexico*. Dallas: Southwest Press, 1933.

Shah, Nayan. *Contagious Divides: Epidemics and Race in San Francisco's Chinatown*. Berkeley: University of California Press, 2001.

Sherratt, Harriott Wight. *Mexican Vistas Seen from the Highways and Byways of Travel*. Chicago: Rand, McNally, 1899.

Showalter, William Joseph. "Mexico and Mexicans." *National Geographic* 25, May 1914, 471–493.

———. "Redeeming the Tropics." *National Geographic* 25, March 1914, 344–364.

Simpson, Lesley Byrd. *Many Mexicos*. New York: G. P. Putnam's Sons, 1941.

Skwiot, Christine. *The Purposes of Paradise: U.S. Tourism and Empire in Cuba and Hawaii*. Philadelphia: University of Pennsylvania Press, 2010.

Smith, Andrea. *Conquest: Sexual Violence and American Indian Genocide*. Cambridge, MA: South End Press, 2005.

Smith, Francis Hopkinson. *A White Umbrella in Mexico*. Boston and New York: Houghton Mifflin, 1892.

Smith, Shawn Michelle. *American Archives: Gender, Race, and Class in Visual Culture*. Princeton: Princeton University Press, 1999.

Sontag, Susan. *On Photography*. New York: Farrar, Straus and Giroux, 1973.

Spivak, Gayatri Chakravorty. "Can the Subaltern Speak?" In *Marxism and the Interpretation of Culture*, edited by Cary Nelson and Lawrence Grossberg, 271–313. Urbana: University of Illinois Press, 1988.

Starr, Frederick. *In Indian Mexico: A Narrative of Travel and Labor*. Chicago: Forbes, 1908.

———. *Indians of Southern Mexico: An Ethnographic Album*. Chicago: The Lakeside Press, 1899.

———. *The Physical Characters of the Indians of Southern Mexico*. Chicago: University of Chicago Press, 1902.

Starr, Kevin. *Inventing the Dream: California through the Progressive Era*. London: Oxford University Press, 1985.

Steele, James W. *To Mexico by Palace Car*. Chicago: Jansen, McClurg, 1884.

Stepan, Nancy Leys. *"The Hour of Eugenics": Race, Gender, and Nation in Latin America*. Ithaca: Cornell University Press, 1991.

Stoler, Ann Laura. *Carnal Knowledge and Imperial Power: Race and the Intimate in Colonial Rule*. Berkeley: University of California Press, 2002.

———, ed. *Haunted by Empire: Geographies of Intimacy in North American History*. Durham, NC: Duke University Press, 2006.

Strange Lands Near Home. Edited by M. A. L. Lane. Youth's Companion Series. Boston: Ginn and Company, 1902.

Streeby, Shelley. *American Sensations: Class, Empire, and the Production of Popular Culture*. Berkeley: University of California Press, 2002.

———. "Joaquín Murrieta and the American 1848." In *Post-Nationalist American Studies*, edited by John Carlos Rowe, 166–196. Berkeley: University of California Press, 2000.

Strong, Josiah. *Our Country: Its Possible Future and Present Crisis*. Rev. ed. New York: Baker and Taylor, 1891.

Tejada, Roberto. *National Camera: Photography and Mexico's Image Environment*. Minneapolis: University of Minnesota Press, 2009.

Tenorio-Trillo, Mauricio. *Mexico at the World's Fairs: Crafting a Modern Nation*. Berkeley: University of California Press, 1996.

Terry, Thomas Philip. *Terry's Guide to Mexico: The New Standard Guidebook to the Mexican Republic*. Boston and New York: Houghton Mifflin, 1909.

Torgovnick, Marianna. *Gone Primitive: Savage Intellects, Modern Lives*. Chicago: University of Chicago Press, 1990.

Torres, Edén E. *Chicana Without Apology: The New Chicana Cultural Studies*. New York: Routledge Press, 2003.

Turner, John Kenneth. *Barbarous Mexico*. Chicago: C. H. Kerr, 1910. Volume referenced throughout this book published by the University of Texas Press, 1969.

———. "The Slaves of Yucatan." *The American Magazine* 68 no. 9 (October 1909): 523–538.

Truman, Ben C. *History of the World's Fair*. Reprint. New York: Arno Press, 1976 (1893).

Tweedie, Mrs. Alec (Ethel B.). *The Maker of Modern Mexico, Porfirio Díaz*. New York: John Lane Company, 1906.

———. *Mexico as I Saw It*. Reprint. New York: Macmillan, 1911 (1901).

Valdés, Dionicio Nodín. *Barrios Norteños: St. Paul and Midwestern Mexican Communities in the Twentieth Century*. Austin: University of Texas Press, 2000.

Vanderwood, Paul J. "The Picture Postcard as Historical Evidence: Veracruz, 1914." *The Americas* 45, no. 2 (October 1998): 201–225.

Vanderwood, Paul J., and Frank N. Samponaro. *Border Fury: A Picture Postcard Record of Mexico's Revolution and U.S. War Preparedness, 1910–1917*. Albuquerque: University of New Mexico Press, 1988.

Vasconcelos, José. *The Cosmic Race/La raza cósmica*. Translated by Didier T. Jaén. Baltimore: The Johns Hopkins University Press, 1997 (original Spanish-language publication, 1925).

von Humboldt, Alexander. *Political Essay on the Kingdom of New Spain*. Translated by John Black. London: Longman, 1811.

von Keck, Irvin. "Mexico of To-day." *The West Coast Magazine* 7, no. 3. From a clipping found at the Autry National Center in Los Angeles.

Walker, Ronald. *Infernal Paradise: Mexico and the Modern English Novel.* Berkeley: University of California Press, 1978.

Weber, Max. *The Protestant Work Ethic and the Spirit of Capitalism and Other Writings.* Edited and translated by Peter Baehr and Gordon C. Wells. New York: Penguin, 2002.

Wells, Mrs. D. B. "A Bit of Mexico Personally Observed." Pamphlet archived at the Braun Research Library, Los Angeles.

Weston, Rubin Francis. *Racism in U.S. Imperialism: The Influence of Racial Assumptions on American Foreign Policy, 1893–1946.* Columbia: University of South Carolina Press, 1972.

Wexler, Laura. *Tender Violence: Domestic Visions in an Age of U.S. Imperialism.* Chapel Hill: University of North Carolina Press, 2000.

White, Trumbull. *Our New Possessions.* Chicago: International Publishing, 1898.

Winter, Nevin O. *Mexico and Her People of To-day.* London: Cassell and Company, 1913.

Woll, Allen L. *The Latin Image in American Film.* Los Angeles: UCLA Latin American Center Publications, University of California, 1977.

Wright, Marie Robinson. *Mexico: A History of Its Progress and Development in One Hundred Years.* Philadelphia: George Barrie and Sons, 1911.

———. *Picturesque Mexico.* Philadelphia: J. B. Lippincott, 1897.

Wyatt, David. *The Fall into Eden: Landscape and Imagination in California.* London: Cambridge University Press, 1990.

Yeager, Gene. "Porfirian Commercial Propaganda: Mexico in the World Industrial Expositions." *The Americas* 34, no. 2 (October 1977): 230–243.

Young, Robert J. C. *Colonial Desire: Hybridity in Theory, Culture and Race.* New York: Routledge, 1995.

Yu, Henry. "How Tiger Woods Lost His Stripes: Post-Nationalist American Studies as a History of Race, Migration, and the Commodification of Culture." In *Post-Nationalist American Studies*, edited by John Carlos Rowe, 223–246. Berkeley: University of California Press, 2000.

Note: an italic *f* indicates a figure on the page cited.